Non-violence —
Central to Christian Spirituality:
Perspectives from Scripture
to the Present

Non-violence —
Central to Christian Spirituality:
Perspectives from Scripture
to the Present

EDITED BY
JOSEPH T. CULLITON, C.S.B.

Toronto Studies in Theology
Volume 8

The Edwin Mellen Press
New York and Toronto

Library of Congress Cataloging in Publication Data

Main entry under title:

Non-violence--Central to Christian spirituality.

(Toronto studies in theology ; v. 8)
1. Nonviolence--Religious aspects--Christianity
--Addresses, essays, lectures. 2. Pacifism--
Religious aspects--Christianity--Addresses, essays,
lectures. I. Culliton, Joseph T. II. Series.
BT736.6.N66 1982   261.8'73   82-7964
ISBN 0-88946-964-4   AACR2
ISBN 0-88946-965-2 (pbk.)

The Edwin Mellen Press
P.O. Box 450
Lewiston, New York 14092

Toronto Studies in Theology   ISBN 0-88946-975-X

Printed in the United States of America

ACKNOWLEDGEMENTS

We gratefully acknowledge the use of quoted material from the following sources:

Specified extracts from "MNS Group Process," by Pete Hill, in DANDELION, Summer/Fall, 1979. Reprinted by permission of New Society Publishers.

Specified extracts from FRANCIS OF ASSISI, OMNIBUS OF SOURCES, edited by Marion Habig. Copyright 1973. Reprinted by permission of Franciscan Herald Press.

Specified extracts from FRANCIS, THE JOURNEY AND THE DREAM by Murray Bodo. Copyright 1972. Reprinted by permission of St. Anthony Messenger Press.

Specified extracts from A MANIFESTO FOR NONVIOLENT REVOLUTION by George Lakey. Copyright 1972. Reprinted by permission of New Society Publishers.

Specified extracts from THE ORIGINAL REVOLUTION: ESSAYS ON CHRISTIAN PACIFISM by John Howard Yoder. Copyright 1972. Reprinted by permission of Herald Press.

Specified extracts from THE POLITICS OF JESUS by John Howard Yoder. Copyright 1972. Reprinted by permission of Wm. B. Eerdmans Publishing Co.

Specified extracts from THE POLITICAL PHILOSOPHY OF MARTIN LUTHER KING, JR. by Hanes Walton, Jr. Copyright 1971 by Hanes Walton, Jr. Reprinted by permission of Greenwood Publishing Corporation.

Specified extracts from MAN'S VISION OF GOD AND THE LOGIC OF THEISM by Charles Hartshorne. Copyright 1941, renewed 1968, by Charles Hartshorne. Reprinted by permission of Harper & Row, Publishers, Inc.

TABLE OF CONTENTS

NON-VIOLENCE: CENTRAL TO CHRISTIAN SPIRITUALITY

INTRODUCTION

by Joseph T. Culliton, C.S.B.

Even the most superficial scan of Western history makes it abundantly clear that Christians have lived neither by the principle of non-violence nor that of pacifism in a consistent, widespread fashion. In fact, the majority of Christians have never recognized that their Christian faith placed any conscientious obligation on them, as a matter of principle, to avoid all violence. This is evidenced by the holy wars and crusades in which they have engaged and the widespread justification given to war in the just war theory.

Today most Christians regard non-violence and pacifism as synonymous. They are unaware that pacifism is usually equated with total non-resistance, whereas non-violence permits a great variety of positive action aimed at preventing evil. Many Christians look at non-violence as simply an attitude or a particular ethical stance adopted by a few scattered Christian sects. They associate it almost exclusively with Quakers, Mennonites and anti-war movements, and see it as something that is narrow and restrictive. Above all, vast numbers of Christians today regard non-violence as peripheral to mainline Christian spirituality. This book challenges these attitudes.

Non-Violence: Central to Christian Spirituality consists of a number of original, scholarly chapters written on the scriptural evidence and the thought of various spir-

itual writers, mystics and theologians selected from a variety of branches within the Christian tradition. The aim
is not simply to set forth the thought of these outstanding
Christian witnesses to non-violence. Each chapter also
shows that the person's thought on non-violence flows from
his profound religious experience or mystical vision (if he
has written from within the contemplative, mystical or
spiritual traditions) or from central tenets of his theological synthesis (if he is a theologian). Each chapter
opens with an introductory section that situates the thinker historically, denominationally and theologically to the
extent that this assists the reader to appreciate his
thought and place in the Christian tradition. In the re-
mainder of each chapter the person's thought on non-violence or pacifism, as the case may be, is set forth in such
a way that its origins and its relation to his overall
vision or synthesis is made clear.

     Thus, individually and as a whole, the chapters show
that throughout the centuries when Christians have born
witness to a life of non-violence, their specific teaching
on non-violence has not been unrelated or accidental to the
central principles of their Christian faith, doctrine and
ethics. Their stance on non-violence has not been an ethical decision only loosely related to the core of their understanding of the Christian life. Nor have they been
limited to members of denominations that some would regard
as far from mainline Christianity. Each of the chapters
makes it clear that Christians who have acknowledged the
call to live non-violently have recognized it as coming
from ideas that are central to their Christian faith, their
mystical experience and vision, and/or their theological
syntheses. Thus the main achievement of this book is that
it demonstrates that non-violence is central to Christian
spirituality, not accidental or peripheral to it.

The unique feature of this anthology, therefore, is not that it simply sets forth the thought of a variety of Christian thinkers on the subject of non-violence. A number of works have already done that. To my knowledge, this work is the only one in English that sets out to show the centrality of non-violence to Christian spirituality. This is a task of particular significance which scholars of most other world religions have already accomplished on behalf of their respective traditions.

It is impossible, of course, to demonstrate that non-violence is central to Christian spirituality without starting with the biblical evidence. Our study of the Old Testament literature certainly lays to rest a host of popular, and even scholarly, opinions regarding God and the violence He seemed to have condoned. The New Testament chapter goes a long way in shedding light on Jesus' answer to the use of violence for purposes of defending oneself, protecting one's own interests and living up to one's social responsibilities. It is of paramount importance that we look directly to the New Testament teaching for insight and not simply try to find new reasons to maintain a modified justification for war. Our chapter on the New Testament extends beyond the scriptures themselves to the early Fathers, because in this, as in other areas of thought, their writings shed light on the scriptural evidence itself.

Once one moves beyond the scriptures, one thinks of so many Christians who have born witness to a life of non-violence on the basis of their faith that any selection will strike some readers as purely arbitrary. No matter what theoretical arguments one presents to justify including one spiritual writer over another, one can find cogent arguments for the opposite decision. Finally selections had to be made, and often for reasons of practicality.

Some central figures from different eras of the past
have been selected to show that non-violence has always
been recognized as of major importance to Christian thought
and action. Maximus the Confessor, the Father of Byzantine
theology, established the foundation for a strong theological stance against violence within that tradition.
Francis of Assisi's contribution in the areas of mystical
theology and theology of peace need no comment. Murray
Bodo's poetic style has done a great deal to bring us into
direct contact with the heart and mind of Francis. The
chapter on George Fox, the founder of the Quakers, intro-
duces us to another tradition within Christianity and to a
spiritual giant who committed much of his life to promoting
peace non-violently.

Most of the chapters focus on twentieth century figures of various traditions. This emphasis reflects what
appears to be an increased awareness of the call to live
non-violently in our century, even though we live in a
world saturated with violence. Like the growth of awareness in many other areas of our religion, consciousness of
the call to live non-violently is developing slowly. Various persons in different traditions and at different times
have come to grips with it and expressed deep insights into
the path of non-violence each in his/her own way. A renewed consciousness of this call seems to be emerging from
many sources within Christianity today. Undoubtedly there
are numerous reasons for this, one of which is assuredly
the fact that modern means of warfare have forced us to
examine ourselves and our religion and seriously ask if we
can continue to justify violence.

The twentieth century writers presented here have been
selected because they represent different traditions and
because each says something unique about non-violence.
They do not all agree, but at times contradict each other

on some points. Inconsistencies can even be found within
the thought of individual writers. No reader will be able
to agree with all the ideas on non-violence nor with all
the theologies presented in this book. The formal teaching
of the work is that non-violence is central to Christian
spirituality. The value of presenting views that both illustrates this teaching and complement each other only im-
perfectly is to show how Christians have to grapple with
issues and grope towards insight into truths inherent in
their faith all along, but only seen by some at any one
time, and then only as through a glass darkly.

Thomas Merton represents the twentieth century Roman
Catholic mystical and contemplative traditions. His
thought also developed out of a knowledge of Catholic social ethics and Eastern mysticism, especially the pacifist
thought of Gandhi. The thought of Martin Luther King Jr.
represents a very different tradition. Yet it has many
contemplative and mystical elements as well as a personal
knowledge of the thought of Gandhi behind it.

Reinhold Niebuhr's thought, in particular, illustrates
the grappling with issues and the evolution of consciousness that is involved in facing non-violence in theory and
practice. He moves from a relatively firm position to a
much weaker one in which he maintains that religious pacifism bears witness to central facets of our faith. Although he cannot bring himself to adopt this form of pacifism, he maintains that it is a Christian ideal and an eschatological sign for the community of faith.

The shift in Niebuhr's thought is made on theological
grounds, but is also heavily dictated by pragmatic considerations as well. So too the thought on non-violence of
Charles Hartshorne, a leading exponent of process philosophy and theology, is directly centered on philosophical/
theological grounds. Nevertheless, pragmatic considera-

tions also play a major role in causing him to qualify it
rather rigidly.

John Howard Yoder, who is undoubtedly the central
spokesman for the Mennonite tradition on this topic today,
is in sharp contrast with Niebuhr and Hartshorne on the
point of pragmatism. Yoder's thought illustrates that
there is a fundamental difference between non-violence and
pacifism or non-resistance. He rejects non-violence because he sees it to be a method or strategy and not a theological stance. As such it can give way to violence when
it proves to be unworkable. In one area Yoder's thought is
similar to Niebuhr's religious pacifism in rejecting all
resistance to violence by Christians. Yoder disagrees with
Niebuhr's pragmatic pacifism which strives to avoid violence because it is judged pragmatically to be the most
productive policy available to the Christian at any time.
Yoder would also disagree with the pragmatic tendencies in
Hartshorne's thought.

Our purpose is not to get waylaid in a lengthy discussion of the merits of pragmatism when applied to a life of
non-violence. Nevertheless, since non-violence is so frequently rejected for pragmatic reasons, it is necessary to
face the fact that pragmatism is neither utilitarianism nor
simply short-term expediency. Pragmatism determines the
validity of an action in terms of its long-term consequences. This means that one does not limit one's inquiry
into the consequences of an act to the scope of either immediate or long-term usefulness to self or others. Examining the consequences of an action pragmatically must extend
far beyond a consideration of all the possible, useful
effects it will undoubtedly produce. Since the most significant consequences of our actions are those that affect
us specifically as persons, the study of consequences
cannot be reduced to the limits of utility. Consequences

develop or destroy our character; they either integrate or fragment us as persons.

In an earlier work, *A Processive World View for Pragmatic Christians*, I have argued that one can justify martyrdom (giving up one's life to maintain one's integrity by bearing witness to the validity of a principle or truth) on pragmatic grounds. In fact, I show that such an act might even be regarded as morally necessary in the light of the pragmatic criterion of examining all the foreseeable consequences of the alternative choices available in a particular situation.

Sometimes people are confronted with a demand to either face execution or perform an act which in their judgment will fragment them and destroy their personal integrity. In such a situation pragmatic criteria for evaluating moral acts may well lead an individual or group to decide that to perform a particular action to which they cannot commit themselves conscientiously is equivalent to destroying themselves. This is to say, that for this individual or group the consequence of performing the act would be to fragment them or destroy their character so that to do it would be tantamount to death. Thus they may decide that accepting physical death at the hands of another is the only meaningful alternative open to them because it alone enables them to maintain their integrity and exercise their freedom.

These facts drastically weaken the so-called pragmatic arguments against a firm, Christian non-violent stand. Nevertheless, they do not necessarily place Christians in the position of having to avoid all non-violent opposition to evil. On the basis of their understanding of the biblical evidence, many Christians feel that the use of a great variety of non-violent strategies is their right.

To delve in depth into the strategies of non-violence

is far beyond our scope. There is a whole corpus of literature describing non-violent strategies and illustrating
the fact that they frequently have an utterly disarming and
devastating effect on aggressors. The use of such strategies makes non-violence a very positive activity although
one in which persons must be prepared to accept much suffering, hardship and occasionally, death. Christian non-
violence does not leave one totally defenseless nor does it
give aggressors an unimpeded opportunity to do whatever
they choose. Non-violence is not directed toward the success of evil, but toward peace, that is, the experience,
externally, of harmonious, ongoing interactions among persons and nations and the experience, internally, of the
peace of Christ. The absence of the former is an obstacle
to the latter.

Our work, in sum, focuses almost exclusively on the
spiritual and theological foundations for non-violence,
rather than on strategies for living non-violently. The
final chapter adds a slightly different dimension to the
book. The Movement for a New Society (MNS) is a Quaker-
based movement committed to building community and working
by non-violent means to bring about radical social change.
MNS maintains that its inspiration and motivation to strive
to promote non-violence have been inherited from its Quaker
forefathers.

The Movement strives assiduously to be thoroughly ecumenical because it is committed to developing universal
community. Much of its literature appears to be almost totally secular in nature. Nevertheless, like many other
modern organizations committed to performing works of service, it is operating on a reserve of spiritual energy that
is solidly Christian, but too infrequently acknowledged as
such. Since commitment to non-violence is meaningless

apart from action that is non-violent, and since the spiritual energy and inspiration behind this Movement's non-
violent action is Quaker Christian, the article enables us
to illustrate how Christian principles regarding non-violence can be put into action.

THE OLD TESTAMENT

by Edward J. Crowley

*As early as the second century A.D. there were
Christians who were repelled by the violent, warlike character of the God of the Old Testament.
A fundamental belief of Christianity is, however,
that the Father of our Lord Jesus Christ is the
God of the Old Testament. Therefore, the rejection of this God raises serious problems for
Christianity. E. Crowley indicates that the Old
Testament need not be a scandal in its approach
to violence if it is correctly understood. This
chapter shows that the wealth of information acquired in this century about the Old Testament
world makes possible a new view of Old Testament
violence.*

"They shall beat their swords into ploughshares, and
their spears into pruning hooks; nation shall not lift up
sword against nation, neither shall they learn war any
more" (Isa 2:4; Mic 4:13).[1] Is this classical prophetic
picture of a peaceful future just an aberration, an unreal-
izable ideal in the harsh world of the Old Testament?

There are the stories of Abraham going to war (Gen
14:14-17), Simeon and Levi slaughtering the men of Shechem
(Gen 34:25), Moses committing murder (Exod 2:11-12), Joshua
devastating the Canaanites (Josh 6:21; 8:21-29; 11:1-23),
and in the book of Judges continuous wars and violence from
without and within. Wars and slaughters continue through
the books of Samuel and Kings.[2] It seems difficult to
explain all this away, to mitigate this mass of violence.

REASSESSMENT

This chapter will assemble some recent interpretations of these, as well as other, biblical texts which will make it possible to see the violence in a different light. These interpretations originally arose, not to deal specifically with the question of non-violence, but to present the best possible historical reconstruction of the incidents dealt with in the texts. The word "reconstruction" is used deliberately. Some readers will object to any reconstruction and will want to read the biblical texts "as they are."[3] To these readers it must be pointed out that such an approach often has to put up at best with enumerating disconnected items, and at worst with leaving obvious contradictions.

Reconstruction on the other hand tries to get at the purposes of conflicting accounts. Frequently the purpose is not so much to describe what happened as to give the significance of what happened. Once such a purpose is taken into account, it often becomes possible to fit formerly conflicting accounts into an adequate general picture. In addition, there is then the added hope of grasping what the authors saw in events and this can bring a particular theological understanding of a text into sharper focus. A good deal of this chapter will concentrate on trying to do precisely this with the accounts in Exodus, Joshua and Judges.

PATRIARCHAL PERIOD

In any study of non-violence in the Old Testament the stories of the "wars of conquest" in the books of Joshua and Judges, along with some incidents in the books of Exodus and Numbers, provide the greatest difficulty. In contrast, the references to Abraham going to war (Gen 14) and Simeon and Levi attacking Shechem (Gen 34) are anomalies in

Gen 12-50. Otherwise, throughout these chapters we see a peaceful penetration of Canaan by the Patriarchs.[4] Even the negotiations between Jacob and the prince of Shechem (Gen 33:18-34:31) have been considered an indication of how peaceful arrangements were worked out between the Israelite tribes and Canaanite city-states during the former's settlement in the land, even though at first sight the outcome this time was not so peaceful.[5]

This interpretation explains why there is no mention of any hostilities at Shechem in the book of Joshua; there are contacts (Josh 8:30-35; 24:1-28) but no conflict. Moreover, there are good arguments for considering the story of Simeon and Levi's violence to be secondary developments in Gen 34, added under the influence of Gen 49:5-7, which speaks of these brothers or tribes as violent and cruel.[6] For the purposes of this study, it can be noted that in the final form of Genesis the exceptional violence of Gen 34 is to be read in the light of the unfavourable reaction of Gen 49:5-7.

EXODUS

The story of the murder of an Egyptian overseer by Moses (Exod 2:11-15) must be examined a little more closely. As G. Mendenhall points out, "the great importance of this narrative for the origins of the religious ideology of ancient Israel is indicated by the fact that it is the only story preserved about Moses between infancy and his experience at the burning bush."[7] Mendenhall thinks that the question of one of the Hebrews in v.13, "Who made you a prince and a judge over us?" is a challenge to force and violence. Moreover, he emphasizes that "early Israel rejected entirely the idea that God had delegated to some autocrat the legitimate power to put human beings to death."[8]

Two other points emphasized by Mendenhall should also be noted. First, in chapter 3 of *The Tenth Generation*, Mendenhall thoroughly refutes the idea that blood feud was a social characteristic of early Israel.[9] Recent linguistic studies require a radical reassessment of previous translations of the Hebrew work *nqm* as vengeance or revenge. In fact, both in Israel and neighbouring societies, power to act for redress or deliverance had been turned over exclusively to the highest authority and in Israel that was God alone. Moreover, it is redress or deliverance, not revenge or vengeance.

Secondly, Mendenhall explains the Exodus and Covenant (Exod 1-24) as the withdrawal from an oppressive situation in Egypt by a group of slave-labour captives, "a mixed multitude" (Num 11:4), who then became united by covenant into a community "based on common objectives rather than common interests--on ethic rather than on covetousness."[10] Central to this was belief in a God with whom they had entered into covenant. From that point on they would not be subject to earthly lords, but to this one Lord alone. Most importantly in this explanation there is no room for violence, either in the beginnings or the goals of this new community.

DIVINE WARRIOR

In fact, a careful reading of Exod 13:17-15:21 indicates no warlike activity by the Israelites. . . . As de Vaux puts it, ". . . according to the text, the Israelites did nothing and . . . Yahweh[11] destroyed the Egyptians while they looked on. It was undoubtedly a war, but it was a war in which Yahweh played the leading part as a warrior."[12] Two questions suggest themselves here. The first, in what way could God be a warrior? The second, is this not merely a transfer of blame for violence from Israel to God?

In regard to the first question, although this will not justify an unquestioning acceptance of a link between the all-holy God and the horrors of war, the idea of God as a warrior is not an unfamiliar one.[13] The New Testament refers to heavenly battles, but in them angels are the warriors.[14] This imagery of angelic warriors goes back to the book of Daniel.[15] But in earlier Old Testament books God himself is the warrior. "In that day the Lord with his hard and great and strong sword will punish Leviathan the fleeing serpent, Leviathan the twisting serpent, and he will slay the dragon that is in the sea" (Isa 27:1).[16] "Awake, awake, put on strength, O arm of the Lord; awake, as in days of old, the generations of long ago. Was it not you that cut Rahab in pieces, that pierced the dragon? Was it not you who dried up the sea, the waters of the great deep, who made the depths of the sea a way for the redeemed to pass through?" (Isa 51:9-10).[17]

ANCIENT UGARIT

In each of these texts, the sea and the various monsters (Leviathan, dragon, Rahab) are embodiments of the chaotic forces subdued in the course of creation and now kept under control by the creator's power. This imagery is only intelligible and meaningful against the background of ancient Near Eastern myth. The sea and its monsters are symbols of chaos in both Babylonian and Canaanite mythology. There is no doubt now after the discoveries at Ras Shamra, ancient Ugarit,[18] beginning in 1929, that Canaanite myths have most directly influenced the biblical tradition. One example will be enough to illustrate how the Bible is related to these 14th-13th century texts from northern Syria. The god of death, Mot, warns Baal not to boast just "because you smote Lotan (Leviathan) the slippery serpent, made an end of the twisting serpent, the

mighty one with seven heads."[19] The similarity of Isa
27:1 to this is indeed striking.

   After this necessary digression, it is now possible to
examine Exod 13:17-15:21 in a new way, a way that will provide a new assessment of the turbulence and violence of
these chapters. As mentioned before, a careful reading of
these chapters shows that Yahweh played the leading part as
a warrior. Exod 14:31 and 15:3 are explicit on this and
the whole poem of Exod 15:1-18 is a song of victory in honour of Yahweh. The later biblical references[20] to the
Reed Sea incident definitely make use of the Canaanite imagery to give "mythical" depth to the event. However, is
this imagery present in these chapters of Exodus, especially in Exod 15 which is considered by F. Cross to have been
written very early?[21]

STORM-TOSSED SEA

   Cross speaks of a "storm-tossed sea that is directed
against the Egyptians by the breath of the deity."[22] He
points out that the sea is not personified or hostile, but
is a passive instrument in Yahweh's control. Moreover, he
is very clear that there is no question of a mythological
combat between two gods. Instead he sees a very strong
impact of historical events on the narrative.[23] But he
also points to a dialectic at work in the development of
Israelite religion, and along with a concern for history
there was a clear line of continuity with the mythopoeic
patterns of Canaanite myth. In fact, Cross states, "The
power of the mythic pattern was enormous."[24] Myth is being put at the service of history to emphasize the fact
that in the liberation of Israel there is a challenge to
mysterious forces of evil that permeate existence. Or as
Cross puts it, the episode at the sea is mythologized in
order to reveal its transcendent meaning.[25]

A comparison of Cross' approach with the analysis of R. de Vaux[26] reveals some contrasts. According to de Vaux, only the song of Miriam (Exod 15:21) is considered to be very early, while the longer poem (Exod 15:1-18) is much later. However, he agrees with Cross that in later biblical texts the miracle at the Sea was described as a victory of Yahweh over the sea and cosmic enemies[27] and that there was borrowing from Canaanite mythology. Moreover, he thinks that "this cosmic transposition is already obvious in Exodus 15."[28]

It must be admitted, however, that the mythical element is much more subdued in Exod 15 compared to Ps 77:17-20 or Isa 51:9-11, written centuries later. The sea in Exod 15, for instance, is not an enemy to be overcome by God, but an ally. In the later poems the sea is a symbol of evil. This heightening of myth in the later material may be considered a progressively more enlightened attempt to probe the mysterious depths of evil from which Israel was delivered.

EXODUS 14

On the other hand, Exod 14 contains no mythical elements. However, a closer study of the chapter is warranted in order to discover other influences at work in the development of the narrative. Such a discovery will, it is hoped, put the violence there in a different light.

Literary critics are in general agreement that there are two different accounts intermingled in Exod 14. In one Moses' rod and outstretched hand "divided" the waters so that Israel crossed on dry ground. Then Moses stretched out his hand again and the waters engulfed the Egyptians. In the other version, the pillar of cloud came between the Israelites and Egyptians, an east wind dried up the sea, then Yahweh looked down on the Egyptians, threw them into

confusion, and clogged the wheels of their chariots. Then
the waters returned and Yahweh overthrew (RSV "routed") the
Egyptians in the sea. In this second account there is no
reference to the Israelites crossing the sea: they were
encamped by the sea, watching the Egyptians approach, (Exod
14:1.9-10) and were told to stay there and just watch
(14:13).

In this second story, Yahweh's "great work" (14:31)
was not the crossing by the Israelites, but the destruction
of the Egyptians, just as in the early song of Miriam in
Exod 15:21 or in the longer poem of Exod 15:1-18. Any attempts to introduce war-like activity by the Israelites
here are completely gratuitous.[29]

As de Vaux points out, each of the two stories in Exod
14 is complete in itself.[30] As just noted, in the second
one it is Yahweh who destroys the Egyptians, using wind,
cloud and fire. In the first one, in contrast, it is Moses
who acts to "divide" the waters, to let the Israelites escape and to drown the Egyptians. Further analysis is needed to deal with the violence of this destruction or drown-
ing.

RIVER AND SEA

It is not worthwhile to speculate on how and why these
two different accounts arose. However, it can be asked why
the first one emphasizes the dividing of the waters, which
is not even mentioned in the second? The answer is available in Exod 15, where in verses 4-10 there is a description of the destruction of the Egyptians in the sea, while
in verses 15-17 there is a reference to a "crossing," which
in the context can only be a crossing of the Jordan.

The relationships between Exod 14-15 and Josh 3-4 are
very difficult to determine, especially due to the fact
that there seem to be several levels of editing in the lat-

ter.[31] However, de Vaux makes a very good case for the
"crossing" in Exod 14-15 being a replica of the crossing of
the Jordan, although it is described with a different vo-
cabulary and with a heightening of the miraculous element
to some extent.[32]

F. Cross too holds that the story of the crossing of
the Jordan has influenced the stories at the Sea.[33] His
study is valuable in reducing the warlike and violent aspects of both chapters 14 and 15 of Exodus. For if he is
right, some of these happenings were events of ritual and
liturgy instead of violent acts on the stage of history.
He is of the opinion that a later ritual, celebrating the
Exodus-Conquest and centered at Gilgal,[34] involved a procession from Shittim,[35] across the Jordan, and then on to
Gilgal. The river was dammed up ("divided") so that Israel
in battle arrray and carrying the ark could pass over on
dry ground. This was a reenactment of the crossing of the
sea as well as the "crossing over" to the new land. The
procession would be followed by a covenant-renewal ceremony
at Gilgal[36]

R. de Vaux, however, does not think there was such an
early liturgy at Gilgal, because by the time Gilgal became
a sanctuary shared by all the tribes (which would be in the
period of Samuel and Saul or even David), the ark, essential to the ceremony, was first with the Philistines, later
at Kiriath-jearim and finally at Jerusalem.[37] Nevertheless, de Vaux admits that Josh 3-5 is cultic in character.
Instead of a liturgy at Gilgal, he thinks there was a sacred discourse recited there where the twelve stones were
displayed. However, de Vaux had earlier stated that the
crossing of the Jordan and the arrival of the Israelites at
Gilgal are actually described as a liturgical procession.

Whether it all began at Gilgal or not, the link in
Josh 4:21-23 between the two crossings (Jordan and Reed

Sea) is reflected in Pss 66:6; 74:13; 114:3.5. Moreover,
there can be no doubt about the cultic influence in the
story of the Israelites crossing the sea on dry ground.
What Cross says of Exod 15:16b-17 could be applied to the
prose account in Exod 14 too: the author "wrote from the
point of view of Israel after the Conquest, or rather from
the point of view of one reenacting the conquest, including
both the episode of the sea and the passing over into the
land to a Palestinian sanctuary."[38] Finally, such cultic
fusing of River and Sea could be fostered by the pairing in
Canaanite myth of Prince Sea and Judge River, chaotic forces to be overcome by Baal.[39]

DIVINE WARRIOR AGAIN

At the beginning of the discussion of Exod 13:17-15:21
it was pointed out that these texts contain no warlike activity of Israel. But what can now be said of God's warlike activity? When the influence of the Gilgal cult on
Exod 14 is taken into account, there remains in chapter 14
exactly the same picture as in Exod 15: a stormy sea directed by Yahweh against the Egyptians. To understand what
is implied in this, it must be emphasized that ancient Israel had a different notion than we of divine activity.
They saw God's activity, not just in what we call the miraculous, but in everything. Anything that happened was
caused by God. Intermediate or secondary causes were less
emphasized. If the Egyptians died in a storm, according to
this way of thinking God had caused it. Our culture of
course still has a survival of such primitive notions in
the horrible legal term "Act of God." Hurricanes, torna-
does, earthquakes, and now nuclear disasters are referred
to as "Acts of God," despite the fact that the natural
causality or the human responsibility involved is well
known. Ancient Israel can readily be excused for their way

of thinking. They had another world view and could make use of a disaster to the Egyptian pursuers to give expression to their conviction that their God was providentially delivering them from danger and oppression. So the violence in Exod 13:17-15:21 is the violence of a stormy sea.[40]

This storm imagery occurs again in descriptions of the "Divine Warrior" in a march of conquest from the southern mountains.[41] But except for the poetry of Judg 5:4-5, most of the very complicated books of Joshua and Judges seem filled with very earthy war and violence.

JOSHUA

In regard to the complications of the books of Joshua and Judges, R. de Vaux states that the problem of the settlement of the Israelites in Canaan and the development of the twelve-tribe system is the most difficult problem in the whole history of Israel.[42] This is very easily overlooked, because at first sight the biblical texts seem to give a very simple description of a quick military conquest. It goes like this: after an apparent initial repulse[43] of an attempt to enter from the south, the twelve tribes under the leadership of Moses make a long detour around the Dead Sea (Num 21-25) and conquer and divide territory east of the Jordan (Num 32). The victorious march across the Jordan and into Canaan continues under the leadership of Joshua (Num 27; 31-34; Josh 1-12). However, even the non-critical reader takes note of the treaty with the Gibeonites (Josh 9) and the seemingly peaceful settlement of the hill country of Ephraim[44] as well as the absence of military operations at Shechem (Josh 24).[45] This seems to indicate the presence of some Israelite tribes inside Canaan before the Exodus.[46]

A further complication is presented by Judg 1:1-2:5:

after the death of Joshua individual tribes still have to
acquire their assigned territories west of the Jordan; in
the book of Joshua this generally had already been done.

So a brief survey is needed of the various hypotheses
or reconstructions that try to deal with the difficulty of
assembling from Numbers, Joshua and Judges a coherent view
of the "conquest" or "settlement." Special note will be
taken of the views of those who see not a conquest but a
peaceful settlement.[47]

PEACEFUL SETTLEMENT

A. Alt, M. Noth, and more recently, M. Weippert give
great emphasis to such a peaceful occupation by the Israelites of the less populated portions of Canaan.[48] They
believe that this occupation, beginning some time before or
after 1300 B.C. and continuing until about 1100 B.C., was
generally uneventful and therefore left no deep impression
on tradition. But in the course of two centuries there
would be some fighting or skirmishing whenever an attempt
was made to extend their territory by seizing land from the
nearby city-states. These military exploits made a greater
impression on their memory than the less spectacular events
of everyday life. Moreover, they claim that the conquest
tradition especially arose from aetiological[49] stories to
explain, for example, why there were ruins at Jericho, why
Ai was called a "ruin," why Gibeonites were employed in an
Israelite sanctuary (Josh 9), or why a cave in the plain of
Makkedah was blocked by great stones (Josh 10:16-27).

ARCHEOLOGY

A number of archaeologists would say that Alt, Noth
and Weippert neglect the evidence from archeology about the
destruction in the second half of the 13th century B.C. of
such Canaanite cities as Debir (for those who identify it

with Tell Beit Mirsim), Lachish, Bethel and Hazor. The Alt group would say, however, that these ruins may have resulted from the repeated struggles that took place between the city-states of Canaan, and, after 1200 B.C., from the attacks by the so-called Sea Peoples. Noth and Weippert emphasize too that no writings have been found in these excavations and therefore there can be no certainty about the cause of destruction.[50] It could be an earthquake, or fire, or attack by some unidentified enemy. The 13th century B.C. was a time of upheavals all around the perimeter of the eastern Mediterranean, and the Israelites simply moved in to take advantage of the disruptions and the resulting political vacuum.

PEASANT REVOLT

Another approach is taken by G. Mendenhall who believes that the Israelite people were largely made up of the peasants who had revolted against the now debilitated Canaanite and foreign rulers in the city-states of Canaan.[51] As mentioned before, a new ideology was provided for this revolt by the arrival of those who had escaped from Egypt.[52] Here Mendenhall contrasts the old paganism concerned about perpetuating the king's control over all his enemies with the new religion proclaiming that no one but God was, or could be, in control.[53] In this view there was war, but it was a war of liberation, not a war of conquest or a war pitting one nation against another. The violence here, as in many modern wars of liberation, is violence addressed to a more violent situation. The new situation, according to Y. Aharoni, is reflected in the absence of fortification in several early Iron Age Palestinian sites.[54]

THE BOOK OF JUDGES

In the book of Judges there are still more than enough wars, or at least skirmishes, even if there may be fewer walled cities. Once again, this may be due to wars being able to scar the memory more deeply. However, it is war to defend territory from outside attackers or to react or overreact to unjust activity from within (Judg 19-21). As to the involvement of the "Divine Warrior" in these conflicts, this would be a survival of more mythological notions of cosmic warfare,[55] noted already in connection with Exod 15. The attempts to give an institutional religious atmosphere to the early wars of Israel is now seen to be an idealized creation centuries after the events.[56]

LATER PERSPECTIVES

With the passage of centuries, another perspective on war is provided by a number of psalms and by the later prophets, including the prophet Joel. From the late 6th century B.C.,[57] Joel's message is: "Beat your plough shares into swords. . . ." At first sight this seems like the cry of a warmonger. However, closer analysis reveals not the horrors of war but divine judgment and deliverance.

In Joel the situation was to change from disaster to triumph when correct worship led to right order (2:18 is the pivotal verse) on "the day of Yahweh" (1:15; 2:1; etc.). Behind Joel 4:41-17[58] there may be a ritual for this "day," consisting of a procession with the ark from the valley up to the temple, as in Ps 24:7-10.[59]

The Kidron valley below the Temple area was the place where the ritual destruction of pagan altars and idols took place in the reforms of Kings Asa and Josiah (1 Kgs 15:13; 2 Kgs 23).[60] The Kidron could then be the valley of Jehoshaphat, the setting for Joel 4:9-15 and the doom of the oppressing nations. There in the valley of decision

(4:14), these nations will be judged for what they did to Israel.

The Kidron valley had had other cultic connections as well: royal enthronement rites had taken place there.[61] Just as the jubilant enthronement procession started from this valley after Solomon's anointing (1 Kgs 1:34-40), this other procession would start from there after a ritual of Yahweh's triumph and judgment. For this procession and enthronement read Psalm 47.[62] As in the march of conquest from the southern mountains, nature is convulsed at the coming of the Divine warrior.[63] Other cosmic, mythological motifs are reflected in the emphasis in Joel 4:18-21 on an ideal, paradisaical future.

JOYFUL RITUAL

As indicated already,[64] Israel's wars were no more holy than any war, ancient or modern. The rituals of war that formerly attracted attention are now seen to be common to the ancient Near East; they could not be the foundation of a distinctive religion. How wrong was Wellhausen then when he said: "The war camp was the cradle of the nation, it was also the oldest sanctuary."[65] On the contrary, war imagery was channelled into the sanctuary and changed into joyful ritual.[66] But this must be taken one step further. What is being expressed in ritual is a theological concept, about the universe and salvation. To use modern terminology, what is being taught in this ancient and colourful imagery is that there is a divine providence mysteriously guiding our universe. When human beings get in step (to use a harmless military phrase) with that providence, violence and war will cease.

NOTES

[1]Translations are from the Revised Standard Version.

[2]For instance, in 1 Kgs 19:15-18 the prophet Elijah is "inspired" to set in motion events that culminate in the bloody purge of 2 Kgs 9-10. There are other prophetically inspired assassinations as well; see, for example, 1 Kgs 14:1-16; 15:25-30; 15:33-16:7.

[3]This desire to read the texts *as they are* becomes impossible when we meet conflicting biblical accounts. For example, the description of the conquest in Judg 1-2 conflicts with that of Josh 1-22. See also footnote 12.

[4]R. de Vaux, The Early History of Israel (Philadelphis: Westminster, 1978), p. 461.

[5]M. Weippert, The Settlement of the Israelite Tribes in Palestine (SBT 2/25; London: SCM, 1971), pp. 18-20.

[6]A. de Puy, "Genèse XXXIV et l'histoire," Revue Biblique 76 (1969), pp. 5-49.

[7]G. Mendenhall, The Tenth Generation (Baltimore: The Johns Hopkins University Press, 1973), pp. 20-21.

[8]Ibid., p. 21.

[9]Ibid., pp. 69-104. See also J. Linsey, Jr., "Vengeance," The Interpreter's Dictionary of the Bible Supplementary Volume (hereafter IDBS) (Nashville: Abingdon, 1976), pp. 932-33.

[10]Mendenhall, ibid., pp. 21-22; see also his article, "The Hebrew Conquest of Palestine," The Biblical Archaeologist 25 (1962), pp. 66-87. Further consideration of his approach will be given in the study of Joshua-Judges.

[11]Yahweh: in Hebrew the most personal name of God.

[12]R. de Vaux, The Early History . . . , p. 383. For a concise historical analysis of Exod 13:17 - 15:21 see pages 370-88 of de Vaux. The approach of G. Mendenhall, (see footnotes 7 - 10) to the Exodus from Egypt and the Settlement in Canaan makes use also of socio-political and socio-economic categories. For a commentary on Exodus that concentrates on literary and theological matters see B. Childs, The Book of Exodus: A Critical, Theological Commentary (OTL; Philadelphia: Westminster, 1974). Childs asserts that undue reliance on historical reconstruction often distorts the text by forcing it into a historical background rather than letting the text give its own clues for interpretation. But as one reviewer of Childs (J. Gammie, Catholic Biblical Quarterly 37 (1975), pp. 561-62) puts it: "Childs' program, however, leaves the reader with the feeling that the passages under review are only

secondarily related to the anguish, searchings, trials and heartaches of flesh and blood people." Gammie adds: "Even if historical (and sociological) reconstructions rarely can escape the burden of being hypothetical, can they really be abandoned by a church which continues to seek from the scriptures guidance for its historical life?" For another view of Childs' commentary see M. Newman, "Moses," IDBS, pp. 604-05.

[13]See P. Miller, Jr., The Divine Warrior in Early Israel (Cambridge: Harvard University Press, 1973) and N. Gottwald, "War, Holy," IDBS, pp. 942-44.

[14]For example, see Rev 12:7-17 where "war arose in heaven, Michael and his angels fighting against the dragon . . . and his angels. . . ."

[15]The same Michael is mentioned in Dan 10:13.20-21 and 12:1.

[16]It is sometimes claimed that Leviathan may refer to Assyria and Babylon and that the dragon refers to Egypt. This substitution of the historical for the mythological began in the targum. In regard to this W. Millar, Isaiah 24-27 and the Origin of Apocalyptic (Missoula: Scholars Press, 1976), p. 55, note 1, remarks: "Many scholars have attempted to establish the identity of the beasts. In Proto-Apocalyptic, however, this is of less concern than the recovery of the creation myth itself and its implication for the study of Israel's religion."

[17]For other examples, see Ps 24 and the phrases "the Lord, mighty in battle" (v.8) and "the Lord of hosts (armies)" (v.10). Hab 3:3-15 is a magnificent poem, filled with imagery from Canaanite myth and describing the coming of the Divine warrior. See also Job 26:12-13: Pss 74:13-17; 77:17-20; 89:9-11.

[18]M. Coogan, Stories from Ancient Canaan (Philadelphia: Westminster, 1978) and J. Gibson, Canaanite Myths and Legends (Edinburgh: Clark, 1978) both provide translations of the Ugaritic texts. Gibson has extensive references to the Old Testament. Any worthwhile biblical encyclopedia or dictionary has an article on Ugarit. The most recent would be J. C. de Moor, "Ugarit," IDBS, pp. 928-31. F. Cross, Canaanite Myth and Hebrew Epic (Cambridge: Harvard University Press, 1973), pp. 91-120 proves what enriching insights into biblical texts (for example, Ps 24; Hab 3; Exod 15) are ready at hand when the biblical imagery is traced back to its Canaanite roots.

[19]For a discussion of the translation of this Ugaritic text, see A. van Selms, "A Systematic approach to CTA 5, I, pp. 1-8," Ugarit-Forschungen 7 (1975), pp.477-82. The dragon of Rev 12:3 and Tiamat in the Mesopotamian

creation epic, *Enuma elish*, also have seven heads.

[20]See again Isa 51:9-10; also Ps 74:13-14.

[21]See Cross, Canaanite Myth . . . , pp. 121-24 and the bibliography on p. 121. He considers Exod 15 one of the oldest compositions preserved by biblical sources, and as early as the late 12th or early 11th century B.C.; but this is still a century or two after the Exodus.

[22]Ibid., pp. 131-32.

[23]Ibid., p. 143.

[24]Ibid., p. 143. See also page 89 for a brief summary of the historical and mythical elements already present in patriarchal religion.

[25]Ibid., p. 144.

[26]R. de Vaux, The Early History . . . , pp. 321, 381-84, 388, with bibliography, p. 381, footnote 55.

[27]In Pss 74:13-14; 89:10-11; etc.

[28]R. de Vaux, The Early History . . . , p. 388.

[29]See the attempt to do this by L. Hay, "What Really Happened at the Sea of Reeds," Journal of Biblical Literature 83 (1964), pp. 397-403.

[30]R. de Vaux, The Early History . . . , p. 383. The entire discussion here of Exod 14 is dependent on de Vaux, ibid, pp. 381-88. See also G. Coats, "The Traditio-Historical Character of the Reed Sea Motif," Vetus Testamantum 17 (1967), pp. 253-65.

[31]The most recent study of these chapters of Joshua is F. Langlamet, Gilgal et les récits de la traversée du Jourdain (Jos iii-iv) (Paris: Gabalda, 1969).

[32]R. de Vaux, The Early History . . . , pp. 384-88 and 598-608, discusses the two "crossings" as well as the cultic influences at work there.

[33]F. Cross, Canaanite Myth . . . , pp. 138-39. H. J. Kraus, "Gilgal, Ein Beitrag zur Kultusgeschichte Israels," Vetus Testamentum 1 (1951), pp. 181-99 is the starting point for later studies.

[34]The precise location of Gilgal is unknown, but it was at the eastern limit of the territory of Jericho (Josh 4:19). There may have been an open-air Canaanite sanctuary there, a circle of raised stones. In any case it was the sanctuary where the ark was placed (Josh 4:18-19; 6:6) and where the first Passover was celebrated in the land of Canaan (Josh 5:10-12). The sanctuary became very popular during the early monarchy and remained a place of pilgrimage until the 8th century B.C. (Hos 4:15; 12:12; Amos 4:4;

5:5). See de Vaux, The Early History, pp. 595-96.

[35]Shittim was probably located about 12 km. east of the Jordan River.

[36]F. Cross, Canaanite Myth . . . , p. 138, especially footnote 95. The reference to Deut 27:1-8 gives some basis for speaking of covenant-renewal at Gilgal. When Deut 27:2 speaks of erecting stones, plastering them and writing upon them all the words of the law "on the day you pass over the Jordan," there seems to be a reference to a covenant ceremony, not at Mount Ebal (as in Josh 27:4) which would be too far from the Jordan, but at Gilgal. It would explain the use made of the twelve stones at Gilgal, which parallel the twelve stones at Sinai (Exod 24:4). However, the feast mentioned in Josh 5:10 is the Passover. If later on the Passover was repeated at Gilgal, the damming of the river at the height of the Spring floods would be difficult. As for other times of the year, de Vaux, The Early History . . . , p. 607 says that "there was no need for a miracle to enable the Israelites to cross the Jordan, which could be very easily forded." However, he adds that something seems to have happened that was looked on as miraculous.

[37]R. de Vaux, The Early History . . . , p. 604.

[38]F. Cross, Canaanite Myth . . . , p. 130.

[39]Ibid., pp. 112-44.

[40]In regard to the cloud and fire, see T. V. Mann, "The Pillar of Cloud in the Reed Sea Narrative," Journal of Biblical Literature 90 (1971), pp. 15-30. Mann holds that this imagery is derived from Canaanite mythology surrounding the storm deity. In reference to a storm being behind the sea event, Mann states: "Such naturalistic explanations, however instructive, can hardly offer a completely satisfactory solution to the problem, even though they may indicate historical circumstances behind literary descriptions" (page 30, footnote 69).

[41]See, for example, Judg 5:4-5; Deut 33:2.26-29; Ps 68:7-9; and Hab 3:3-15.

[42]R. de Vaux, The Early History . . . , p. 475 and pp. 635-36.

[43]Num 14:40-45; however, Num 21:1-3 seems to indicate a victory of some kind at some time; see R. de Vaux, ibid., pp. 527-28.

[44]R. de Vaux, ibid., pp. 635-40.

[45]See the earlier discussion of Gen 34 about contacts with Shechem in the time of the Patriarchs.

[46]R. de Vaux, The Early History . . . , p. 669.
Referring to Josh 24, he writes: "We may therefore conclude that Joshua was addressing a group of Israelites who
had not yet accepted the religion of Yahweh." See also
pages 370-76 on several exoduses, some earlier groups being
expelled, others fleeing later on from Egypt. Also see
pages 744-49, where de Vaux discusses the hypothesis that
some of the tribes had never gone down to Egypt.

[47]For a "Conquest" view see Y. Kaufmann, The Biblical Account of the Conquest of Palestine (Jerusalem:
Magnes, 1953). See more recently A. Malamat, "Conquest of
Canaan: Israelite Conduct of War According to Biblical
Tradition," Encyclopaedia Judaica Year Book 1975/76 (Jerusalem: Encyclopaedia Judaica, 1976), pp. 166-82 (with bibliography). Malamat's approach "hopes to reaffirm the ten-
ability of much of biblical tradition and therefore re-
trieve it from the clutches of current criticism." This
presumes as already answered the question of what the traditions of the Bible itself really were.

[48]See M. Weippert, The Settlement . . . (see footnote 5 above); reference to the various works of Alt and
Noth may be found in Weippert, who, however, modifies their
approach to some extent.

[49]The presence of aetiology does not necessarily indicate the presence of fiction, especially when the aetiology only touches on certain aspects of a narrative. The
most recent work on aetiology is F. Golka, "The Aetiologies
in the Old Testament," Vetus Testamentum 26 (1976), pp. 410-
28 and 27 (1977), pp. 36-47.

[50]M. Weippert, The Settlement . . . , pp. 128-29,
points out that there are stele fragments to shed light on
the period of Assyrian expansion in the 8th century B.C.;
compared to this the 13th-12th centuries B.C. are the "dark
ages." This comparison shows that scepticism on the place
of biblical archaeology should not be developed into a dog-
ma just because of difficulties in connection with the "conquest."

[51]G. Mendenhall, "The Hebrew Conquest of Palestine,"
The Biblical Archaeologist 25 (1962), pp. 66-87 and The
Tenth Generation, pp. 19-31 and passim. See footnote 7
above. See aso N. Gottwald, "The Hypothesis of the Revolutionary Origins of Ancient Israel: A Response to Hauser
and Thompson," Journal for the Study of the Old Testament 7
(1978), pp. 37-52. The articles by Hauser and Thompson and
a response to them by Mendenhall as well are all contained
in the same volume.

[52]The treaties with Gibeon and Shechem (see footnotes 44 and 45 and Jos 9 and 24) would then reflect the

linking up of the exodus group with those who had defected
from their old overlords.

[53]G. Mendenhall, The Tenth Generation, p. 25.

[54]Y. Aharoni, "Nothing Early and Nothing Late:
Re-writing Israel's Conquest," The Biblical Archaeologist
39 (1976), pp. 55-76. R. de Vaux, The Early History . . . ,
pp. 488-680 examines all the traditions on the settlement in
Canaan.

[55]P. Miller, The Divine Warrior . . . , pp. 5-6.

[56]See G. Jones, "'Holy War' or 'Yahweh War'," Vetus
Testamentum 25 (1975), pp. 642-58 and N. Gottwald, "War,
Holy," IDBS, pp. 942-43. The so-called "sacral" elements
in Israel's wars are also found in the war customs of
Israel's neighbours.

[57]For the date and a thorough analysis of the book
see G. Ahlström, Joel and the Temple Cult of Jerusalem (SVT,
vol. 21; Leiden: Brill, 1971).

[58]3:14-17 in RSV. See notes in RSV at 2:28 and 3:1.

[59]G. Ahlström, Joel . . . , p. 76. See the related
imagery of the march of conquest from the southern mountains (footnote 41 above). Recall too the ritual of Gilgal, as described by Cross (see footnote 33); in Joel 4:18
there is even a link between the temple and Shittim (see
Josh 3:1). See further W. Millar, Isaiah 24-27 . . . ,
pp. 82-95 for a study of "The Divine Warrior Hymn and the
Processional Way in the Royal Theology of Hebrew Tradition."

[60]On the connections of the Kidron valley with "To-
pheth" and the valley of Hinnom, see O. Wintermute, "Sites,
sacred," IDBS, pp. 827-29; also L. Bailey, "Gehenna," IDBS,
pp. 353-54.

[61]1 Kgs 1:9.33. On "sacred springs" see O. Wintermute, "Sites, sacred," IDBS, p. 827.

[62]See F. Cross, Canaanite Myth . . . , p. 111.
P. Hanson, The Dawn of Apocalyptic (Philadelphia: Fortress, 1975), pp. 304-08 lists eighteen psalms with a similar thematic pattern of threat, combat, victory, procession and celebration of Yahweh's eternal reign. If a procession in the Kidron Valley was impossible after the destruction of 587 B.C. (see Neh 2:14), then Joel could be using imagery based on a pre-exilic ritual.

[63]Joel 4:15-16. See footnote 41 above. Especially
compare Hab 3:3-15.

[64]See Jones and Gottwald, footnote 56 above.

[65]Quoted in Jones, Vetus Testamentum 25 (175),
p. 642.

[66]Limitations of space make it impossible to discuss warfare in the period of the monarchy or the contemporary "pacifism" of the prophets (see, for example Isa 11-12; 49). It should be noted, moreover, that the prophets frequently refer to the "Divine Warrior" turning in judgment on his chosen people.

THE NEW TESTAMENT AND EARLY CHURCH

by Robert J. Daly, S. J.

By examining the witness of the New Testament and Early Fathers, R. Daly provides a renewed and clarified description of their teaching on non-violence and pacifism. In doing so he highlights the weak biblical basis for the just war theory and the crusading mentality. He argues that the early Christians were pacifists committed to living non-violently and sets forth the biblical basis for a "modified non-violence" understood as a very positive reality intimately related to the central ideal of love. While indicating that Christians are called to resist evil in society, he shows how non-cooperation with evil is consistent with the prohibition against resisting one who is evil.

Part One will treat the New Testament witness in a fairly direct way that does not presume extensive familiarity with biblical exegesis. Part Two will sketch the understanding and witness of the Early Church. Part Three will take up the New Testament material again, or at least a core selection of it, in the manner of a critical exegete.[1] The mutually reinforcing conclusions of these three parts will, I trust, set out clearly the earliest Christian foundations for discussing the place of non-violence in Christian spirituality.[2]

ATTITUDES TOWARD WAR, PEACE AND
NON-VIOLENCE IN THE NEW TESTAMENT

The question of the legitimacy of the use of force is
one of the relatively few living questions to which the New
Testament seems to give direct, practical answers. But
even here--not surprisingly when one considers the variety
of backgrounds and concerns that readers can bring to the
Bible--Christians can find radically different answers to
their questions.

Three basic attitudes characterize much of Christian
reflection on this subject.[3] The early Church was mainly
non-violent and, at times, consciously *pacifist* (i.e.,
no circumstances justify a Christian use of force).[4] From
the time of Constantine the *just war* theory dominated
(i.e., under certain circumstances, when all other means
have failed, a discriminate use of force, as the lesser
evil, may be employed). In the middle ages, the
crusading mentality became dominant (i.e., force may or
should be used in the cause of religion). Since that time,
and to this day, all three positions, in different times
and places, and often in ways that resist easy classification, have been found among Christians.

Moreover, proponents of all these positions claim support in the New Testament. If one is convinced, as most
Christians are, of the basic unity of the New Testament
message in matters necessary to salvation, and if one is
further convinced that one's attitude toward violence is a
matter of fundamental Christian importance, then it is
clear that some way must be found to resolve these contra-
dictory readings of the New Testament. A conflation of
some typical arguments often used in support of these three
positions might read as follows.

The *pacifist* points to the Sermon on the Mount with
its beatitudes (Mt 5:3-10) and love commandment (Mt 5:38-48;

Lk 6:27-36); he/she will point to the same teaching in Paul
(Rom 12:14-21), and quote the words of Jesus: "Put your
sword back into its place, for all who take the sword will
perish by the sword" (Mt 26:52; cf. par.) If he/she has
some acquaintance with New Testament theology, the pacifist
might also try to point out that the Servant Christology of
the New Testament period is consistent only with a position
of pacifism and non-violence.

The *just war* advocate will quote: "Render to Caesar
the things that are Caesar's" (Mk 12:17 parr), and suggest
that Paul's exhortation to obey secular rulers (Rom 13:1-7)
is talking about obedience to a totalitarian military dictatorship. He will remind us of Jesus's praise for the
centurion (Mt 8:5-13; Lk 7:1-10; cf. Acts 10), of John the
Baptist exhorting soldiers to be, in effect, good soldiers
(Lk 3:14), and point out that Jesus' parable of the king
"going to encounter another king in war" (Lk 14:31-32)
seems to take war for granted. Finally, he/she will not
fail to point out the significance of Paul's acceptance of
a military escort in order to foil a plot against his life
(Acts 23:12-35).

The advocates of *crusade* point to Jesus' forcible
cleansing of the temple (Jn 2:13-22; Mk 11:15-19;
Mt 21:12-17; Lk 19:45-48) and to several strong sayings of
Jesus, such as "Do not think that I have come to bring
peace on earth; I have not come to bring peace, but a
sword" (Mt 10:34), and: "Let him who has no sword sell his
mantle and buy one" (Lk 22:36), and: "The law and the prophets were until John; since then the good news of the
kingdom of God is Preached, and every one enters it violently" (Lk 16:16; cf. Mt 11:12).

Is the New Testament hopelessly confused, self-contra-
dictory? Or is it possible to approach the New Testament
on a deeper level than mere proof-texting, and find there a

basic and consistent thrust in its teaching? Scripture
scholars overwhelmingly agree that there is such a basic
thrust in the New Testament, and it is quite clearly in the
direction of pacifism and non-violence. The traditional
just war and crusading proof-texts simply cannot stand up
under the light of an even rudimentary exegesis.

"JUST WAR" TEXTS EXAMINED

Popular homiletic application aside, neither the words
over the coin of tribute: "Render to Caesar the things
that are Caesar's" (Mk 12:17; Mt 22:21; Lk 20:25) nor their
context can be made to bear the meaning that anything more
is being talked about here than Caesar's taxes. We are not
even told whether Jesus actually paid Roman taxes. Further, whether or not one takes these as historical words of
Jesus, their intended meaning seems to be ironic. With its
graven image of Caesar, the coin of tribute was itself an
offense against Jewish Law, and yet it is readily produced
upon Jesus' request. His words, then may mean nothing more
than the ironic suggestion that they simply return to its
origin this sacrilegious coin. In the context of Luke's
gospel, this passage suggests criticism rather than support
of Roman rule.[5]

Romans 13:1-7 certainly exhorts Christians to be obedient subjects and avoid revolution or sedition. This passage is about the use of force, and the appropriate Christian reaction to it, by those charged with maintaining civil order. To go beyond this, and argue that this text justifies war or the use of force on the grand scale (as indeed some Christians did argue in Nazi Germany), especially
in the light of the non-violent teaching of the previous
chapter (Rom 12:14-21), is to go wholly beyond the evidence
of the text.

At a time when the administration of the empire and the duties of public service were generally in the hands of the military, John the Baptist's instructions to soldiers (Lk 3:14) and the relatively frequent appearance of soldiers in the narratives of the Gospels and Acts say nothing directly about the legitimacy of war. Regarding Jesus' praise for the centurion (Mt 8:10; Lk 7:9), it is his *faith* and not his profession that is being praised.

To adduce the Lukan parable of one king going to war against another (Lk 14:31-32) in support of the just war theory offends not only against widely accepted norms for interpreting the prables,[6] but also against common sense. It would be equivalent to using Jesus' comparison of the coming of the Son of Man to the coming of a thief in the night (Mt 24:42-44; cf. Lk 12:39-40) as a justification for thievery in the night.

However, Paul's ready acceptance of a military escort is more to the point (Acts 23:12-35). The obvious implications are that Paul and Luke approve at least of the secular state using the amount of force which is necessary to maintain public order and protect the innocent (which is also the clear meaning of Rom 13:1-7). If one is searching for a basic New Testament position, this seems to modify somewhat the apparent absoluteness of the New Testament rejection of the use of force.

"CRUSADE" TEXTS EXAMINED

All four evangelists narrate the cleansing of the temple (Jn 2:13-22; Mk 11:15-19; Mt 21:12-17; Lk 19:45-48). John, who alone mentions that Jesus used a whip of cords (Jn 2:15), serves as the star witness for many who seek legitimation for the use of force in the cause of religion. But this uniqueness, coupled with the fact that John is also unique in locating the incident at the beginning rath-

er than at the end of Jesus' public ministry, suggests that
John's intention was less to communicate historical detail
than to emphasize Jesus' zeal to purify the house of God.
In any case, despite the impression given by some translations, the whip of cords was apparently applied not to people but only to the sheep and goats. Thus, if one were to
insist on some kind of direct practical application, which
does not seem to be what the evangelist intends, one might
see in the passage a model for direct-action, non-violent
protest which is careful to avoid personal injury. To find
there support for the use of force in the cause of religion
goes wholly beyond the content and intention of the text.

A frequently quoted crusading text is Jesus' statement: "Do not think that I have come to bring peace on
earth: I have not come to bring peace, but a sword"
(Mt 10:34). However, one of the verbal variants with which
Luke records the same logion is the replacement of "sword"
with "divisions," specifying, as he sometimes does, a nar-
rower range of interpretation than what is suggested in the
text of Matthew.[7] The New Testament commonly uses
"sword" in a symbolic sense. That Matthew also had the
symbolic sense "division" in mind is indicated by the fact
that both he and Luke record the logion as going on to
speak of the intra-familial dissension that inevitably a-
rises when only some members of a family become Christian.[8]

The evangelists' awareness of the pain of these dis-
sensions must have been particularly strong, for they were
writing at a time when relations between Judaism and the
new Christian communities had already degenerated into mis-
trust and enmity. It seems to be a classic case where the
situation-in-life of the early communities is decisive for
interpreting the meaning of a recorded saying of Jesus.
Also at play is the Semitic mode of heightening the poign-

ancy of an unwanted tragic effect by expressing it in terms
of purpose. A paraphrase of the saying could end something
like: ". . . but the tragic effect of my coming has been,
alas, dissension."

The famous two-sword passage, which played such an important role in medieval exegesis and political theology,[9] is also cited to support crusades. At the end of
Luke's account of the Last Supper, we read:

> And he said to them, "When I sent you out with no
> purse or bag or sandals, did you lack anything?"
> They said, "Nothing." He said to them, "But now,
> let him who has a purse take it, and likewise a
> bag. And let him who has no sword sell his man-
> tle and buy one. For I tell you that this scrip-
> ture must be fulfilled in me, 'And he was reckon-
> ed with transgressors'; for what is written about
> me has its fulfillment." And they said, "Look,
> Lord, here are two swords." And he said to them,
> "It is enough" (Lk 22:35-38).

To interpret this as a call to arms, as a brief glimmer of
light on the real Jesus, Jesus the revolutionary, whose political propensities have generally been quite successfully
expurgated by the evangelists, runs counter to the overwhelming weight of evidence available to us.[10] Furthermore, "practically all commentators take the reference to
purse, wallet and sword figuratively,"[11] i.e., as an attempt to prepare the disciples for the trials and opposition that their lives of service will occasion.

Behind this passage may also be something like Jose-
phus' description of the life-style of the Essenes, that
"they carry nothing whatever with them on their journeys,
except arms as a protection against brigands" (*Jewish War*
II, No. 125). This fits in well with what was apparently
the original situation-in-the-gospel of this passage:

Jesus' instructions to the missionary disciples (Lk 9:1-5;
10:4; Mk 6:7-11; Mt 10:1-14).[12] A plausible reason for
Luke to relocate this incident into the situation of the
Last Supper may have been his embarrassment or perplexity
at the conduct of the disciples. For the mention of the
two swords does prepare the reader somewhat for the shock
of seeing one of Jesus' closest followers so misunderstand
Jesus as Suffering Servant and the internal meaning of the
Eucharist as to try to defend him with the sword. Thus
Jesus' reaction: "It is enough" (Lk 22:38; cf. 22:49-51)
stands out more clearly as a formula of dismissal (i.e.,
"enough of this"--cf. Deut 3:26) spoken, likely enough,
with irony and exasperation.

Finally, the striking logion about taking or entering
the kingdom of heaven by force (Mt 11:12; Lk 16:16) is a
notorious *crux interpretum*: no reliable exegete presumes
to know for certain what it means. Norman Perrin's
suggestion that is means that "the time of God's activity
as king is now, and that the form of this activity can be
envisaged in terms of conflict" which can, in the short
run, "issue in defeat as well as victory" is probably not
far from the mark.[13] In any case, to draw from this
saying conclusions which run counter to the main thrust
of New Testament teaching is wholly out of place.

NON-VIOLENCE AND PACIFISM IN THE NEW TESTAMENT

To sum up, a careful reading of those texts which have
commonly been brought forward in support of the crusade
mentality reveal not support but actually opposition to
this position. But some of the texts brought forward in
support of the just war theory are not quite so easily dismissed. Lk 3:14, Acts 23:12-35 and Rom 13:1-7 fall into
this group. When one places them in the context of the
whole New Testament and its pervasive commitment to what we

today call pacifism and non-violence, they recede into the
background and do little more than remind us that the New
Testament witness on this point is not wholly unequivocal.

This is admittedly an over-simplified way of dealing
with "uncomfortable" texts. But it may not be without significance that none of these three texts claim to be giving
either the actual words or the direct teaching of Jesus.
When we ask if there are such words and direct teaching,
the answer is obvious. The words of Jesus in the beatitudes and in his preaching of the universal application of
the love commandment in the Matthaean Sermon on the Mount
and its Lukan parallels (Mt 5:3-12, 38-48; Lk 6:20-23,
27-36) come through with the highest possible authority and
clarity. Exegetes disagree about whether, or to what extent, the exact words of Jesus are recoverable from these
texts, but there is fairly wide agreement that it is the
message of Jesus that is coming through loud and clear.

René Coste, for example, is summarizing a broad consensus of gospel criticism when he affirms:

> It is an incontestable fact that Christ did
> preach nonviolence, both as a condition and a
> consequence of the universal love that he taught
> us. To pretend, as is sometimes done, that his
> directives are only meant to be applied to indi-
> vidual or ecclesial relationships is a supposi-
> tion that is nowhere justified in the writings of
> the New Testament. Evangelical morality embraces
> the whole of human activity: only methods of ap-
> plication may differ according to the various
> levels at which it operates. The Christian, more
> than anyone else, is bound to use only peaceful
> means, both in his collective relationships and
> his individual ones. Otherwise, he is not faith-
> ful to the demands made by his master.[14]

The obvious meaning of words such as "Love your enemies, do good to those who hate you, bless those who curse you, pray for those who abuse you" is there for anyone who can read. This meaning is heightened still further by the added injunction: "To him who strikes you on the cheek, offer the other also" (Lk 6:27-29; cf. Mt 5:39, 43-44). And the correctness of this obvious meaning is confirmed by the way Jesus lived, steadfastly refusing to use or to allow anyone else to use force in his cause. He showed by his actions and his life-style that the Suffering Servant Christology of the New Testament was not a mere theory but the expression of a concretely lived way of life.

THE EARLY CHURCH

Even when in disagreement with each other, Christians have generally agreed in granting special authority to the life and practice of the early Christians. These first followers of Jesus clearly understood non-violence to be what Jesus preached, and they generally lived up to it. To be a Christian meant to be non-violent. In the late second century when we begin to find evidence of Christians in the army, the meager indications that we have suggests that this may have been considered a proper occupation for a Christian only as long as it did not involve fighting (a soldier's normal duties were the peaceful functions of public administration and civil service). Apparently, Christians usually refused to take part in public life, as Celsus complained in his polemic against the Christians in the late second century. Part of this may well be just typical anti-Christian rhetoric, but Origen does accept the fact of the charge.[15] The main reason for Christians acting this way seems to have been their awareness of the incompatibility of violence and bloodshed with love.[16]

Tertullian, the North African lawyer-convert writing
in the late second and early third century, claims to be
representing the basic Christian moral stance as he refuses
to allow Christians to participate in the ceremonial crown-
ing of soldiers.

> To begin with the real ground of the military
> crown, I think we must first inquire whether war-
> fare is proper at all for Christians. What sense
> is there in discussing the merely accidental,
> when that on which it rests is to be condemned?
> Do we believe it lawful for a human oath to be
> superadded to the one divine, for a man to come
> under promise to another master after Christ, and
> to abjure father? . . . Shall it be lawful to
> make an occupation of the sword, when the Lord
> proclaims that he who uses the sword shall perish
> by the sword (Mt 26:52)? And shall the son of
> peace (Mt 5:9) take part in the battle when it
> does not become him even to sue at law (I Cor
> 6:1-8)? And shall he apply the chain, and the
> prison, and the torture, and the punishment, who
> is not the avenger even of his own wrongs? Shall
> he, forsooth, either keep watch-service for oth-
> ers more than for Christ, or shall he do it on
> the Lord's day, when he does not even do it for
> Christ Himself?[17]

In the blatant legalism of this passage we can recognize in Tertullian the early ancestor of those who would
base their pacifism on the prohibition of killing, or on
the inconsistency of pacifism with the "law" of love. But
Christianity does not mix well with legalism, nor is it
well served by reducing it to a set of rules. The Christian way of life is far too sacred and profound a reality
to base it upon a legalistic interpretation of some chosen

texts as Tertullian does when he writes that "Christ in
disarming Peter ungirt every soldier" (*On Idolatry* 19).
This does not serve well the Christ who so steadfastly set
his face against excessive legalism. But, legalism or not,
his preaching does represent the faith of the primitive
church. It is interesting to note, however, that there are
indications even in Tertullian's own writings (e.g., *The
Apology* 5; 37; 42) that this pacifism of withdrawal from
worldly involvements is apparently no longer practiced by
all Christians.

Around AD 249, Origen, originally from Alexandria but
then teaching in Palestine, wrote a detailed refutation of
a piece of anti-Christian polemic written by the pagan,
Celsus, some seven decades earlier. Celsus, who was apparently quite well informed about Christianity, had bit-
terly complained that Christians, by their policy of withdrawal from involvement in secular affairs, were shirking
their civic and moral responsibilities. It is interesting
that Origen, probably the most gifted and influential
Christian writer of his day, does not deny the charge. In
a passage pregnant with ramifications for the later Christian development of the just war theory, he justifies the
Christians' behaviour:

> In the next place, Celsus urges us "to help the
> king with all our might, and to labor with him in
> the maintenance of justice, to fight for him; and
> if he require it, to fight under him, or lead an
> army along with him." To this our answer is,
> that we do, when occasion requires, give help to
> kings, and that, so to say, a divine help, "put-
> ting on the whole armor of God" (Eph 6:11). And
> this we do in obedience to the injunction of the
> apostle (Paul), "I exhort, therefore, that first
> of all, supplications, prayers, intercessions,

and giving of thanks, be made for all men; for
kings, and for all that are in authority" (1 Tim
2:1-2); and the more any one excells in piety,
the more effective help does he render to kings,
even more than is given by soldiers, who go forth
to fight and slay as many of the enemy as they
can. And to those enemies of our faith who require us to bear arms for the commonwealth, and
to slay men, we can reply: "Do not those who are
priests at certain shrines, and those who attend
on certain gods, as you account them, keep their
hands free from blood, that they may with hands
unstained and free from human blood offer the ap-
pointed sacrifices to your gods; and even when
war is upon you, you never enlist the priests in
the army. If that, then, is a laudable custom,
how much more so, that while others are engaged
in battle, these too should engage as the priests
and ministers of God, keeping their hands pure,
and wrestling in prayers to God on behalf of
those who are fighting in a righteous cause, and
for the king who reigns righteously, that whatever is opposed to those who act righteously may
be destroyed!" And as we by our prayers vanquish
all demons who stir up war, and lead to the violation of oaths, and disturb the peace, we in
this way are much more helpful to the kings than
those who go into the field to fight for them.[18]

Note Origen's open admission of the Christian's obligation to support, albeit only by spiritual means, those
who are "fighting in a righteous cause." He solved the
practical dilemma by envisioning that the Christianization
of the world would bring with it, proportionately, the e-
radication of war. Living in the interior of an empire

largely at peace, it was possible for him to reason this
way. He could admit that some wars might be necessary or
"righteous," but he conceived of them basically as non-
Christian or sub-Christian phenomena in which Christians
themselves could never actually take part.

Augustine, however, was not so easily rid of the problem; for Origen's expectations were not, in fact, borne
out. One may indeed question how genuinely "Christian" the
empire had really become, but the fact remained that there
were no one but Christians left to defend it. While rejecting the "imperial theology" associated with Eusebius,
and remaining quite negative towards any sacral conception
of the empire, when the attacks came Augustine naturally
tended to assume justice to be on the side of the Romans
(which later historians can at least challenge), and to
think that justice was more to be hoped for from a Christian than from a non-Christian government (conveniently
overlooking the fact that some of the barbarians had already been converted to Christianity). He concluded that
Christians could, and in some cases should, defend the empire under the direction of lawful authority. Still, Augustine's interpretation of the Sermon on the Mount as *personally*--i.e., at least in the private sphere--obliging
Christians to lives of non-violence did not change from
that of earlier Christians. But there had been a change in
his view of human life; it had become much more sombre. He
pointed out, sorrowfully, that the non-violence preached by
Jesus was an ideal to which we were, with equal certainty,
unable to attain in this life.

In Augustine's attempt to develop a theory of the legitimate use of force, the Platonizing tendencies of his
thought, among other factors, disposed him to emphasize an
intensely inward ethic and to locate the center of morality
more in attitudes than in acts. This helped him to recon-

cile somewhat the incompatibility which the early Christians felt between love and outward violence. This is
strikingly illustrated in the following group of texts:

> If it is supposed that God could not enjoin war-
> fare because in after times it was said by the
> Lord Jesus Christ, "I say unto you, Resist not
> evil . . . (Mt 5:39)," the answer is that what is
> here required is not a bodily action but an in-
> ward disposition (*Against Faustus* XXII 76; CSEL
> XXV 1 p. 674). Moses in putting to death sinners
> (Exod 32) was moved not by cruelty but by love.
> So also was Paul (1 Cor 5:5) when he committed
> the offender to Satan for the destruction of the
> flesh (*Against Faustus* XXII 79: CSEL XXV 1 p.
> 680-81). Love does not preclude "a sort of kind-
> ly harshness" (*Letters* 138, *Fathers of the
> Church* 20 p. 46); nor does it preclude that se-
> verity which compassion itself dictates (*On the
> Lord's Sermon on the Mount* I xx 63; Migne PL 34,
> 1261). No one indeed is fit to inflict punish-
> ment save the one who has first overcome hate in
> his heart. The love of enemies admits of no dis-
> pensation (*On the Lord's Sermon on the Mount* I
> xx 69-70; Migne PL 34, 1264-65); but love does
> not exclude wars of mercy waged by the good
> (*Letters* 138; *Fathers of the Church* 20
> p. 46-47).[19]

Consistently, Augustine refused to allow self-defense
to the private citizen, since, in this case, the motive
would be self-love, not love of neighbor (cf. *Letters* 47,
5; *On Free Will* I 5). In this he was closely following
his mentor, Ambrose, who stated:

> I do not think that a Christian, a just and wise
> man, ought to save his own life by the death of

another; just as when he meets with an armed robber he cannot return his blows, lest in defending
his life he should stain his love toward his
neighbor. The verdict on this is plain and clear
in the books of the Gospel. "Put up thy sword,
for every one that taketh the sword shall perish
with the sword" (Mt 26, 52). What robber is more
hateful than the persecutor who came to kill
Christ? But Christ would not be defended from
the wounds of the persecutor, for He willed to
heal all by His wounds.[20]

Thus, although Christian theorizing about the just war doctrine has often been unaware of it, Augustine saw his
teaching as consistent with the non-violent ideals of the
Sermon on the Mount.

But, perhaps even more significantly, in terms of the
development of Christian attitudes, two considerations, one
historical and the other anthropological, suggest that the
traditional Christian conception of the just war theory
which historians generally trace back to Augustine may be
flawed at its very roots. Historically, Augustine was
writing at the time of the barbarian invasions and was
grappling with the problem of whether it was allowable, or
even obligatory, for "Christian" Rome to defend itself.
But a modern historian can now make a fairly strong case
that the Romans were not victims of unjust aggression, and
that justice may well have been more on the side of the
barbarians. The systemic import of this is devastating
(for the theory could still be valid even if its historical
development was occasioned by false judgements about what
was just in a given case). The systemic flaw is that each
side in a conflict almost inevitably believes that it, and
it alone, is the unjustly aggrieved party. Secondly, modern theological anthropology is much more integral than the

dichotomized matter-spirit, body-soul relationships familiar to Augustine. It is much harder for most Christians
today to maintain that men and women in the heat of battle,
even of a just and necessary war, can be guided by the dis-
positions of love. But if this cannot be maintained, a
foundational assumption of Augustine's theory has been de-
molished.

Summing up the evidence from the New Testament and the
early Church, the central understanding that Christians are
pacifists committed to the practice of non-violence clearly
prevails. But there is also clear evidence, perhaps going
back to the New Testament itself, that Christians were not
always able to live up to this ideal in every way. Faced
with this reality, Augustine chose to exempt the public
sphere from the full demands of the Sermon on the Mount.

In historical retrospect, one can hardly claim that
the Augustinian solution, and all the various ways in which
it has been understood and applied, has been a great success. For despite its principles and accomplishments,
Christendom does not seem to have been much the less belli-
cose for having been Christian. For, within the basic Augustinian framework, the Christian could, and often did,
conceive of himself in his actual war-making as doing a
Christian thing. Christian nations could, and usually did,
glorify war and joyously celebrate victories as national
triumphs. Granted our flawed moral natures, we may have to
admit that war or systemic violence may perhaps never be
wholly eradicated from human affairs. But if we are
consistently Christian, how can we see war or violence as
anything but a *de facto* denial of our Christianity, as
one of the ultimate human scandals, to avoid which almost
anything should be readily endured.

THE NEW TESTAMENT LOVE COMMAND
AND THE CALL TO NON-VIOLENCE

A few aspects of our presentation, however, still leave something to be desired. For one thing it relies a bit too heavily on the negative: do not be violent, avoid war, etc. Quite rightly we sense that fidelity to Christ must be an essentially positive reality. And as we struggle to find ways to live the modified non-violence that practical Christian realism demands of us,[21] we tend to focus on one, central, over-riding ideal which we call the love command. But it can be misleading to all it the *law* of love, for genuine love cannot ever be commanded in the strict sense of the word.

A different approach which, conceptually at least, might help us out of this impasse would be to focus the obligatory aspects of Christian life less on the "law" of love and more on the missionary command to preach the good news. The central New Testament command would thus be centered more on the missionary command to "make disciples of all nations . . . teaching them to observe all that I have commanded you" (Mt 28:19-20), to be "witnesses to Jesus to the end of the earth" (Acts 1:8), to be "ambassadors for Christ" with his message of reconciliation (2 Cor 5:19-20), i.e., *to preach the good news of Jesus Christ.*[22] (This is, of course, theological reflection which goes beyond the direct meaning of the texts we have quoted.) In any case, the missionary command heightens the Christian obligation to non-violence. For against those who would like to impose religion one can ask how it is possible, if one has really listened to the gospels, to think of being a witness to the true Jesus by means of force or violence.

Another way of approaching the same point is to point out that emphasis on love as *commanded* might push us too strongly in the direction of a purely heteronomic ethic in

which one acts virtuously simply because one is so commanded. I.e., the motive for an ethical act comes *entirely* from outside, in this case, from God. When pushed to
extremes, this view ends in what can be called a theonomic
moral positivism, a position not only at odds with popular
modern views of human autonomy and human dignity, but also
quite inconsistent with a mature understanding of what it
means to be created in God's image and likeness (Gen 1:26)
and to have God's own Spirit dwelling within us.

     These and similar motives (although I cannot pause
here to speculate in what particular combination) were undoubtedly behind some modern attempts, e.g., those of Bultmann and Braun, to locate the essence of the love command
in the subject who is to love. But these too are unsatis-
factory: they tend toward the extremes of a purely auto-
nomic ethic which is quite difficult to reconcile with
Christian faith. But, most decisively, such interpretations don't seem to be reconcilable with those texts of
Matthew, Luke and Romans which are a Christian's primary
source for the love command.[23]

     The second major aspect of this presentation which
needs comment is that, at best, it might not be very satisfactory to a critical biblical scholar. I have spoken dis-
paragingly of proof-texting, and yet what I have done so
far might itself be described as just a highly sophisticat-
ed form of proof-texting. Nor have I demonstrated that my
approach has escaped the possible short-comings of a merely
literal reading of the text. I claim that my reading of
the New Testament is consistent with at least a modest exe-
getical consensus, and that this consensus is reasonably
accessible to the non-exegete. Lest the reader be simply
asked to take my word for this, it seems appropriate to
take a few pages to show how a critical exegete might approach those New Testament texts which are the central, di-

rect witness to Christ's teaching on non-violence: Mt
5:38-48; Lk 6:27-36; Rom 12:14, 19-21. These are the texts
which tell us to love our enemies, to pray for those who
persecute us, not to resist one who is evil, and to return
good for evil.

After confirming the reliability of the text itself,
the exegete turns to source criticism to see what can be
determined about the prior history and the process of formation and tradition behind these texts as we now have
them. The earliest text is from Paul in Rom 12:14, 17,
19: "Bless those who persecute you; bless and do not
curse. . . . To no one render evil for evil, but provide
good things. . . . Do not avenge yourselves, beloved, but
give place to the wrath." Written in the late 50's, Paul
to the Romans clearly contains the same teaching as Matthew
and Luke whose gospels took their final form some twenty
years later. The verbal variation, however, suggests that
Romans gives us an independent example of tradition derived
from Jesus and formulated in a manner distinctive of Paul.

But what seems to be most significant is that the Matthaean and Lukan texts form part of the hypothetical Q document.[24] Happily, the beginning of the wider context
which is needed to resolve the ambiguities and tensions
which a study of Q alone suggest (cf. note 24) is to be
found within the New Testament, within the gospels themselves; for it is from Mt 5:35-38 and Lk 6:27-36 that we
know Jesus' teaching on non-violence. It is these gospels, not a hypothetical Q, that the Christian church re-
veres as God's word. This is not to dismiss Q as unimpor-
tant, for it provides us with an invaluable means toward
reconstructing some of the sayings of Jesus. If a significant number of these sayings could be reconstructed beyond
all doubt, their authority and normativity would be recognized by most as unparalleled. However, such a reconstruc-

tion is not within our grasp. Thus it is that the gospel witness to and interpretation of the words and works of Jesus, as received by the Christian community of faith, must serve as our basic starting point. Q, and what we can reconstruct of its "theology" helps us to interpret the gospels, but the gospels themselves in their contexts remain the authoritative and inceptively normative sources for Christian Life.

Now what we can piece together of the Lukan and Matthaean communities which produced these gospels gives us a picture in which community expectations of an imminent Parousia remained fairly strong; but is also gives us a picture of communities beginning to settle down for the long haul. Further, the way Matthew and Luke incorporate the Q material and material from other sources suggests that they are conflating earlier "theologies" into their own redactional framework (cf. Edwards 150). Thus, the practical exhortation of gospels produced in this context cannot be dismissed by us as mere interim-ethic, no more than it was so dismissed by the early Christians. Our inquiry thus comes down to two interrelated (and not necessarily completely different) questions: What did Mt 5:38-48 and Lk 6:27-36 mean in their respective gospel contexts? What do they mean for us today?

Following very closely Schottroff's exposition, we can remark first that the existential interpretations of Bultmann and Braun fail to do justice to the gospel texts. One must rather look to an interpretation which is not so much interested in what goes on internally in the heart of the one who loves, but rather looks to the effect that loving one's enemy and renouncing violence will have in the heart of the enemy. This view takes love of the enemy as a concrete social event. As Schürmann explains: "Here is required that ultimate, creative goodness which makes all

malice disappear . . . such love takes evil to its heart
and crushes it to death."[25] But most importantly, this
does not seem to be a universally applicable ethical rule
but rather is the attitude expected of Christians when they
encounter resistance. It can be practiced only by the weak
toward the strong, and only those who are involved in resistance can teach or demand it. When it is recommended
from outside it is perverted into a demand to give up resistance (Schottroff 13).

This understanding of love for the enemy can be easily
verified as a valid interpretation of Mt 5:38-48 and
Lk 6:27-36, for the passage is indeed addressing the problem of the enmity between Christians and their persecutors,
and it is quite clear that the early Christians were socially at a disadvantage in this conflict. But if love of
enemy is understood in this way--i.e., not as passively accepting but actively seeking to turn evil into good, to
change, to convert the enemy--how can we explain it in relation to the clear prohibition of resistance in Mt 5:39-41
and Lk 6:29? In other words, why is resistance forbidden,
and at the same time an active love of the enemy enjoined?

Some solve this by seeing the prohibition of resistance as an attack on the zealot position, rejecting the
idea of violent rebellion against the Romans. But for this
interpretation to make sense, we would have to be able to
see the text as being formed at a time when the enemies
(persecutors) of the Jews were the same as the enemies
(persecutors) of the Christians. From what we know of the
formation of the gospel traditions, this does not seem possible. But this interpretation still makes an important
point which will be a key element in any adequate solution: the combination of the prohibition of resistance and
the injunction to love the enemy has political implications. In order to determine what these might be, one

should be able to distinguish what is here being preached to the Christian community from the various ways in which "love of enemy" could be conceived in non-Christian antiquity.

Some of these parallels in non-Christian antiquity are: (a) The attitude and reactions of the underdog, the person who does not resist evil or avenge him/herself because he/she is powerless to do so. This seems to fit the actual social situations of those being addressed in Mt 5:38-48 par, 1 Pet 2:18-25 and by the early Christian (ca. AD 177) apologist Athenagoras. None of these Christian texts pay any attention to the social relation of dependence which did not give the Christian any other realistic option than to submit to injustice peaceably and non-violently. Does this mean that we, too, should ignore social differences and interpret Mt 5:38-48 par as inculcating a universal ethic intended for everyone under all circumstances?

(b) The renunciation of revenge by the powerful is a constant theme in classical ethics. But this theme is always talking about the benefits of clemency, patience and leniency by one who is in power. Mt 5:38-48 par presupposes a fundamentally different situation which cannot be prescinded from if we wish to avoid misunderstanding and misusing this text.

(c) Antiquity also knows of the non-violent protest of the powerless, associated especially with the figure of Socrates, and made popular in a variety of legendary embellishments. But the common theme here is that the philosopher accepts even the physical abuse of his tormentors in order to proclaim the rottenness of society. This is quite different from what is going on in Mt 5:38-48 and Lk 6:27-36 (cf. Schottroff 15-23).

What one can draw from all this is the importance of knowing the concrete social situation of the authors and

audience of a text in order to discern accurately what is
the meaning and intended message of that text. For since
biblical texts are not just of divine provenance (doctrine
of inspiration) but are also human productions, we cannot
ignore the concrete social situation of their original human authors and audience.

Close analysis of the Matthaean and Lukan call to non-
violence, renunciation of revenge and love of the enemy enables us to reconstruct the general nature of the common
tradition behind Mt 5:38-48 and Lk 6:27-36, but not the o-
riginal order of these injunctions. It seems clear that
the tradition behind both evangelists defined "your enemies" as "those who persecute you." It seems equally clear
that the parallel material in the rest of the NT (e.g., Rom
12:14; 1 Cor 4:12-13; 1 Pet 2:12, 23, 3:9, 16, 4:4, 14)
teaches the same thing, and understands "doing good to,"
"praying for" and "blessing" one's enemies in a thoroughly
active and even "aggressive" sense. I.e., "the command to
love the enemy is an appeal to take up a missionary attitude towards one's persecutors, to convert them from their
enmity and bring them into the fold of the Christian community. This is the meaning of Rom 12:21: "Do not be
overcome by evil, but overcome evil with good" (Schottroff
23).[26] Despite verbal variations, this attitude of active, converting love that a Christian is expected to show
towards enemies of the community seems to be very much the
same in all levels of the New Testament tradition. Its authority and normativity, in terms of biblical foundations
for basic Christian attitudes, could not be much more firmly established.

Taking social distinctions into account, we can see
that this "desire of the powerless for the salvation of
their enemies is the precise opposite of the desire of the
ruling classes to integrate their enemies or rebellious

subjects into their dominion after they have defeated them"
(Schottroff 24). Thus, whether or not the identification
of enemies with persecutors goes back to the historical
Jesus, the essential meaning of the Dominical teaching is
that we should love our enemies, i.e., work to make them
our brothers and sisters in the Lord, even when they are
truly our enemies. And thus again, "Insistence on the love
of enemy has a public and implicitly political dimension
because it explicitly refers to the identity of the social
group" (Schottroff 25).

With this meaning of love for one's enemy (=the active
desire of the powerless for the salvation of their persecutors) fairly well established as the basic New Testament
meaning, the combination of love for the enemy with non-
violence or non-resistance in the face of injustice—for
these appear together in all levels of the tradition—
appears to be an insoluble enigma. For if love of one's
enemy is a genuinely *active* love, as explained above,
this is inconsistent with a passive, non-violent acceptance
of an enemy's unjust demands. It seems that we must, as
Schottroff (25-27) suggests, go beyond what can be established by exegesis alone and see non-resistance in these
texts as applying specifically and concretely in the area
of politics, and most specifically to the area of insurrec-
tional or revolutionary politics. Christians are not revolutionaries. But non-cooperation with evil (e.g. Martin
Luther King, Jr.) is consistent with the prohibition
against resisting one who is evil (Mt 5:39); for this prohibition is not a fundamental rejection of every type of
resistance. In other words, as Tertullian puts it, Christians are, and precisely as Christians, factors of resistance in society.[27] They resist injustice and oppression.
They are impelled to this by their active and aggressively
missionary love by which they strive by non-violent yet

quite active means to bring all, including their enemies, into the one flock of Christ.

It is in this way, or at least in a way very similar to this, that it seems we must try to make sense of the way the various strata of the New Testament have presented the "love command" side by side with the call to non-violence. It also seems to be the predominant way in which the early Christian writers also understood the relationship between non-violence and love. It is an active, missionary, 'aggressive' love that makes sense of the whole picture. The "command" part of the love command can be thus quite logically and comfortably associated with the command to "make disciples of all nations" (Mt 28:19). Love is the motivating heart of this commandment. Non-violence, its inseparable corollary, specifies the mode and style of its fulfillment.

NOTES

[1]Parts One and Two comprise, for the most part, a revised summary of my own article: "The New Testament: Pacifism and Non-violence," American Ecclesiastical Review, 168 (1974), pp. 544-62. For Part Three I rely extensively on L. Schottroff, "Non-violence and the Love of One's Enemies," Essays on the Love Commandment (trans. R. H. and I. Fuller; Philadelphia: Fortress, 1978), pp. 9-39. For numerous criticisms and suggestions which have improved almost every page of this article, I am indebted to the generous assistance of my colleague at Boston College, Dr. Pheme Perkins.

[2]I am presuming that most of my readers will agree with me that Christian doctrine, life and pracatice should be at least foundationally biblical; i.e., that its ultimate, real center and foundation is biblical, regardless of whether or not the connection to that foundation is explicit, or consciously made. This means that Christians should seek to ground in the Bible, esp. the New Testament, at least the values, attitudes and action-principles of their Christian lives.

[3]Following the convenient classification of R. Bainton, Christian Attitudes toward War and Peace (Nashville-- New York: Abingdon, 1960), esp. pp. 13-16.

[4]Pacifism, since it implies a conscious stand on the issue, is not synonymous with non-violence, especially among the early Christians who, because of their social position, did not have an option to use force or not.

[5]Cf. R. J. Cassidy, Jesus, Politics and Society: A Study of Luke's Gospel (Maryknoll, New York: Orbis, 1978), pp. 54-62.

[6]The "meaning" of a parable is widely recognized as centered on its main point or central focus. In this case, as is indicated by the parable of the tower-builder which is paired with this one, the central focus is on prudent and realistic preparation for accepting the cost of discipleship. For successful popular treatments of the parables, see C. H. Dodd, The Parables of the Kingdom (London: James Nisbet, 1935, repr. many times) or J. Jeremias, The Parables of Jesus (rev. ed.; New York: Scribner's, 1963). For a quick outline of modern parable interpretation, see D. M. Stanley and R. E. Brown, "The Parables of Jesus" in "Aspects of New Testament Thought," The Jerome Biblical Commentary (Englewood Cliffs: Prentice-Hall, 1968), Nos. 78:133-45, Vol. II, pp. 788-90.

[7]Another instance of this, also in the so-called Q material (the 230-250 lines in Matthew and Luke comprising

sayings of Jesus and found, in varied order but in basically the same or similar wording) is the Lukan "Be merciful,
even as your Father is merciful" (Lk 6:36) in contrast to
the Matthaean "You, therefore, must be perfect, as your
heavenly Father is perfect" (Mt 5:48).

[8]Cf. R. A. Edwards, A Theology of Q: Eschatology,
Prophecy, and Wisdom (Philadelphia: Fortress, 1976),
pp. 127-28.

[9]Cf. G. E. Caspary, Politics and Exegesis: Origen
and the Two Swords (Berkeley--Los Angeles: University of
California, 1979).

[10]The evidence is largely the internal evidence of
the gospels themselves carefully examined in the light of
our extra-biblical knowledge of the history of the times.
Cf. O. Cullmann, Jesus and the Revolutionaries (New York:
Harper and Row, 1970); M. Hengel, Was Jesus a Revolution-
ist? (Philadelphia: Fortress, 1971); Victory over Violence: Jesus and the Revolutionists (Philadephia: Fortress, 1973); G. R. Edwards, Jesus and the Politics of Violence (New York: Harper and Row, 1972).

[11]C. Stuhlmueller, "The Gospel According to Luke,"
The Jerome Biblical Commentary (Englewood Cliffs: Prentice-
Hall,1968), No. 44:160, Vol. II, p. 159.

[12]In general, Luke is quite ready to change the situation-in-the-gospel of a passage in order to heighten its
kerygmatic effect. E.g., the quarreling of the disciples
which occasioned Jesus' teaching on leadership in terms of
self-sacrificing service is changed from its apparently o-
riginal gospel context immediately after the third predic-
tion of the passion (Mk 10:32-35 par) to the situation immediately following the institution of the Eucharist (Lk
22:24-27).

[13]N. Perrin, Rediscovering the Teaching of Jesus (New
York and Evanston: Harper and Row, 1967), p. 77.

[14]R. Coste, "Pacifism and Legitimate Defense," Con-
cilium 5 (1965), p. 87.

[15]Cf. Origen, Against Celsus, Bk. VIII, chaps. 68-75
(ANF, IV, pp. 665-68). Our knowledge of Celsus' work comes
solely from Origen's refutation of it, written about AD
249. English translations: F. Crombie, Ante-Nicene Fathers (Grand Rapids: Eerdmans, 1956 repr.), IV, pp. 395-
69: H. Chadwick, Origen: Contra Celsum (Cambridge, 1953).

[16]Cf. Bainton, pp. 61-78.

[17]De Corona (On the Soldier's Crown), p. 11; ANF,
III, pp. 99-100. Granted that Tertullian's primary concern here is with the problem of idolatry in the military

rather than with force and non-violence, the passage speaks for itself and obviously appeals to an already existing Christian attitude.

[18]Against Celsus, VIII, chap. 73; ANF, IV, pp. 667-68.

[19]Cf. Bainton, p. 97.

[20]Ambrose, Duties of the Clergy, IV, p. 27; Post-Nicene Fathers, X, pp. 71-72.

[21]It would seem that Christian non-violence must necessarily be a modified non-violence. For example, could a Christian refuse to use force if it was needed to restrain a child from seriously harming itself in a fit of infantile rage?--or refuse to applaud the policeman who used the necessary minimum force to keep an anti-social person from harming others?

[22]Cf. H.-W. Bartsch, "The Foundation and Meaning of Christian Pacifism," New Theology No. 6 (ed. M. E. Marty and D. G. Peerman; London--New York: Macmillan, 1969), pp. 185-98.

[23]Cf. L. Schottroff, pp. 9-12.

[24]The "two-source theory," favored by the great majority of exegetes, states that the gospels of Matthew and Luke, besides material that is unique to each of them, drew upon two other common sources or documents: Mark and the Q document, a collection of Jesus' sayings. This collection of sayings accounts for some 230 to 250 verses in Matthew and Luke which are so similar (and often identical) in content and style that exegetes commonly assume that a common document lies behind them. The existence of the extra-canonical Gospel of Thomas, a collection of 114 sayings of Jesus which may well have been based on a collection similar to Q, tends to support this theory. Exegetes have been familiar with this hypothesis for over a century, but only recently, after the flowering of redaction criticism in the last three decades, has there been a concerted effort to study the theology of Q and to reconstruct the religious situation of the communities which formed this collection of Jesus' sayings (cf. R. A. Edwards, A Theology of Q). A prominent feature of this situation, as reflected in Q, is the pervasiveness of eschatology. For example, Howard Kee's Division of Q into themes or subjects finds 1 narrative, 3 parenetic and 37 eschatological themes (cf. H. C. Kee, Jesus in History New York: Harcourt, Brace and World, 1970, pp. 62-103, as cited by Edwards p. 25; cf. also pp. 32-43). Also quite prominent in Q, and especially in Mt 5:38-48 and Lk 6:27-36, are motifs and forms of exhortation from the wisdom tradition (Edwards, pp. 58-79). A reconstruction of the religious situation of the community

which gathered the sayings of Jesus into the Q collection
would describe a group whose whole vision of reality was
both colored by their imminent expectation of Jesus' return, but also tempered by the worldly-wise traditions and
forms of expression of the wisdom tradition. But here we
must be careful; for this reconstruction is itself a hypothesis built upon another hypothesis (the two-source or
documentary theory). Thus, this evidence alone cannot support the often-made conclusion that the non-violent ethic
of the Sermon on the Mount was an interim-ethic with little
relevance for the modern world. But neither can one ex-
clude eschatology from a careful consideration of the New
Testament. To resolve this tension, a wider context than
just the New Testament texts is needed. That is why, in
our initial sweep, we discussed the understanding and practice of the early Church.

[25]H. Schürmann, Das Lukasevangelium I (HTKNT 3;
Freiburg: Herder, 1969) pp. 344, 349, as cited by Schottroff, p. 12.

[26]In actual fact, the relationships of the early
Christian minorities to their sometimes persecuting enemies
were profoundly complicated; and the spotty evidence we
have allows only conjectual conclusions as to the extent to
which the persecutions may have been engendered by missionary activity on the part of the Christians.

[27]Tertullian, Apology 37; ANF, III, p. 45; cf.
Schottroff, p. 27.

MAXIMUS THE CONFESSOR
(580 - 662)

by Charles C. McCarthy

C. McCarthy shows clearly that Maximus, the Father of Byzantine theology, grounds his radical opposition to violence on such central themes as God's love and the process by which one comes to participate ever more fully in God's life and love. One becomes God-like by living as God lives. In this theology, violence is never treated effectively as an isolated form of evil. It must be understood in relation to sin, freedom and the disciplines of love and detachment. Since non-violence is either total or non-existent, it requires a new consciousness and a new mind-set and life-style. Maximus' non-violent spirituality in many respects parallels that of St. Francis, George Fox and Thomas Merton.

HISTORICAL BACKGROUND

St. Maximus the Confessor was born in 580 A.D. in Constantinople. He lived for 82 years. Between his birth and death lies a physical life of which relatively little of fact is known. As with many who gain renown after their deaths, the life of St. Maximus as it is popularly known today is permeated with pious legend. Therefore, we must be content with knowing only a few of the larger and fewer of the smaller events of his physical life. Yet this is sufficient, for the information we have confirms that this man, who is known as the "Father of Byzantine Theology" was no mere academic speculator. What we have of his life ver-

ifies what we have of his writings. He wrote primarily
about a reality that was above all else alive in him. What
we know of his life testifies to this axial fact. Thus we
can enter into his teachings knowing that what we are reading is not the work of a compulsive theological wordsmith,
but rather the innermost thoughts of a person who in the
end chose to die with the mind he had rather than live with
a different one.

St. Maximus was born into an upper class family. His
formal education was of the highest quality. When it was
completed, he took employment at the imperial court, and
soon after 610 Emperor Heraclitus named him his First Sec-
retary. However, in 614 he resigned from this prestigious
position and entered the monastery at Chrysopolis.

By 618 he had at least one disciple, a monk named
Anatasius who was to stay with him until they were both
martyred more than forty years later. In 625 he left his
first monastery and went to the Monastery of St. George at
Cyzicus. It is from this monastery that his earliest writings come. In 632 he moved to the Monastery of Euchratas
in Carthage. The abbot of this monastery was Sophronius, a
significant figure because he was one of the first to recognize the problems involved with monothelitism,[1] the
heresy which would eventually be responsible for taking
Maximus' life. It is during this stay in Africa that
Maximus completed two of his major works--*Questions to
Thalassius* and *Ambigua*.

Maximus appears to have stayed in Africa until 646 at
which time he went to Rome to continue his efforts for dy-
othelitism.[2] Pope Martin I called a Lateran Council in
649 in order to confront monothelitism. The Council at
which Maximus was present as a monk rejected monothelitism. When the Emperor Constans, himself a monothelitist,
heard this, he arrested the Pope and Maximus in 653. Pope

Martin I was tried in 654 and was sentenced to exile in Cherson where he died in 655.

The trial of St. Maximus began in 655. Consistent with the course of suffering his Master had to endure, Maximus was first subjected to trumped-up and artificially inflated crimes against the state. When this course of action by the Emperor proved fruitless, he was sent into exile for six years. In 662, at the age of 82, he was hauled back to Constantinople where a Church Council of hierarchs, more loyal to the Emperor and Rome than to the Church of Christ, anathematized and condemned him. The traditional sentence of mutilation of those members by which "false" doctrine was expounded was carried out. Maximus' tongue was cut out and his right hand was amputated. He was then carted about the city of Constantinople; so, like his Master, the people he was trying to serve could mindlessly ridicule him on cue from the state and the ecclesiastical politicoes. After this exercise of legalized meanness and "justified" punishment, he was sent off to exile in Lazica where he died on August 13, 662 A.D.

GOD'S LOVE AND THE PROCESS OF DEIFICATION

Having seen the historical milieu in which Maximus lived and developed his theology, we shall zero in immediately on the central theme from which he derived his thought on non-violence. It is the goodness, and above all, the love of God.

> God alone is essentially good, and only a man who imitates God is good in the disposition of his soul; for this man's chief aim is to unite the wicked with Him, who is essentially good and thus make them good. To this end, being reviled, he blesses; being persecuted, he suffers it; being defamed, he brings comfort; being slain, he prays

for his slayer. He does all, lest he fall from
his chief aim--love.[3]

"For he who has love has God himself, for 'God is
Love'. To Him be glory unto ages of ages. Amen."[4] With
these words St. Maximus, the Father of Byzantine Theology,
summarizes and concludes his spiritual classic, *Four Centuries on Love.* These words could equally be a summary
and conclusion for his entire theology. Indeed, they encapsulate Byzantine spirituality. For above all realities,
experiences and concepts in Byzantine spirituality, the
reality and experience that "God is Love" reigns supreme.
No aspect of theology, no dimension of liturgy, no practice
of spirituality is outside this fundamental insight. All
existence is a mystery in the perduring embrace of Love.
"God is Love" is the paradigmatic notion of Byzantine theology.

The second most important idea in the Byzantine spiritual tradition is one which might strike the Western mind
as absurd, if not blasphemous. The idea is that of "deification." The formula which has been universally employed
to embody this idea is "God became man, so that man may become God."[5] St. Maximus, in explaining the concept of
deification, says:

> In the same way in which the soul and the body
> are united, God should become accessible for par-
> ticipation by the soul and, through the soul in-
> termediary, by the body, in order that the soul
> might receive an unchanging character, and the
> body immortality; and finally that the whole man
> should become God, deified by the grace of God-
> become-man, becoming whole man, soul and body, by
> nature and becoming whole God, soul and body by
> grace.[6]

To "become partakers of the divine nature" (2 Pt 1:4) is the reason why men and women were created and the reason why God became a human being. Deification is so central to Byzantine spirituality because it represents the purpose and meaning of all human history.

If God is Love, another way of formulating the notion of deification is by saying that Love became man so that man could become love. However, the only way to become love is by loving. One can no more become a loving person by hating than one can become a truthful person by lying. There must be consistence between the end to be achieved and the means of achieving it. One becomes God-like by living like God lives. The living God is living Love. To love, according to Maximus, is not merely to live like God or to imitate Him; to love is to participate in the very life of God here and now. Participation here is the way to participation hereafter. "The mystery of Christ is the mystery of Love."[7]

It is not exclusively through our own activities that we are deified. The process of deification occurs when we freely choose to use our own energy in obedience to the un-created divine energy of love, which is the divine will, which is God. The synergy of these two energies finds its ontological root in Jesus Christ, the man who is God--the Person in whom this cooperation or synergy between divine will and human will is perfected. To follow Christ, then, is not merely to follow an external ethic; it is to liter-ally live in Christ, to be one with the new reality of Im-mortal Love made accessible to all people. Thus, it natur-ally follows that when Jesus is asked what is the way to eternal life, He simply proclaims, "Love!" "Love the Lord your God with your whole heart, whole mind and whole strength and love your neighbor as yourself" (Lk 10:25). The Kingdom of God is the Kingdom of Love. Love is both the Kingdom and the way to the Kingdom.

But what is this love? Of what does it consist? How
can one judge whether one is living it? After all, the a-
trocity cannot be imagined that at some time and place has
not been committed in the name of love.

It is the understanding of Byzantine theology that
Jesus Christ is the icon or image of the Father--the image
of God who is Love. The person who sees and hears Jesus
Christ, sees and hears the Father. "Christ is the icon of
the invisible God," says Paul (Col 1:15). Therefore,
St. Maximus, in the sixteenth paragraph of his *First Century on Love*, writes:

> 'If you love me, keep my commandments' says the
> Lord (John 14:15). 'This is my commandment, that
> you love one another as I have loved you' (John
> 15:12). Thus he who does not love his neighbor,
> does not keep the commandments; and he who does
> not keep the commandments can not love the
> Lord.[8]

Here Maximus is stating with precision and clarity the
concrete meaning and daily practical implications of the
great commandment of love that was proclaimed by God Incarnate. To love God means to love your neighbor. To love
your neighbor means to love him/her as Jesus would have
loved him/her, and as Christ does love him/her now.
Christ, not the law; Christ, not the social custom; Christ,
not secular wisdom, is the standard by which one determines
whether one is loving God and neighbor.

The only commandment unique to Christ in the entire
New Testament is the one just quoted above: "Love as I have
loved." Love Incarnate is the living Icon to which anyone
who wishes to do God's will must constantly refer in order
to determine what the love of God and neighbor means in
each situation in life. To love as Christ loves is the sum
and substance of the Christian life. It is the purpose of

every life, the goal of every moment of life. It is the
means to be employed at every instance of life in order to
accomplish every task. Any act, which is not an act of
love as Christ defined love by word and deed, is an act
which is morally worthless (cf. 1 Cor 13).

If, therefore, one wishes to burn witches or engage in
the mass slaughter of war in good Christian conscience, all
one has to do is prove to oneself that the loving Christ
would have burned witches or engaged in the mass slaughter
of war. But if one cannot see our Lord thinking, speaking
or acting in a particular way, then one obviously cannot
"love as He loves" by thinking, speaking or acting in such
a fashion. When one does not love as Christ loves, one
neither loves God nor one's neighbor. When one does not
love as Christ loves, one cannot grow in Divine life. The
name for the act of refusing to grow in Divine life, for
refusing to love as Christ loves, is sin.

SIN: REVOLT AGAINST LOVE

In Byzantine spirituality, sin is a revolt against
God, a revolt against Love. Sin is a thought, word or deed
not in conformity with the mind, the spirit and the heart
of Christ. The origin of sin is freedom, which is also the
necessary condition for love. Christian love is free love
or it is not Christian love. Maximus states that human beings are morally free: "Since man was created according to
the image of the blessed and supra-essential deity, and
since, on the other hand, the divine nature is free, it is
obvious that man is free by nature, being the image of the
deity."[9]

Sin has no other source than the freedom of the human
being who sins. The problem of evil is the problem of the
evildoer. In Byzantine spirituality, original sin does not
mean that a baby is born full of evil and inherited guilt.

There can be no sin, original or personal, no revolt a-
gainst the God of love, without the individual's personal
and free choice.   Indeed, human nature incurs the consequences of Adam's sin which is mortality or death.   "The
shadow of death is human life," says St. Maximus.[10] Having become mortal, Adam and Eve conceived mortal children
and "because of death all men have sinned" (Rom 5:2).   Human beings inherit mortality (death) from the fall and from
this flows fear of non-being, fear of death.   From fear
flows sin, unChrist-like love, self-love streaming from the
instinct of bodily self-preservation.

Thus, in Byzantine spirituality the baptism of a baby
is not to forgive sins which it has never committed, but to
communicate to the new-born child the immortal life which
Christ brought into the world by His resurrection.   The
guarantee of immortal life liberates human beings from the
fear of death, and therefore, from the tremendous pull of
sin, the pull of self-love, that emanates from the instinct for bodily self-preservation.

In Byzantine spirituality, however, immortality does
not remove freedom so that the "origin of sin" remains.
Human beings may be offered by Love (God) all that makes
love possible.   They may be offered Love itself, but it is
a gift and can only be offered.   It cannot be imposed.   A
person always remains free to say "yes" or "no" to a union
in Love.   In the end, without the agreement of the will of
the person and the will of God, salvation is not possible.
People are made in God's image, which means that they are
free for as long as they exist.   Even if a person is to be
forever, this will not change.   But how far a person ad-
vances into or separates him/her self from God's likeness,
i.e. from loving as God loves, from being like God, depends
on how the person exercises his/her moral freedom.

Christ's resurrection can liberate us from death and sin if we allow it to do so. But under no circumstances does Christ's resurrection liberate us from freedom. For to take away freedom would be to simultaneously take away the possibility to love. Once freedom and love are no longer part of human existence, life, even immortal life, is at best a compulsive movement from one meaningless now to the next in an eternal Disneyland. Men and women deify themselves through the gift of Love. Only by freely loving as Christ loves can humanity be united in a communion of love with Love itself.

But to love as Christ loves requires doing the very first word that Christ spoke at the beginning of his public ministry: "Repent" (Mt 4:17). Repentence is not mere sentimental sorrow of sins. It is a radical change of mind and fundamental change of heart. It means becoming a new person by putting on the mind of Christ and thereby loving what Christ loves and as Christ loves. St. Maximus sees that to live the life that Christ invites us to live requires that we freely enter into the discipline of love. This discipline of love is necessary, not because discipline saves, but because love saves. However, the love that saves is so contrary to the values and desires that society nurtures in its people, that only the most serious work to put off one's old mind and put on the mind of Christ can possibly be effective. Maximus understands that the human mind is a bloody and sinful mess, and that the bloody and sinful human activities and institutions that abound are the organic bad fruit of this mindstyle which has chosen to do other than love as Christ loves. He has no prescription on how minds that overflow with anger, vainglory and cupidity can create institutions that are anything other than reflections of themselves.

St. Maximus is concerned with the mind, the soul and
the spirit of the person. He recognizes that a person becomes what he/she thinks and desires, and on a larger
scale, that a community becomes what its individual members
think and desire. Thus, each person must enter into the
process of converting his/her mind and heart into the mind
and heart of Christ. The discipline of love which he discusses amounts to insights and suggestions on what it is
necessary to do and to avoid in order to move more deeply
into the life of God and thereby participate more fully in
the salvation of the world.

THE DISCIPLINE OF NON-VIOLENT LOVE

Because of the scope of this article, I shall limit my
discussion of Maximus' reflections on the discipline of
love to those that relate specifically to the problem of
violence. This is, regretfully, a somewhat artificial
treatment of his spirituality, because he sees an irrevocable connection on many levels between other forms of evil
and violence.

> Let no man deceive you by the thought that you
> can be saved while serving lustful pleasure . . .
> [because] a mind that falls away from God and
> forms friendship with material things, surrender-
> ing to lustful pleasure, becomes bestial and
> fights with men for such things.[11]

Sin generates a further propensity to sin, and therefore,
in reality, sin cannot be compartmentalized. Violence is a
manifestation of evil and cannot be effectively treated or
understood as an isolated form of evil independent of
pride, greed, lust, envy, resentment, despair and sloth.

For St. Maximus, loving God with one's whole heart,
whole soul, whole mind and whole strength is everything.
All flows from this great commandment, including the second

of the great commandments, to love one's neighbor. The first sentence of St. Maximus', *Four Centuries on Love*, reads: "Love is that good disposition of the soul in which it prefers nothing that exists to the knowledge of God."[12] Knowledge here does not mean the fruit of abstract speculation, but knowledge in the biblical sense of knowing and being known through a communion of love. "But," continues Maximus, "no man can come to such a state of love if he be attached to anything earthly."[13]

"[H]e who has torn the mind away from love of God and from His presence and lets it attach to anything sensory prefers the body to the soul"[14] and "self love, the mother of passions, is love of the body."[15] "What a man loves, he desires to grasp with all his strength and all that obstructs him in this he pushes aside, lest he lose it." Thus a love of God "casts out every passion which hinders this end."[16] "Passions taking hold of the mind attach it to material objects and separating it from God force it to be occupied with them. On the other hand, love of God, when it takes possession of the mind, severs its bonds, persuading it to value neither objects of the senses nor even temporal life itself."[17]

NON-VIOLENCE REQUIRES DETACHMENT

It would be very easy and very wrong to relegate Maximus to the level of a non-realist who simply espouses a doctrine of passive pietism. One of the most obvious meanings of non-violence is the voluntary relinquishing of the protection of violence. What are the dynamics of consciousness and conscience that are necessary in order to genuinely accept this way of existence, this way of living without the protection of violence? Certainly most people who espouse or reject non-violence do not equate non-violence with the total rejection of violence in human af-

fairs. They may reject the more obnoxious and brutal forms
of violence. They may reject all violence that is not socially condoned. Or, they may reject all violence that does
not seem to serve, advance or protect their earthly
interests. For instance, the pacifist church, which calls
on the police power of the state to protect its personal
and real property, possesses worldly prudence, but is not
non-violent. Maximus says that "Love of God disposes a man
to scorn all transitory things"[18] including temporal
life, and that without this state of detachment, which
flows from the total love of God, non-violence is impossible.

"If one loves someone, one strives to please him in
all possible ways. Thus if a man loves God he will certainly strive to do what pleases Him.[19] . . . To love
Him is to keep His commandments.[20] . . . But if you are
indeed keeping the commandment of loving your neighbor, why
do you implant in yourself the bitterness of annoyance a-
gainst him? It is not clear that instead of active love
you prefer the transitory and in protecting it you wage war
against your brother?"[21]

The love of the transitory always results in war a-
gainst someone, because some neighbors knowingly or unknow-
ingly assist others in a particular love of the transitory,
while other neighbors inhibit them. Those who provide assistance, usually receive love; those who hinder such love,
usually receive hatred. Only the love of God can result in
love of all neighbors, for no neighbor can separate one
from the love of God; and all neighbors, even the violent,
can provide assistance in one's progress in the love of God.

Transitory things in themselves are not evil. It is
the way the individual apprehends and judges them that
causes problems. People develop according to what they
think and according to how they respond to what is thought.

"An object is one thing, a representation another, passion yet another. An object is, for example, a man, a woman, gold and so forth; a representation a simple thought of some such object; passion--either an irrational love or un-discerning hatred of one of these things."[22] "The mind of a lover of God arms itself not against things and their representation, but against the passions connected with the representation. In other words, it rises not against the man nor against a woman who has offended it, nor against their image, but against the passions connected with these images."[23] "The whole struggle against the demons con-sists in separating passions from representations."[24]

Dissolve the desires of hate and lust, and such acts as murder and adultery will never happen. Nurture the de-sires and passions of hate and lust, and murder and adul-tery will ultimately occur. The conquest of the enemy, evil, in all its forms, is a conquest of the enemy within.

When you see that your mind acts rightly and
justly amidst worldly thoughts, know that your
body will remain pure and free of sin also. But
if you see your mind occupied by sinful thoughts
and do not stop it, then know your body too will
not fail to succumb to them.[25]

For St. Maximus the struggle against evil cannot be piecemeal. Human freedom ultimately resides in one's abil-ity to choose which thoughts one will retain and with what disposition they will be retained. The Christian life, that is to say, the effort to put on the mind of Christ, is a very active, intense use of intellect and will. It is an ongoing commitment to choose a particular mindstyle, a mindstyle consistent with the mind of Christ. As the Christian mindstyle is chosen, the Christian lifestyle will automatically follow.

As things are the world for the body, so representations are the world for the mind. As the
body of a man commits adultery with the body of a
woman, so the mind of a man commits adultery with
the represenation of a woman. . . . In the same
way he revenges himself through a mental image of
his body on a mental image of the man who has offended him. It is the same with all other sins;
for what the body does in deed in the world of
things, the mind does in the world of images.[26]

There is a danger of interpreting Maximus as only offering another form of "Christianized" stoicism, that joy-
less good news of "not this--not that," that meaningless
universe of detached lovelessness. In "Christian" stoicism
the primary value is control. In St. Maximus' thought, the
prime and only value is love. "If we truly love God, by
this very love we shall banish passion. And to love Him
means to prefer him to the world."[27] This preference
amounts in the first instance to preferring thoughts of Him
and his will to passionate representations of the transitory.

"Therefore," St. Maximus says, "one must observe his
mind."[28] Non-violence requires that one first be vigilant
and watchful of one's own inner self. Thus when one's inner perception of a brother who has offended you is that of
bitterness, guard against rancour in yourself. The way of
those who remember injuries leads to death, because to remember an injury is also to become a transgressor. Maximus
encourages Christians to pray for those toward whom they
feel rancour. By doing so they separate their distress
from the memory of the wrong and arrest in themselves the
movement of the passion. Such passion is banished from the
soul by feelings of friendliness and affection. Kindness,
humility and efforts to live at peace with someone who bears

malice against you will free that person from his/her passion.[29]

NON-VIOLENCE: TOTAL OR NON-EXISTENT

How total is the non-violence which St. Maximus espouses?

He who loves Christ is certain to imitate Him as
much as he can. And Christ never ceased doing
good to men; was long suffering in the face of
ingratitude and revilement; and when He was
scourged and put to death, He endured this, im-
puting evil against no one. These three actions
are acts of love for the neighbor, without which
a man deceives himself if he asserts that he
loves Christ or that he will gain His kingdom.[30]

It is hard to imagine a clearer statement regarding the
centrality of non-violence to Christ's teaching and to the
Christian life here and hereafter. The totality of the requirement of non-violent love under all circumstances is
evident when Maximus says, "Christ does not wish you to
feel hatred or malice, anger or bitterness against anyone,
in whatever manner or for anything. The four Gospels
preach this to all men."[31] "He who abandons love for any
such reason has not yet understood the aim of Christ's
commandments."[32]

Non-violence is either total or it is non-existent.
An ethic of justified violence, that is, violence made acceptable when certain conditions are present, is not non-
violence. It is precisely at the moment when violence is
justified for some reason or other that non-violence becomes an operational option. Non-violence is a total approach to all life--internal and external, private and public.

> The friends of Christ love all men sincerely, but
> are not loved by all. Friends of the world nei-
> ther love all, nor are loved by all. Friends of
> Christ keep the bonds of love to the end; but
> friends of the world love only until some discord
> arises between them about some earthly thing.[33]

What St. Maximus is indicating here is that Jesus Christ
authorizes no-one, under any circumstances, to substitute
violence, by whatever name, for love.

The non-violence being spoken of by Maximus is far removed from the "non-violence" which a nationally-known
peace activist spoke of recently. When the "non-violent
leader" was asked if he thought the hundreds of people he
was urging to occupy government property were, in fact, believers in non-violence, he said, "I just hope that they
believe in it enough to be non-violent while they are on
government property." For Maximus, such non-violence would
not be non-violence. It would just be a method of doing
evil under the guise of non-violence. It would be the ab-
surdity of evil trying to conquer evil.

St. Maximus himself said "no" to civil and ecclesiastical authorities when he felt "no" had to be said. He also suffered imprisonment and torture for his stand. But
his "no," his imprisonment and his torture were the result
of an entire mindstyle and lifestyle. Two months or two
years in jail for "non-violent" civil disobedience is
child's play compared with a life commitment to the discipline of non-violent love. Without such personal commitment by all who engage in acts of non-violent civil disobedience, it is hard to see how non-violent civil disobedience is possible. Without this commitment it is also
hard to see how non-violent civil disobedience is not
fraudulent non-violence--a way of appearing holy and loving
and Christ-like while willfully retaining a disposition of
the soul that is unholy, unloving and unChrist-like.

Evil, fear and death are all phenomena that can make personal and collective life on earth a living hell. St. Maximus, like most who have committed themselves for a lifetime to Christ's teaching of non-violent love, is extremely sensitive to these phenomena. He is also one who does not ignore or forget them by speaking of them euphemistically in order to excuse his own immorality. He does not employ theological legerdemain in order to say that war can be God's will, that preparation for slaughter can be preparation for love.

> No one must distort the word of God to indulge his moral negligence; it is better to confess one's weakness, not concealing God's truth, lest, together with transgressing His commandments, we become guilty of intentionally misinterpreting the Word of God.[34]

Christ does not just condemn illegal violence; He condemns legal violence. Christ does not simply condemn sordid violence; He condemns romantic violence. Christ does not merely condemn personal violence; He condemns social violence. Christ does not only condemn external violence; He condemns internal violence. Christian non-violence is the rejection of violence at all levels because violence is evil; it is against the will of God as revealed by God Himself, Jesus Christ.

Whether it is done in the name of self-interest, self-defense or social responsibility, violence in thought, word or deed is incompatible with loving as Christ loves. Maximus knew the power that human institutions such as the family, state, religion and school have to nurture mindstyles and lifestyles of selfishness and retaliation. He knew the transitory loves to which the human heart can give itself. He knew the extremes to which people will go in order to get or to protect the totally perishable realities

they love. It is precisely because Maximus was under no
self-created or socially-created illusions about the power
of evil that he was so unambiguous about the effort that
has to be made and the price that has to be paid to love as
Christ loves.

THE NORM: NON-VIOLENT LOVE

Yet, St. Maximus' spirituality is not difficult to understand. Its five essential points are: a) God is Love,
b) God became man so that man may become God, c) Love became man so that man could become Love, d) The only way to
become Love is by loving, and e) Love as Christ loved.
"Relate all happenings to the ultimate end,"[35] advises
St. Maximus. The ulimate end of existence is deification,
achieving eternal union with Holy Immortal Love. Non-violent love in thought, word and deed is the way to this end
--there is no other. So, when Maximus says, "Do not wound
your brother, even with insinuations, lest you receive the
same in return and thus banish a loving disposition from
both"[36] and "Do not regard as well-meaning those who repeat to you words which engender in you vexation or enmity
against a brother--even if they appear to speak the truth.
But turn away from such, as from deadly snakes,"[37] he is
talking about more than the power of positive thinking. He
is speaking of how to build the eternal Commonwealth of
Love.

That lesser commonwealths can be built on truth as the
carrier of enmity, on vexation, on insinuations and on
other wounds is obvious. But to relate all happenings to
whether a transitory commonwealth of snakes will arise or
be sustained is, for Maximus, the folly of idolatry. It is
equivalent to raising the purely transitory to the level of
an ultimate criterion by which to judge the correctness of
thought, word or deed. The five principles that encapsulate

St. Maximus' spirituality are easy to understand, and provided one is willing to accept a Christianity with a cross,
they are possible to apply and to execute on a daily basis.   Nevertheless, one has to have one's priorities
straight. One must seek first the Kingdom of God, the Commonwealth of Love.

For Maximus, "the holy place, the temple of God is the
human mind."[38] It is here that the demons "have devastat-
ed the soul by passionate thoughts, have erected the idol
of sin."[39] Here also is the primary battleground on which
the war against evil must be fought. Refuse to fight evil
here and all is lost. Actions that are not the fruit of
having put on the mind of Christ, that are not the fruit of
Christ-like love, are simply sound and fury signifying
nothing (1 Cor 13). "For God's judgment," says Maximus,
"looks not only on what is done, but also on the intentions
with which it is done."[40]

Yet, for Maximus, not simply intention, but also "what
is done," is of importance. Putting on the mind of Christ
is not some sort of mind-game or accidental peak experience. The only way one can know if one has, in fact, put
on the mind of Christ is if one is living "a love testified
by deeds."[41] To St. Maximus, a person who is living a
mindstyle or a love that is not testified by deeds, is a
stranger to love and "'a stranger to love is a stranger to
God, for God is Love'"(1 Jn 4).[42]

The spirituality of non-violence of St. Maximus the
Confessor is probably not the first form of Christian non-
violence to which people are normally attracted. But as
other forms of non-violence show themselves to be unable to
do battle effectively with the powers of darkness, the
power and wisdom of the non-violent spirituality of
St. Maximus may become more visible. "He loves all men"
says Maximus, "who loves nothing human."[43] There is, of

course, no end to the distortions to which such a statement
is subject. But, in reality, does it not mean something as
simple as dropping all allegiance to the transitory and
loving God with one's whole heart, whole soul, whole mind
and whole strength, so that when one does this, love of
neighbor--all neighbors--must and will follow.

The non-violent spirituality of St. Maximus is totally
predicated on the understanding that the microcosmic deed
of love is all that humanity has to work with in its struggle against evil and that this same deed of love is all humanity needs to work with in order to be all it was created
to be. For where Love is God is, because God is Love. For
where Love is, there is the only Power capable of conquering evil and death, the ultimate sources of all the bad
news in the universe.

One of the most extraordinary Christian characters in
world literature is Dostoevski's Byzantine staretz,
Fr. Zossima. He is the epitome of Byzantine spirituality,
a truly impressive literary embodiment of the Truth of
Christianity. Fr. Zossima is probably best known in a popular sense for his statement that "Love in action is a
harsh and dreadful thing, compared with love in
dreams."[44] But there is another reflection that the staretz made that summarizes and encapsulates the spirituality
of non-violent love of the "Father of Byzantine Theology"
and on which it would be appropriate for this exposition of
his thought to conclude:

> At some thoughts a person stands perplexed, above
> all at the sight of human sin, and he wonders
> whether to combat it by force or by humble love.
> Always decide: 'I will combat it by humble
> love.' If you resolve on that once and for all,
> you can conquer the whole world. Loving humility
> is a terrible force: it is the strongest of all
> things and there is nothing else like it.[45]

"Loving humility is a terrible force." It is the Power of
God to those who love as Christ loves, to those who dare to
convert to the mind of Christ instant after instant after
instant.

NOTES

[1] The theology that Christ was not as the Council of Chalcedon had stated "true God and true man," but, in fact, had one will (divine), not a human will and a divine will.

[2] The doctrine that Christ had two wills, and therefore, had to make choices as all human beings must.

[3] St. Maximus the Confessor, "Four Centuries on Love," The Early Fathers from the Philokalia, ed. by E. Kadloubovsky and G. E. H. Palmer (London: Faber and Faber Ltd., 1954) IV, p. 90.

[4] Ibid., IV, p. 100.

[5] For example: St. Irenaeus, "Adversus haereses," V, Preface, PG 7, col 1120; St. Athanasius, "De incarnatione verbi," 54, PG 25, col 192B; St. Gregory Nazianzen, "Poema dogmatica," 10, 5-9, PG 37, col 465; St. Gregory of Nyssa, "Oratoria catechetica magna," 25, PG 45, col 65D. All these references to "God became man that man might become God" can also be found in: In the Image and Likeness of God, edited by Vladimir Losskey (Crestwood, N.Y.: St. Vladimir's Seminary Press, 1974).

[6] St. Maximus the Confessor, "Ambigua," PG 91, Col 1237AB.

[7] Lars Thunberg, Microcosm and Mediator: The Theological Anthropology of Maximus the Confessor (Lund: C. W. K. Gleerup, 1965), p. 20.

[8] Maximus, Four Centuries on Love, I, p. 16.

[9] St. Maximus the Confessor, "Disputations with Pyrrho," PG 91, col 304C.

[10] Maximus, "Four Centuries in Love," II, p. 96.

[11] Ibid., II, p. 63.

[12] Ibid., I, p. 1.

[13] Ibid., I, p. 1.

[14] Ibid., I, p. 8.

[15] Ibid., II, p. 8.

[16] Ibid., II, p. 7.

[17] Ibid., II, p. 3.

[18] Ibid., II, p. 58.

[19] Ibid., III, p. 10.

[20] Ibid., I, p. 16.

[21] Ibid., III, P. 15.

[22] Ibid., III, p. 42.

[23] Ibid., III, p. 40.

[24] Ibid., III, p. 41.

[25] Ibid., III, p. 52.

[26] Ibid., III, p. 53.

[27] Ibid., III, p. 50.

[28] Ibid., III, p. 79.

[29] Ibid., III, pp. 89-90.

[30] Ibid., IV, p. 55.

[31] Ibid., IV, p. 84.

[32] Ibid., IV, p. 81.

[33] Ibid., IV, p. 98.

[34] Ibid., IV, p. 85.

[35] Ibid., IV, p. 24.

[36] Ibid., IV, p. 32.

[37] Ibid., IV, p. 31.

[38] Ibid., II, p. 31.

[39] Ibid., II, p. 31.

[40] Ibid., II, p. 37.

[41] Ibid., I, p. 39.

[42] Ibid., I, p. 38.

[43] Ibid., III, p. 37.

[44] Feydor Dostoevski, The Brothers Karamazov, Book II, Part 4.

[45] Ibid., Book IV, Part 2.

FRANCIS OF ASSISI

(1181 - 1226)

by Murray Bodo, O.F.M.

*Opposition to violence is at the core of St.
Francis' spirituality in a twofold sense. As
mystic one can attain union with Christ only
through forgiveness and reconciliation, both of
which foster peace. As martyr (witness to
Christ) one must do violent battle with those interior forces that prevent peace and reconciliation with self, neighbour and God. Since violence and fear, its root, are internal, the way
to peace is the way to peace of soul in Christ.
M. Bodo demonstrates that in St. Francis' spirituality non-violence is prophetic, not pragmatic.
Its aim is not efficacy, but the manifestation of
the fundamental truth that violence is an obstacle to the love and peace of Christ.*

INTRODUCTION

The twelfth century was coming to an end. The year
war 1181, a time of the rise of city states, of brutal wars
between towns and constant conflict between papal and imperial forces. In the small Italian city of Assisi one of
the world's greatest peacemakers was born to Pietro
Bernardone and Lady Pica. At his baptism his mother named
him John, but he was later renamed Francis by his father
who was away in France at the time of the christening.
Francis' father was a wealthy Assisi cloth merchant, and
the boy Francis grew up surrounded by material prosperity
and comfort. A popular leader among his peers, well-liked

for his joviality and generosity, he loved to sing and to party with his friends.

As a young man Francis was inspired by the songs of the French troubadours and dreamed of becoming a knight. When he was 21, this dream came true and Francis went to battle in a war between Assisi and the neighboring city of Perugia. He was captured at the battle of Ponte San Giovanni and spent a year in a Perugian prison, where his constant good humor and optimism made him something of a celebrity among his fellow prisoners.

After his return to Assisi, Francis became ill and was bed-ridden for over a year. When he finally recovered, his previous desire to become a knight was again enkindled, and he set out for war with the papal army in Apulia. That night in the city of Spoleto, he had a vision which was the beginning of his gradual process of conversion. He returned to Assisi the next day and began to pray in a cave outside the city. The following year, while praying before the crucifix in the little chapel of San Damiano, a voice spoke to him: "Francis, go and repair my church." Taking these words literally, Francis immediately hastened to his home, took some bolts of cloth from his father's shop and rode to the nearby city of Foligno. There he sold the cloth and the horse for money to repair the church of San Damiano.

Francis' father was enraged over this prodigal transaction, and in a dispute over the money and what he viewed as Francis' religious fanaticism, Pietro had his son summoned before the Bishop of Assisi. There, in a dramatic and heart-breaking scene, Francis renounced his father and his earthly possessions. He put on a hermit's garb and began to live a life of gospel poverty, spending himself nursing the lepers, repairing churches, and living in imitation of the poor Christ.

It was not long before Francis' holiness began to in-
spire others to follow him in his way of life. When his
disciples had reached 12 in number, he and his brothers
journeyed to Rome to seek approval of his Order of Lesser
Brothers. Pope Innocent III granted verbal approval for
the brothers to live in strict gospel poverty, and the
First Order of St. Francis began. In the year 1212 Clare
di Favarone, a young noblewoman of Assisi, joined Francis.
St. Clare was the first woman to follow Francis, and around
her clustered a community of cloistered nuns who lived at
St. Damiano and who took inspiration for their Rule of Life
from Francis.

The first brothers lived lives of penance and travelled throughout Europe and the Middle East preaching the
gospel of peace through conversion and penance, mystical
union with God, and love for all creatures. Francis himself journeyed to Damietta in Egypt. There he was received
by the Sultan but was unsuccessful in his attempt to convert him to Christ. In 1220 Franics resigned as head of
the Order, but he continued to be its spiritual father and
inspiration. He revised the Rule of his Order and secured
its approval from Pope Honorius III in 1223. The following
year, while praying at the mountain retreat of La Verna,
Francis received the sacred stigmata, the bodily marks of
the passion of Christ. Two years later, on the evening of
October 3, 1226, he died in the little chapel of the
Porziuncola on the plain below Assisi. He was canonized in
1228.

St. Francis was a poet and mystic. His poem, *The
Canticle of Brother Sun*, is a classic of medieval poetry.
His love of nature, his communication with animals and
birds, his total commitment to the Gospel, his gentleness
and extreme poverty, his love for the poor and rejected,
and above all, his simple, heroic love of Jesus Christ have

made him one of the most beloved saints of all time. The
classic work about Francis and his companions is *The
Little Flowers of St. Francis*, written by a Franciscan
friar about the year 1330.

FEAR AND VIOLENCE

There is a story from *The Little Flowers of St.
Francis* about Francis taming a ferocious wolf in the town
of Gubbio. A few years ago I wrote the following passage
about that legend. It contains most of what I know of St.
Francis' response to violence within himself and others:

> As soon as he heard the news of the wolf of Gub-
> bio, Francis felt sympathy for the wolf. There
> was something of the wolf in all of nature, that
> ravenous hunger, that restless pursuit, that bar-
> ing of the fangs, so symbolic of what was wild
> and violent in all of us. But he saw in the wolf
> not so much the stalker as the stalked. Everyone
> feared wolves and disliked them, and he saw in
> the eyes of wolves a fear, a hunted look, an an-
> ger and hostility that wanted to devour every-
> thing in sight in order to avenge their own hurt
> and alienation. Wolves after all, were like
> men. If you feared them, they eventually turned
> into what you were afraid they were anyway.[1]

For Francis of Assisi violence was not something "out
there" that he had to resist with some active or passive
technique. Violence is of the human heart. It is in
everyone, and the way to peace is the way to peace of
soul. It means first of all acknowledging one's own potential for evil and that of others, then embracing[2] it and
allowing the grace of God to redeem it. Yet one's potential for sin and violence can never be totally erased, for
one is always free to reject the grace of God.

Recently, in an interview with the eminent psychiatrist, Karl Menninger, I asked what thread, if any, runs through all his published works. In a response that spoke to the Franciscan soul within me, he said simply, "The vein of evil, self-determined maybe, irradicable." It is precisely this vein of evil within himself and others that Francis sought to allow the Lord to redeem through selfless love, through supernatural charity, and through a gradual process of reconciliation with his inner and outer world.

One incident in his life, particularly, illustrates how he came to be reconciled with that fear which is the root of the violence people do to themselves and others. This was a crucial event in Francis' life, because in his Last Testament he singles it out as the true beginning of his life in the Lord. He writes: "When I was in sin, the sight of lepers nauseated me beyond measure; but then God himself led me into their company, and I had pity on them. When I had become acquainted with them, what had previously nauseated me became a source of spiritual and physical consolation for me."[3]

Here we have the central symbol and reality in the psychology of St. Francis. In embracing what is seemingly repulsive within yourself and others, you achieve a deep inner reconciliation; you discover the true beauty and goodness that lies beneath the appearance of things. The great charism of St. Francis was his love for those who are seemingly unlovable or who return love with hatred and contempt. Only true charity can transform evil and overcome fear. For perfect love, as John indicates, casts out fear; and fear is the root of violence in ourselves and others.

The poet, Rainer Maria Rilke, has beautifully expressed this central insight of St. Francis in a short piece entitled "The Dragon-Princess."

But fear of the inexplicable has not alone impov-
erished the existence of the individual; the relationship between one human being and another
has also been cramped by it. . . . And only if
we arrange our life by that principle which coun-
sels us that we must always hold to the difficult, then that which now seems to us the most
alien will become what we most trust and find
most faithful. How should we be able to forget
those ancient myths that are at the beginning of
all peoples, the myths about dragons that at the
last moment turn into princesses; perhaps all the
dragons of our lives are princesses who are only
waiting to see us once beautiful and brave. Perhaps everything terrible is in its deepest being
something helpless that wants help from us.[4]

THE CAVE

Reconciliation, or the transforming of dragons into
princesses, is a long process and for Francis it took place
only through, with and in the Lord. At the beginning of
his conversion from an outer, superficial man to an inner
man of the spirit, Francis, accompanied by a friend his
age, used to go to a cave outside Assisi to pray. Entering
the cave was a major turning point in Francis' life. In
the cave he came to grips with his own demons, with that
darker side of his nature, that sinfulness which needed
facing and purifying. He learned in the cave that the person in union with Christ need neither fear evil nor deny
it, for in reliance on Christ and in His spirit, the battle
with one's own sin can be won. Evil, which is the fundamental source of violence, comes from the human heart, but
that same heart is purified in a violent battle with itself.

His first biographer, Thomas of Celano, describes St.
Francis' experience in the cave in the manner of an epic
hero burrowing into the depths of the earth in search of a
treasure that is acquired only after combat with dragons
and demons and all those inner forces of evil that one must
face in order to be free. He writes:

> He often took with him [his friend] to remote
> places, . . . telling him he had found a certain
> precious and great treasure. . . . There was a
> certain grotto near the city where they frequent-
> ly went and talked about this treasure. The man
> of God . . . would enter the grotto, while his
> companion would wait outside for him; and filled
> with a new and singular spirit, he would pray to
> his father in secret. . . . He prayed devoutly
> that . . . God would direct his way and teach him
> to do his will. He bore the greatest sufferings
> in mind and was not able to rest until he should
> have completed in deed what he had conceived in
> his heart; various thoughts succeeded one another
> and their importunity disturbed him greatly. He
> was afire within himself with a divine fire and
> he was not able to hide outwardly the ardor of
> his mind; he repented that he had sinned so
> grievously and had offended the eyes of God's
> majesty, and neither past evils nor those present
> gave him any delight. Still he had not as yet
> won full confidence that he should be able to
> guard himself against them in the future. Conse-
> quently, when he came out again to his companion,
> he was so exhausted with the strain, that one
> person seemed to have entered, and another to
> have come out.[5]

In a brilliant analysis of this passage from Francis'
first biographer, the French Franciscan Eloi Leclerc makes
the following significant observations: For St. Francis,
as for the epic hero, in the depths of the cave there is
always some priceless treasure lying in wait if he is courageous and wise enough to seek it.   Guarding the treasure,
there is also a monster of some kind with whom the hero
must battle.   To bury oneself in the cave is, therefore, to
accept struggle, fear and death.   The dark depths are those
of the soul; the cavern is an archetypal image relating the
soul to its own archeology and that of mankind, past and
present.   Therefore, the ultimate victory, the resurrection, unites the hero, not only to himself, but to others
as well.   Thus, a new wholeness, a further integration is
achieved each time one enters the cavern of one's soul to
do battle with those dark forces which are the source of
all violence.[6]

From the moment of his rebirth in the cave outside
Assisi to the end of his life, St. Francis responded to
violence in himself and others by forgiving and by preaching forgiveness.   He asked people to enter into themselves
in order to see there the source of evil, because only then
can they seek, once again *within* themselves, the remedy
--forgiveness and pardon--which alone bring peace.

> And if we do not forgive perfectly, Lord, make us
> forgive perfectly, so that we may really love our
> enemies for love of you, and pray fervently to
> you for them, returning no one evil for evil,
> anxious only to serve everybody in you.[7]

The cave of the self is also a place of resurrection,
of beginnings and gestations.   It is there within that we
also find our own essential sacrality and that of others.
We discover individually that we are precious and good, and
that our previous violence was a projection of the evil in

our own hearts. Prior to this acknowledgment, we simultaneously hated and denied the evil within and struck out at
evil in others in the hope of ridding our own hearts of
what we denied was there. We supposed that evil was something wholly apart from us, refusing to recognize that its
springs were in our own hearts as well.

Acknowledging our own evil prevents us from being alienated from others. St. Francis' thought here parallels
that of other Christian pacifists. For instance, Thomas
Merton wrote that:

> The world as pure object is something that is not
> there. It is not a reality outside us for which
> we exist. . . . It is a living and self creating
> mystery of which I myself am a part, to which I
> am myself my own unique door. When I find the
> world in my own ground, it is impossible to be
> alienated by it.[8]

Then it is possible to be reconciled with the world, which
is what really began within Francis during that crucial
year of the cave.

FRANCIS AND WAR

St. Francis spent his year in the cave at about age
24. God had prepared him for this inner conversion by several visions and dreams which had occurred shortly before
that time. All of these related to his desire to become a
knight and acquire glory by living as perfectly as possible
the knightly code of chivalry. Yet, every time he set out
for war, God frustrated his plans.

The first such occurrence was in a war between Assisi
and its rival city, Perugia, in 1202, when Francis was 21
years old. He was taken prisoner by Perugian soldiers at
the battle of Ponte San Giovanni, and spent a year ill in
bed. Nevertheless, undaunted by this long, mysterious ill-

ness, he set out again for war in Apulia. However, before
he left

> He saw in a dream his father's house changed into
> a marvelous palace filled with arms. The bales
> of cloth had disappeared, and were replaced by
> magnificent saddles, shields, lances, and all
> kinds of knightly harness. Moreover, in one room
> of the palace a beautiful and charming bride was
> waiting for her bridegroom. Francis, thunder-
> struck, was wondering what all this could mean
> when a voice revealed to him that the soldiers
> and this beautiful lady were reserved for him.
> He awoke with happiness, since this vision, as he
> thought, could only be symbolic of the success he
> was to achieve.[9]

The dream, however, was all misinterpreted, as Francis
was to learn shortly after he set out for war. He was on
the road for only a day when he stopped for the night in
the city of Spoleto. There the mysterious voice spoke to
him again in his sleep:

> "Francis, is it better to serve the Lord or the
> servant?"
> "Oh, sir, the Lord, of course."
> "Then why are you trying to turn your Lord into a
> servant?"
> And Francis, trembling in recognition, replied,
> "Lord, what do you want me to do?"
> "Go home, Francis, and think about your first vi-
> sion. You have seen only the appearances and not
> the heart of glory and fame. You are trying to
> make your vision fit your own impatient desire
> for Knighthood."
> And Francis, shaken and fully awake, understood
> now that . . . impatience had driven him to act

too quickly and that he must wait and listen and
purify his heart to hear deeper words than he had
imagined. . . .

    The road back to Assisi seemed to shake be-
neath him. . . . He was returning to Assisi on
the Roman Flaminian way. The Roman legions had
marched this same way. . . . They had stopped
and drunk from the sacred spring of Clitunno near
Foligno. They had asked the water nymphs there
to strengthen them in battle. . . .

    As Francis passed that same clear pool of
water, the dream of glory drained from his heart,
and war and victory were empty words rattling in
his brain. . . . Something told him he was leaving the Roman way forever.[10]

So he was, for what followed was that purifying experience
in the cave. Never again would war be something glorious
for Francis. In fact, he would spend the rest of his life
making peace instead of war, reconciling people to themselves and to one another.

FRANCIS THE PEACE-MAKER

    One well-known incident in the life of St. Francis
speaks dramatically of what he did in lesser ways every day
of his life to transform his own dragons into princesses,
to overcome fear and violence in himself and others. This
incident is his encounter with the Sultan of Damietta in
Egypt. I once wrote an imaginative narrative of that
event, incorporating into it the famous peace-prayer of St.
Francis, which although not written by Francis himself,
certainly conveys his spirit:

    He was terrified when he had finally been ushered
    into the Sultan's presence, . . . But he marched
    steadily forward, never dropping his eyes and
    staring openly into the Sultan's iron eyes. . . .

The Sultan spoke first.

"Well, little man, I see you have courage. . . ."

Francis said nothing.

"I see you also have manners. I like that."

There was a long pause, embarrassing only to
the courtiers who shifted from foot to foot and
coughed tensely.

"Well, holy man, what do you want of me?"

"Only to bring you peace, great one."

The Sultan smiled.

"But I like war, little Italian. . . ."

"But great prince, I am not talking about peace
as the opposite of war. I speak of peace in your
heart. . . ."

"And what, to a warrior, can bring more inner
peace than victory on the battlefield?"

"Prayer, O child of Allah."

"Prayer? And do I not pray every day to Allah?"

. . . .

"But I want to share with you a prayer I learned
by fighting the great battle with myself, by
conquering one by one the demons in my own
heart. . . ."

"Then pray it for me now. . . ."

Francis knelt down and lifted up his eyes beyond
the dais to a small opening in the tent that let
the light in.

"Lord, make me an instrument of your peace.
Where there is hatred let me sow love
Where there is injury, pardon
Where there is darkness, light
Where there is despair, hope
And where there is sadness, joy.

O Divine Master
Let me not so much seek to be consoled
As to console
To be understood as to understand
To be loved as to love.
For it is in giving that we receive
It is in pardoning that we are pardoned
And it is dying that we are born to eternal life."

The Sultan said nothing. He seemed moved. . . .
In a soft voice, so that only Francis could hear,
he said,

"Oh, little beggar and man of dreams. . . . Unfortunately, the world understands only two
things: power and violence. Some day, your
prayer says to me, the world will be turned upside down by little men who fast and pray and who
die rather than take up the sword. Till then
God's will is performed through violent men like
me."

"Will you, Lord Sultan, pray for that day?"

"I will do more, honest man, I will let you walk
out of this camp alive, so that *you* can pray
for that day. I pray that after I am gone from

this earth (but not before) Allah will change his mind
and use meek instruments like you and that this great
army of peace-loving beggars will outnumber the forces
of hatred and violence. Go to your dreams, brave little man."[11]

Francis was more than a man of dreams. He pursued
peace with the same doggedness with which he pursued God
himself. In fact, the two were intimately united in
Francis' mind. Over the portal of his hermitage on Mount
Subasio the friars have placed these words: "*Ubi Deus,
ibi Pax*," (Where God is, there is peace). That was what
the little poor man, Francis, believed and lived. "What he
said was very simple and without art--it only concerned one
thing, namely, peace as the greatest good for man, peace
with God by keeping his commandments, peace with man by a
righteous conduct, peace with oneself by the testimony of a
good conscience."[12]

Francis himself expressed the *source* of this peace
in language that is filled with a wonderful sense of gener-
ativity:

A person is . . . [the] bride . . . [of Christ]
when his faithful soul is united with Jesus
Christ by the Holy Spirit; we are his brothers
when we do the will of his Father who is in heav-
en (cf. Mt. 12:50), and we are mothers to him
when we enthrone him in our hearts and souls by
love with a pure and sincere conscience, and give
him birth by doing good.[13]

A PROPHETIC VOICE

St. Bonaventure said of St. Franics that whenever he
preached, he began by wishing his hearers peace. He would
say to them, "*God* give you peace." Bonaventure maintained that this was a form of greeting which Francis had

learned by a revelation. "He was moved by the spirit of
the prophets and he proclaimed peace and salvation."[14]

That Francis' voice was prophetic rather than utili-
tarian places him at the center of a major contemporary
stance toward non-violence. Thomas Merton summarizes his
own attitude and, I believe, Francis of Assisi's as well,
in this poignant paragraph:

> Non-violence is not for power but for truth. It
> is not pragmatic but prophetic. It is not aimed
> at immediate political results, but at the mani-
> festation of fundamental and crucially important
> truth. Non-violence is not primarily the lan-
> guage of efficacy, but the language of *Kairos*.
> It does not say, "We shall overcome" so much as
> "This is the day of the Lord, and whatever hap-
> pens to us, *He* shall overcome."[15]

Francis himself in his last will and testament summarizes
succinctly his total response to violence and proclaims the
prophetic dimension of peace to the world: "*God* give you
peace'."[16]

Indeed, it is only peace as a *gift of God* that can
effect peace in and among people. Reconciliation takes
place in the presence of God and is effected through his
power. It is this peace of God which Francis commands his
brothers to take with them as they travel as pilgrims and
strangers through the world. In the third chapter of his
Rule of Life Francis says,

> And this is my advice, my counsel, and my earnest
> plea to my friars in Our Lord Jesus Christ that
> when they travel about the world, they should not
> be quarrelsome or take part in disputes with
> words or criticize others; but they should be
> gentle, peaceful, and unassuming, courteous and
> humble, speaking respectfully to everyone, as is

expected of them. . . . Whatever house they enter, they should first say, "Peace to this
house". . . .[17]

And in his fifteenth admonition to his brothers he writes,
"They are truly peacemakers who are able to preserve their
peace of mind and heart for love of our Lord Jesus Christ,
despite all that they suffer in this world."[18]

FORGIVENESS: THE KEY TO PEACE

Once again to preserve one's peace of mind means first
of all that one is able to forgive. Karl Menninger told
me, in the interview mentioned earlier, that he believed
vengeance to be the psychological and spiritual root off
much trouble and unrest in the world. Francis also understood this to be one major source of violence in his own
century. In the second last stanza of his great poem, "The
Canticle of Brother Sun," Francis sings,

All praise be yours, my Lord, through
those who grant pardon
For love of you; through those who endure
sickness and trial.
Happy those who endure in peace,
By you, Most High, they will be crowned.[19]

There is no more beautiful and tender commentary upon this
stanza and what it means than Francis' own words in a letter to a minister of the Order:

I should like you to prove that you love God and
me, his servant and yours, in the following way.
There should be no friar in the whole world who
has fallen into sin, no matter how far he has
fallen, who will ever fail to find your forgiveness for the asking, if he will only look into
your eyes. . . . And should he appear before you
again a thousand times, you should love him more

than you love me, so that you may draw him to
God.[20]

Forgiveness draws others to God, and God gives peace.

COSMIC PEACE THROUGH RECONCILIATION

The desire for reconciliation is the non-violent charism of Franics of Assisi. It was a desire so profound and
so all-embracing that it included all of creation as well.
Francis entered into the elements of the universe and became one with them. Mother earth became his sister, fire
his brother; water was also sister water, and air was
brother wind. For Francis, the person who is at peace with
him/her self has somehow reconciled his/her own person with
the whole universe. The wisdom of Francis on this point is
borne out by the thought of Carl Jung, who writes:

> The empirical truth never frees a man from his
> bondage to the senses; it only shows him that he
> was always so and cannot be otherwise. The sym-
> bolic truth, on the other hand, which puts water
> in place of the mother and spirit or fire in
> place of the father, frees the libido . . . of-
> fers it a new gradient, and canalizes it into a
> spiritual form. Thus man, as a spiritual being,
> becomes a child again, and is born into a circle
> of brothers and sisters; but his mother has be-
> come the "communion of saints," the Church, and
> his brothers and sisters are humanity, with whom
> he is united anew in the common heritage of sym-
> bolic truth.[21]

That man, that child born again, is Francis of Assisi,
and his own rebirth was a cosmic reconciliation that began
in the cave of the self and ended in God. Francis ascended
to the Most High by reconciling himself with all of creation: sun and moon and stars, the four elements of the uni-

verse (earth, water, air and fire), and all people. Then
moving steadily onward by means of pardon, forgiveness and
embracing death, Francis arrived in God and realized that
the whole cosmos is mirrored in his own heart, that is,
that every outside reality has its counterpart inside the
self. By really and symbolically embracing the world of
outer space, Francis is reconciled with his own inner space
and everything contained within it.

This is how he sings it in the great poem of his life,
the poem he wrote the year before his death, that in which
he summarizes everything he had become, everything he knew:

Most high, all-powerful, all good, Lord:
All praise is yours, all glory, all honour
And all blessing.

To you alone, Most High, do they belong.
No mortal lips are worthy
To pronounce your name.

All praise be yours, my Lord, through all that
You have made.
And first my Lord Brother Sun,
Who brings the day; and light you
give to us through him.

How beautiful is he, how radiant in all his
splendour!
Of you, Most High, he bears the likeness.

All praise be yours, my Lord,
through Sister Moon and Stars;
In the heavens you have made them, bright
And precious and fair.

All praise be yours, my Lord,
        through Brothers Wind and Air,
And fair and stormy, all the weather's moods,
By which you cherish all that you have made.

All praise be yours, my Lord,
        through Sister Water,
So useful, lowly, precious and pure.

All praise be yours, my Lord,
        through Brother Fire,
Through whom you brighten up the night.
How beautiful he is, how gay!
        Full of power and strength.

All praise be yours, my Lord, through
        Sister Earth, our mother,
Who feeds us in her sovereignty and produces
Various fruits and colored flowers and herbs.

All praise be yours, my Lord, through those who
        grant pardon
For love of you; through those who endure
Sickness and trial.

Happy those who endure in peace,
        By you, Most High, they will be crowned.
All praise be yours, my Lord, through
        Sister Death,
From whose embrace no mortal can escape.

Woe to those who die in mortal sin!
        Happy those she finds doing your will!
        The second death can do no harm to them.

Praise and bless my Lord, and give him thanks,
And serve him with great humility.[22]

No wonder the Greek poet, Nikos Kazantzakis, could say
that he loved St. Francis

. . . because by means of love and ascetic discipline his soul conquered reality--hunger, cold,
disease, scorn, injustice, ugliness (what men
without wings call reality)--and succeeded in
transubstantiating this reality into a joyous,
palpable dream truer than truth itself. He discovered the secret so sought after by medieval
alchemists: how to transubstantiate even the
basest metal into pure gold. Why? Because for
Francis the "philosopher's stone" was not something inaccessible and external to man . . . it
was his own heart.[23]

For Franics of Assisi peace was a gift of God which he
made real in his life by a life-long process of reconciliation with the dark forces within himself, with other people and with the elements of the whole cosmos. Peace was
the fruit of an inner process of purification which began
and ended in God. As the philosopher, Max Scheeler, said
so beautifully,

It was left to one of the great artificers of the
spirit in European history to make the memorable
attempt of uniting and harnessing this [a non-
cosmic personal love-mysticism of universal com-
passion], within a single life-stream, to the an-
imistic sense of union with the being and life of
Nature. This was the very remarkable achievement
of the saint of Assisi.[24]

This achievement is Francis' gift to those who seek peace,
to those for whom the pursuit of non-violence is a personal
odyssey as well as a dream for all people everywhere.

VIOLENT NON-VIOLENCE

The non-violent way to peace is, indeed, as St. Francis believed and lived, the same as the way to peace of soul. Neither can ever be achieved apart from God; and paradoxically, neither can be achieved apart from doing violence to oneself.

"The Kingdom of heaven suffers violence and only the violent bear it away."

[Francis] lived in an age of violence, an age when to die in battle was a glorious passing. In conformity with his times, he too had twice ridden off to battle to prove himself a man. But with his conversion came the realization that war and violence mocked the Gospel of Jesus and that a man proved nothing by going to war.

He had wanted to confront people with the peace of Jesus in a way that would be convincing. So he did it violently. He did violence to himself and he did violence to his age by turning upside down what man believed in. He wanted to be a knight. So he became a beggar and acted like a knight. He wanted honor and fame. So he tore it out of his heart and put on shame and anonymity. He wanted to conquer the world. So he let Christ conquer him.[25]

Francis of Assisi was a mystic and a "martyr." He was a mystic because he taught and lived the truth that mystical union with God is impossible without love, forgiveness and reconciliation. He was a "martyr" because he did violence to himself and suffered violence to himself in order to cast out fear and the sinful violence it breeds in the heart. Francis knew that there can be no intimate life in Christ without peace and that violence is an obstacle to

peace in Christ. For him, non-violence is simply the re-
moval of the overwhelming obstacle to peace in Christ, a
process that paradoxically involves doing violence to oneself, directing one's violent impulse toward uprooting the
sinfulness in one's own heart. In living this paradox St.
Francis found peace, and it is only by living the same gospel paradox that we shall find peace, that gift of God,
which is the beginning of the end of violence in ourselves
and in others.

NOTES

[1] Murray Bodo, Francis, the Journey and the Dream (Cincinnati: St. Anthony Messenger Press, 1972), p. 71.

[2] By "embracing" I do not mean we must love our evil or potential for evil, but that acknowledging it in ourselves must be without self-hatred or despair. It must include the possibility of redemption.

[3] Marion Habig, ed., Francis of Assisi, Omnibus of Sources (Chicago: Franciscan Herald Press, 1973), p. 67.

[4] John J. L. Mood, ed., Rilke on Love and Other Difficulties (New York: W. W. Norton and Co., 1975), pp. 98-99.

[5] Habig, pp. 234-35.

[6] Eloi Leclerc, The Canticle of Creatures: Symbols of Union (Chicago: Franciscan Herald Press, 1979), pp. 137-47.

[7] Habig, p. 160.

[8] Thomas Merton, Contemplation in a World of Action (Garden City, N.Y.: Doubleday Image Books, 1971), pp. 154-55.

[9] Omer Englebert, St. Francis of Assisi (Chicago: Franciscan Herald Press, 1965), p. 65.

[10] Bodo, pp. 6-7.

[11] Ibid., pp. 87-90.

[12] Johannes Jörgensen, St. Franics of Assisi (Garden City, N.Y.: Doubleday Image Books, 1955), p. 60.

[13] Habig, p. 96.

[14] Ibid., p. 647.

[15] Edward Guinan, ed., Peace and Non-Violence (New York: Paulist Press, 1973), p. 127.

[16] Habig, p. 68.

[17] Ibid., p. 60.

[18] Ibid., p. 83.

[19] Ibid., p. 131.

[20] Ibid., p. 110.

[21] Carl Jung, Symbols of Transformation, trans. R.F.C. Hall, Collected Works, Vol. 5., New York, 1956, p. 226, quoted in Leclerc, p. 171.

[22] Leclerc, pp. xvii-xviii.

[23]Nikos Kazantzakis, Report to Greco (London: Faber
and Faber, 1965), pp. 378-79.

[24]Max Scheeler,   The Nature of Sympathy,   trans.
P. Heath, New Haven, 1954, p. 87, quoted in Leclerc,
pp. xii-xiii.

[25]Bodo, pp. 155-56.

GEORGE FOX

(1624 - 1691)

by Joseph T. Culliton, C.S.B.

*There is a unique quality and content to the
peace testimony of George Fox, balanced as it is
by the Puritan theology and ethics of his day and
his own mystical experience of the inner light.
J. Culliton develops extensively the historical
context in which Fox's opposition to violence develops and establishes that his stand against it
flows from the depths of his spirituality. His
teaching on suffering love and the Lamb's War
strike a common chord with Francis of Assisi,
Thomas Merton and John Howard Yoder. The power
of the indwelling Spirit in people is central to
Fox's spirituality and his non-violence is summed
up in "war is against the Spirit."*

HISTORICAL CONTEXT

To appreciate the peace testimony of George Fox one
must achieve a balance between Fox the mystic and Fox the
Puritan. Many of his thought forms and ethical positions
are largely derived from Puritan teaching; however, many of
his teachings express his reaction against both the Presbyterianism and Puritanism of his day.[1] Thus we must situ-
ate Fox and the early Friends within the long struggle for
religious reform and freedom that took place in England in
the seventeenth century.

The reform of which we speak developed along two
lines. The first is the central Puritan movement toward
Presbyterianism which sought to reform church organization,

life and church-state relations on biblical and Calvinist
lines. The second is the much broader movement of Puritans
who became Independents, Separatists, Congregationalists
and more radical spiritual reformers in their search for a
free religious life. This latter movement, which was heavily ethical, cut across ecclesiastical and political lines
and deeply influenced the whole of English spirituality and
culture.

Although King James I preferred to rule through bishops, Puritan influence steadily increased during his reign,
especially in the parishes. Thus, when Charles I came to
the throne in 1624 the Puritan movement included most of
the active ministers and laymen in England. They strove to
reform the nation and church in terms of Puritan beliefs
and ethics. However, through King Charles, Bishop Laud
gained power over the Church of England. The rigid conformity he demanded forced Puritans to choose between giving up their pattern of church life or rejecting the nation
they sought to reform.[2]

Until the opening of the Long Parliament in 1640, Puritans suffered under Bishop Laud and found it impossible to
accomplish their goal of imposing Presbyterianism on England. The establishment sought to maintain the unity of
the nation through the unity of the one Church. Within
this one national Church, Independents sought a degree of
autonomy for individual congregations and the number of
Separatist churches increased in spite of official opposition.

From 1640 on, Puritans were able to foster their revolution by uniting their cause with Parliament's fight to
restrict the power of the King. Parliament imprisoned
Bishop Laud and expelled other bishops from the House of
Lords. The Solemn League and Covenant abolished episcopacy
and imposed the full Presbyterian system with all its ri-

gidity, intolerance and discipline. Yet, in spite of its
favoured position and even its establishment by ordinance,
Presbyterianism could not secure itself.

Oliver Cromwell raised the regiments of the New Model
Army on a basis of individual commitment to the Puritan
cause. By 1646 the army was dominated by Independents and
gave support to the Separatist and Baptist churches. After
the second civil war, Cromwell's party expelled the Presbyterian majority from Parliament and in 1649 the Rump had
Charles I executed for treason. In 1653 Cromwell replaced
the Rump with the Parliament of Saints which represented
the Puritan cause.[3] Thus we see during the Commonwealth
a degree of toleration that created a situation of relative
religious liberty for most minorities. In fact, at times
unrestrained sectarianism flourished. When restraints or
persecution arose, they did so because the action of the
more radical reformers appeared to be a threat to the unity
of both the religious and political establishments.

1660 saw Charles II and the Restoration. Within the
next few years a series of Acts restored the Anglican
Church and restricted all worship to that of the Common
Book of Prayer. Puritans were expelled from national and
local governments, the military, universities and pastor-
ates. Most lost prestige and property and were simply reduced to dissenters and non-conformists.

Friends, of course, fell under this legislation so
that arrests and unjust imprisonments began in large numbers. The Quaker Act was passed when they were falsely
suspected of being involved in a Fifth Monarchist plot
against the government. Laws requiring the taking of oaths
were also used against them. Thus a period of severe persecution continued until the Toleration Act was passed in
1689.[4] These few facts sketch the *political context* in
which George Fox lived and developed his peace testimony.

Next, we shall examine his personal life and the *religious milieu* in which he matured.

Fox was born in July, 1624, in Leicestershire. His parents were simple, religious country folk who brought him up as a Puritan "in the way and worship of the nation."[5] He apprenticed to a shoemaker and wool dealer and received little formal education beyond the study of scripture. At age 19 he felt called to a very personal search for God. He left home and began a period of spiritual desolation, extreme temptation and near despair as he travelled from place to place consulting clerics, scholars and the faithful of many congregations in a long search for God and truth. He experienced a deep sense of personal sin and gained neither consolation nor light from either professors or clergy. He found the latter to be weak and spiritually ineffective because they had no genuine experience of God.

Shortly before he began his preaching in 1647, in the silence within himself, Fox experienced the Divine presence. He had an immediate experience of the "divine seed" or "inner light" of Christ in him and realized that Christ was present speaking to him from within. He also realized that such experience was available to all believers. Through similar recurring experiences, meditated on in the light of scripture, Fox came to know Christ experimentally. The knowledge he gained through these "openings" he regarded as certain, revealed knowledge as opposed to mere "notions" about God. Rufus Jones maintains that on the basis of these mystical experiences, understood in conjunction with the scripture, Fox's faith took stable form.[6]

Mystical experience similar to that of Fox flourished in the first half of seventeenth century England. From his formative years Fox had direct contact with a great variety of Anabaptists, Congregationalists and Seekers who also centered their lives on their direct experience of God's

presence. However, it is very difficult to assess their
influence on him because he did not openly acknowledge
ideas reaped from his religious milieu. He regarded them
as mere "notions" until they became part of his own inner
religious experience. Then he disregarded their human origin and saw them as revelations or "openings" of light from
the Spirit within him.[7]

One of the leaders of the Familists, Henry Nicolas,
was known for mystical experience, for waiting in silence
for the Spirit and for rejecting oaths, capital punishment
and war. This group also moved beyond the letter of the
Bible and doctrinal formulae to the effective, direct experience of God in their lives.[8] Fox's Journal gives
little detail about his relations with the Seekers until
1652, yet it indicates that from 1643 to 1647 his life was
that of a Seeker. These people, who withdrew from the institutional churches, maintained a deep devotion to
Christ. They interpreted their own experience of the
Spirit and sought further light and/or a future prophet to
lead them. The young Fox was certainly influenced by their
lives, and in turn, from 1652 on, whole groups of Seekers,
already prepared for his message, became Quaker communities.[9]

Members of the Anabaptist movement also appear to have
had an early influence on Fox. His uncle Pickering was a
Baptist. Certainly he knew and was influenced by the Anabaptist's lengthy pacifist tradition. Quaker pacifism has
been placed in an historic succession which includes Felix
Mans, Conrad Grebel and Menno Simons.[10] In fact, Ernst
Troeltsch maintains that the Quaker religion "represents
the final expression in its purest form of the Anabaptist
movement."[11] In 1647 Fox spoke at a meeting of Baptists
at Broughton and associated himself with a community of
separated Baptists at Nottinghamshire. This group later

accepted his message and formed the first community of "The
Children of Light."

The Renaissance emphasis on pacifism and the dignity
of persons was also part of the seventeenth century atmosphere in which Fox lived. It too must have influenced him
at least unconsciously. However, whereas Renaissance humanism was based on the universality of reason, Fox's humanism was based on the universality of the indwelling
light of Christ.

Fox and early Friends did not separate morality and
religion or ethics and theology. Thus, to understand Fox's
ethics one must turn first to the implications of his own
experience, especially implications of his religious experience of the "inner light." Fox was a Christ-centered
person. To understand and live the Christian life for him
meant living according to Christ's light. In this sense,
therefore, his direct experience of Christ's presence is
central or foundational to his peace testimony. All else
either arises out of or is closely related to one's inner
life, that is, to the power of Christ enlightening and
strengthening one from within.[12]

Affirming the centrality of the inner light, however,
is only one half of the picture. Fox also developed many
principles and motives for living non-violently. This development frequently occurred when specific political situations forced him to clarify his position. His Puritan
theology and ethics deeply influenced his testimony. In
fact, experience of the inner light has no meaning unless
the spiritual power it gives is expressed in moral action
directed toward fighting the evil within and converting the
nation.

THE INNER LIGHT

The core of Fox's doctrine of the inner light is to be found in passages where he quotes, paraphrases and develops Jn 1:12-13 and Jn 3:34-36. Christ, who is the express image of the substance of God, existed before the world was created. The world was made by Him. In Christ is life and his life is the light of all people. Christ gives all who believe in his name, that is, all born not of flesh, but of God, power to become sons of God. He is the light of the world. Everyone is offered his light, and all have the capacity to receive, accept and love it. Christ, is, therefore, the light of God in all people who come into the world; all receive a measure of grace regardless of their sin. Those who believe have eternal life; those who reject Christ have God's wrath on them.[13]

Christ does not destroy, but fulfills the law, by being the internal light of God in believers. The ordinances of the New Covenant are internal--written in our hearts. The Holy Spirit is the Teacher of the New Covenant, and the internal light and life of Christ are one. The dominant characteristics of the New Covenant are light, love and peace. Those who receive them receive an anointing, a new heart that is one with that of Christ and the saints.[14]

One cannot ignore or despise the inner light and yet profess God. Nor can one maintain that the written letter of scripture is the word and that the texts themselves are the Gospel. God is the word, light, power and Spirit. The letter is simply a declaration of these realities. Christians, who already possess the ingrafted word within them, must wait patiently in the indwelling light. As they grow in it, it opens the scriptures more fully to them. Not the letter, but the ingrafted Word, which Christians are called to hear and live, is a power that saves their souls (Jm 1:21-22).[15] Here Fox develops a fundamental Puritan

teaching that the grace of God is essentially an inner
moral power. The inner light transforms the believer and
gives a readiness to act morally and to lead others to do
the same.

Faith is essential in order that one possess the peace
of Christ and a good conscience. By faith in the inner
light one is translated from death to life and given victory over sin. Only if one purifies one's conscience by
faith can one witness unity, victory over enmity and other
fruits of faith which work by love. Through faith one possesses truth and is at peace with God.[16] Light and faith
possess a divine power and efficacy. Fox rejects the "notion" of those who claim that people cannot overcome the
body of sin while on earth, and quotes 1 Jn 5:4 and
Col 2:11 to instance the veracity of his position.
Rom 6:22 and Rom 7:6 also reveal that the divine power of
faith purifies the heart and gives victory over the world.
It is by the power of God that we put off the body of sin
and are liberated to serve in the newness of the Spirit.[17]

Christ who is Ruler, Counsellor and Prince of Peace is
in us. If Moses laid down purifications necessary for a
holy war (Num 31), how much more must Christians be inward-
ly holy to fight the spiritual war in the New Covenant?
Fox emphasizes that Christ is Ruler, Lord and King of the
entire universe. He is the Second Adam who has been given
all power to overcome, judge and punish all evil and to re-
ward good. He is presently establishing his kingdom on
earth in and through those who dwell in Him. Thus, they
have power to overcome adversaries without the use of violence.[18] Fox's faith in Christ's sovereign rule over
history is a fundamental theme on which he builds his argument against war.

The inner light requires moral earnestness of the believer. The light informs one's conscience, teaches right-

eousness and holiness and keeps one from lying, swearing, hatred and acts that cause disharmony. It also reveals the fact that human wisdom is sensual and devilish. Where such knowledge and love predominate, there is perversity, envy, selfishness and back-biting. The inner light alone leads to self-denial and control of earthly affections. It manifests the errors of the wicked and enables the believer to take up the cross daily.[19]

In Fox's thought on the inner light we already find two important themes that had emerged in Puritanism by the time of the Parliament of Saints, namely, that of spiritual inspiration and moral earnestness directed toward attaining social justice. This theological and ethical stance set Friends apart from orthodox Presbyterianism, and aligned them more with Cromwell's brand of Puritanism which combined an emphasis on social equality and the work of the Spirit. Radical Puritanism linked conversion and the Spirit in such a way as to emphasize conscious emotional experience and direct impulses to act and speak. This prepared the way for the Friend's form of worship.[20]

Since many Puritans needed to be re-assured of God's power of conversion in them, they often emphasized intensity of personal experience in a manner similar to that of Fox. The similarity between the thought of Familists, Seekers, Independents and some radicals such as the Ranters and that of Fox is also evident in their understanding of the indwelling Spirit's role in moral action. However, since these ideas pervaded spiritual Puritanism, one cannot trace Fox's thought to specific origins. Theological and ethical positions which became foundations underlying his peace testimony were held in common with many other Puritans. The specific conclusions drawn from these starting points were what made Fox's overall ethical stance and peace testimony unique.[21]

UNITY, PEACE AND HONOUR FOR ALL:
CONSEQUENCES OF THE INNER LIGHT

Because the light is one and reconciles believers to God, its consequence is achieving unity and love. The light gathers their hearts together and enables them to experience their former estrangement from God's life. It draws them from under the occasion of all outward laws and helps them walk in the one Spirit so that they neither envy nor fulfill the lusts of the flesh. Believers are baptized into the Body of Christ, which provides them with a compelling reason to care for, suffer with and honour one another. Dwelling in the word removes the occasion of divisions and wars as it brings people back to the original state before conflicts and wars began. It destroys that lustful nature which is the occasion from which wars arise (Jm 4:1-2).[22]

Here we find at the core of Fox's thought a fundamental, Puritan dualism between good and evil, light and darkness, the Spirit and the flesh. Fox was thoroughly convinced of the basic sinfulness of mankind because of the fall and equally convinced of the need for strong discipline and reliance on spiritual weapons in waging spiritual warfare against sin within oneself. If one lives by one's own spirit, depraved nature, which brings forth lust, covetousness and disobedience, acts as a source of war. Friends must keep up the inner struggle against temptation and condemn fallen nature within themselves as part of their larger calling to overcome evil and war outside of themselves.

On the basis of biblical evidence Fox shows that where there is unity in the Spirit there is peace. The first step toward achieving peace is simply dwelling in the light so that grace may increase in oneself. Fox maintains that there are numerous sects within Christianity because Chris-

tians do not drink from the one Spirit in which the fellowship of the Prince of Peace exists. Yet all Christians are
bound to keep his peace and seek the peace of all men
because they are baptized in the one Spirit.[23]

Christ is God's everlasting covenant of peace with
mankind. God has not only made all people of one blood, He
has given Christ as a covenant of light, life and peace.
No-one who plots, betrays, injures or destroys the life of
another can live in Christ's covenant. Thus once again Fox
opposes taking up arms in principle because it is a false
and destructive way of opposing evil.[24]

2 Cor 13:11 commands the believer to be perfect and to
live in peace. If Christians are of good conduct and of
one mind, God's peace will increase in them. Jn 13:35 and
15:8 urge Christians to love one another and to love enemies as Christ loves all people. To the extent that believers do not live in peace and do not love their enemies
they make non-believers deny that they are followers of
Christ.[25] The Christian obligation to foster peace is
fundamental and inseparable from the command to love God
and neighbour, including enemies and persecutors. This is
part of what Fox refers to as the Royal Law of Love, a very
fundamental belief on which he based his peace testimony.

Fox affirms that Friends, in fact, love all people
simply because they are people, God's creation and brothers
and sisters in their common descent from Adam. As well,
they love individuals as they come to be sons of God by
adoption. People have a twofold common basis for loving
everyone because God created all people and wills that all
turn to Him and live. For this He gave his Son. By loving
everyone Fox maintains that he honours everyone in the
Lord. He accuses others of not honouring all people; one
does not strike or hurt a person one honours.

Lk 10:27 commands Christians to love all people as they love themselves, and Lk 6:31 tells them to do to others as they would have others do to them. Persons who love and esteem their neighbours will not abuse and shed their blood. Christians of false conscience esteem and respect others because of advantage. Jm 2:12 warns against such behaviour. The true light in one's conscience demands equity and justice. Those who sin against the poor and show human respect to the mighty neither fear God nor honour the king. They dishonour king, nation and government (1 Pt 2:17). The unjust, proud person does not fear God and so cannot honour anyone because humility goes before honour.[26]

OUTSIDE THE LIGHT IS DESPAIR, LUST AND MURDER

Fox contrasts the first birth in the fallen Adam with the second birth into the kingdom of God. The former leads to a life in profane nature outside the light and is characterized by strife, persecution, lust and killing. The latter is characterized by love and peace. Life in the Prince of Peace is life in Christ, the second Adam, who never fell. Fox urges believers to come out of Adam in the fall to the seed of God in their own selves.[27] That is to say, Fox saw the world as an active evil that opposed the Spirit. Thus he strove to bring people out of the world and into the church through daily perseverance in moral action.

Those living outside the light tend to presumption which leads to despair and the destruction of justice. The actions of Cain, Esau, David and Judas reveal that persons who reject the light first kill justice within themselves, then despair and kill the just outside of themselves. Esau is a symbol of the profane or carnal spirit and nature in all people. Christians recognize this spirit in others,

yet frequently fail to see it in themselves. If this spirit is followed, it kills the Spirit in them. Esau, who
sought his profane liberty with the sword, wanted to maintain the election, but could not do so. In like manner,
those who profess Christ by word, but destroy the effects
of Christ in themselves will be condemned.[28]

Those who cause strife are not children of God:
"Blessed are the peace-makers, for they shall be called the
children of God" (Mt 5:9). Christ insisted that his kingdom was not of this world. His disciples did not fight to
preserve Him nor did He, even though He possessed all
power, use it to defend himself against his persecutors.
In like manner, when Fox was beaten unjustly, he neither
resisted nor struck back.

Those who fight belong to the kingdom of this world.
Gamaliel's intervention in Acts 5:38-39 shows the futility
of outward fighting: "Let them alone, for if this counsel
or this work be of men, it will come to nought; but if it
be of God, ye cannot overthrow it; lest haply ye be found
even to fight against God." As well, 2 Cor 10:2-5 and
Eph 6:10-17 indicate that the Christian uses not carnal,
but spiritual, weapons which will destroy all imaginings
and ambitions that exalt themselves against the knowledge
of God. Outward war is a blind man's war because it accom-
plishes nothing but spiritual defeat.[29]

In a letter to Friends in Barbadoes Fox described in
detail the spiritual armour and weapons of the Christian.
Summarily stated, they consist of truth, salvation, righteousness, the power of God, the sword of the Spirit, the
word of God (which is one of life, wisdom and reconciliation) and faith.[30]

These spiritual weapons are the only weapons available
to believers who are called to love and serve their neighbour. On the other hand, those who destroy their neighbour

are without even natural affections (Rom 1), because they
destroy the good nature in themselves from which natural
affection flows. Nature, before the fall, was one, had
natural affections and did not destroy itself. Sin led
mankind out of the truth which destroyed the integrity of
nature. In turn, sinful people destroy nature outside of
their isolated selves. Outside the light persons can neither know the divine truth nor love the brotherhood, let
alone love their enemies.[31]

THE POWER OF LAW, MAGISTRATE AND CIVIL GOVERNMENT

Those who live by the Spirit are not subject to external law because the light and word of God in them take
away the occasion or need of outward laws in their
lives.[32] Proper external ordinances are of significance
to the righteous, however, because the very occasion of
laws "is a praise to them that do well, and a terror to the
evil-doers."[33] In this teaching Fox relies upon
1 Pt 2:13-14. Law is good in its place if it is used
against the unrighteous and lawless. God wills that evil-
doers be punished and that liberty ought not to be used as
a cloak for malice. Peter gave an example to believers by
obeying all laws that opposed evil, yet opposed unjust laws
that were contrary to the command of God.[34]

There is no doubt that within strict limits Fox recognized the power of the magistrate's sword to use force in
punishing evil-doers. When administered properly by good
men in conjunction with righteous laws, the sword is an instrument of God. It is at one with the Spirit because it
is meant to lead sinners out of darkness to the light. In
order that they might be instruments of the Spirit, Fox
calls magistrates to open themselves to the truth and to
that of God in all men, to exercise their power to punish
evil-doers justly, and to lead people away from profanity,
but never to persecute people for their religion.[35]

In exercising authority Fox exhorts both Christian and non-Christian rulers to at least do unto others as they would be done by, if they cannot observe the full law of the Gospel to love all people.[36] From very early in his ministry Fox declared that participation in the army was against his principles. However, during those years in which Friends regarded the Commonwealth as a potential instrument of God in establishing the kingdom, Fox did not encourage soldiers, who were frequently put on police duty, to leave the army. He advised them as John the Baptist advised the Roman soldiers: "Plunder no one, accuse no one falsely, and be content with your pay" (Lk 3:14). It was the Restoration and the legislation of the Cavalier Parliament that moved Fox openly to declare an outright incompatibility between the faith of all Friends and military service. No Friend must enter the army or take other work requiring violence.

In calling secular rulers to stop abusing the power given them by God to maintain order and keep peace, Fox exhorts them "to answer the principle of God in all people."[37] In searching out the will of God in humility and truth and acting according to it, the whole of creation is "ordered again to the glory of God."[38] Answering that of God in others and ordering everything to the glory of God are used by Fox as principles and motives for living non-violently.[39]

Far from being an anarchist, Fox recognized the state as an ordinance of God and benefit to people wherever it is justly administered. Governors are called by God to administer justice to all, to keep civil peace and to judge and punish evil-doers. To fulfill these duties faithfully and to avoid unlawful abuses of the sword, rulers must receive God's help by living and ruling under the Spirit. Citizens must assist them by keeping the peace and paying taxes. In this teaching Fox relied heavily on Rom 13:1-7.

William Penn maintained that Fox was a staunch sup-
porter of the state, particularly in his refusal to fight,
because he could not take up arms against it.[40] Hugh
Barbour also claims that the Friends' peace testimony was a
great contribution to statecraft. In situations where the
ideals of different parties are clearly antagonistic, fear
and deadlock of consciences can be overcome without compro-
mise of principles because the Friends' refusal to use violence against opponents gives the latter a firm basis on
which to tolerate Friends.[41]

THE ROYAL LAW OF LOVE AND THE LAMB'S WAR

Fox and the early Quakers developed their own version
of the Puritan theocratic ideal. Puritans believed that
God rules both church and state by means of his elect.
Thus, by the power of his grace they strove to reform and
purify England for God's glory. The kingdom had already
been established in England through their reformation, and
they were responsible for actively bringing it to comple-
tion. They maintained a strong apocalyptic hope and complete faith in the eschatological victory of Christ over
all evil. Victory cannot be achieved, however, apart from
suffering.[42]

Fox developed what he referred to as the Royal Law of
Love. This law expressed the divine command to love all
people even to the point of extreme suffering under persecution. One who lives in the light has been called into a
covenant of peace with Christ and neighbour. Thus, one
must obey the command to love one's enemies, accept
suffering as a gift of God and means to victory, and bless
and pray for those who persecute you.

To show that suffering and persecution are the lot of
true followers of Christ just as they were the lot of
Christ himself, Fox frequently refers to Jn 15:18-27;

16:33; 2 Cor 1:5-7 and 2 Tim 3:12.[43] During severe persecutions he encouraged Friends to be patient and to even
rejoice in their tribulations, because they are a test of
faith and proof of membership in the church. When Friends
suffer, it is Christ who suffers, and He will not allow
more to come one's way than one can bear.[44]

Christians can expect to be persecuted because their
kingdom and teaching oppose earthly wisdom and desires.
Friends must practice endurance and not be provoked by persecution because that leads to enmity and hatred, and who-
ever hates another is already a murderer (1 Jn 3:15).

To persecute a person regarding religion implies power
over that person's faith; yet Paul denies this power to
anyone. People who force others to act against their consciences sin against them and Christ. Both Jews and Christians are separated from God because their prophets and
priests have shed blood over religion. Such activity is
not according to the mind or power of Christ. In fact, it
is a cause of shame and scandal before non-Christians.[45]

Fox's teaching on suffering love took on a unique dimension because it was an integral part of what he describes as the Lamb's War. Thus, it became a means to victory. Christ is both the suffering lamb of the Gospel and
the triumphant lamb of Revelations; He triumphs through his
sufferings. Friends represent Christ and do his redemptive
work in accepting suffering and persecution because these
are means of constantly struggling against inner and outward evil in all its forms.[46]

The Lamb's War is certainly fought with spiritual
weapons against all who oppose the Spirit, but first and
foremost it is an inner struggle against all that is not of
God within each believer. Victory comes through faith,
obedience and fidelity to the word of God.[47] Fox was en-
thusiastic about victory because "they that suffer with

him, shall reign with him."[48] Friends are already participating in the victory because through their suffering
love they are helping to achieve it. Christ working in
them has already come, and yet is coming to claim total
victory. Fox saw the final eschatological victory of the
Lamb and his army as bringing history to an end.[49] Very
frequently he emphasized the Day of the Lord when Christ
will judge and punish the unrighteous. However, T. Canby
Jones states that after 1660 Fox spoke less of God's wrath,
vengeance and judgment.[50]

Jones also points out that the Lamb's War was a program of social and religious revolution.[51] We shall conclude our discussion of this war by mentioning a few of the
non-violent strategies early Quakers used against their enemies. They disrupted church services and challenged and
denounced ministers they regarded as false. They refused
to take oaths and broke the Conventicle Acts and Quaker Act
in assembling for worship. They confronted leaders of government or wrote long tracts to them asking for justice and
exhorting them to reform. They sent lists to London enumerating the abuses they suffered daily. They rejected
commissions in the army and refused to leave prison until
the judge acknowledged having commit them under false
charges.[52] These strategies, along with the use of all
the spiritual weapons discussed earlier, gave them very
positive, active methods of bringing about ethical and religious reform.

WAR IS AGAINST THE SPIRIT

From the beginning of his ministry, Fox refused to use
force even to protect himself. The evidence indicates that
from the very beginning he held the principle that violence
was against the indwelling Spirit. Nevertheless, this
principle was only developed and spelled out in detail over

a period of years, and then frequently under the pressures of specific political events that required it. These facts explain a certain inconsistency (allowing Friends to remain in the army for a number of years) and a certain tension between sectarianism and universality in his position. These points are very minor, however, in view of the over-all development of his thought.

One of Fox's recorded statements that war is against the Spirit was made at Derby while in prison in 1650. At that time he refused a commission in a militia, and as a consequence his prison term was extended.[53]   Again, in 1651, a Justice Bennett sent constables to offer him a commission. He refused it twice, along with the money, and was committed as a "close prisoner, without bail or main-prise."[54]

In 1654 Fox wrote a letter to Oliver Cromwell assuring him that he would never draw carnal weapons against him or the government. He maintained that he had been sent by God to witness against violence and all works of darkness in order that he might bring people to the light and out of the occasion of all wars.[55]

In the final years of the Commonwealth there was much plotting and civil disorder. Some Quaker youth were tempted to take up arms, so in 1659 Fox wrote two declarations to Friends denouncing violence. In these letters he stressed that Christ's kingdom is not of this world. It is peaceable and those who live in strife have no part of it. One is deceived if one pretends to fight for Christ. Only by the sword of the Spirit within can believers attain Christ's peace. Those who fight and do not love enemies are outside his doctrine and life and are not heirs of his peace. War and fighting cannot produce peace because the power of the Spirit alone is capable of achieving it.[56]

The Restoration in 1660 destroyed all hope of a Puritan Commonwealth, and subsequent legislation reduced Friends to little better than outlaws. When Quakers were falsely accused of participation in a Fifth Monarchy plot to overthrow the government, Fox immediately developed what has been called the Declaration of 1660.[57] This document contains his most systematic, detailed rejection of war. Since most of the themes set forth in it have been developed above, I shall discuss only a few of its highlights.

In principle and practice Friends seek the peace and good of all. Wars proceed from uncontrolled ambition and desires; people kill to get what they otherwise cannot have (Jm 4:1-2). But Christ has redeemed us from this fallen state and brought us out of the occasion of war. Friends deny all outward strife because he that lives by the sword shall die by it (Mt 26:52; Rev 13:10). They act in imitation of and obedience to Christ who rejected violence even as a means of self-defense. The use of violence is inspired by the devil, the author of violence, and so is an act of disobedience and betrayal of Christ.

The Spirit moves Friends to seek peace and reject violence. Because the Sprit is constant, it can never move them to use violence to achieve either secular or religious victory. Fighting is contrary to the Spirit of Christ, his doctrine and the practice of his apostles. Only by the power of God's word in the hearts of people will the kingdoms of this world become the kingdoms of God. Friends' swords are broken into ploughshares as they await the effective power of God bringing people to love and unity. Thus, eventually "nation shall not lift up sword against nation, neither shall they learn war any more" (Is 2:4; Micah 4:3).

It is evident that George Fox's peace testimony is not simply an isolated ethical decision made independently of

his mystical experience of Christ and his Puritan ethics
and theology. On the contrary, it flows from something
much deeper and more central to his entire spirituality.
Although his thought is certainly biblical, it is not based
on a literal interpretation of a few biblical texts. Fox's
direct experience of the indwelling Spirit is foundational
to his pacifism because Christ and the power of his Spirit
are the center of his spiritual Life. His principles and
motives for living non-violently form at least the framework of a Christian ethic regarding war. These principles
are also related to Christ and the Spirit. The only "violence" acceptable to Fox is that spiritual violence the
Christian must do to him/her self in order to control in-
clinations that oppose the Spirit and lead to strife.

Certainly Fox's spirituality, and the peace testimony
that is central to it, led to the way of the cross. Nevertheless, it also lead to both spiritual and temporal victory. As Hugh Barbour indicates, the non-violence of the
Quakers during the intense persecution after 1661 won the
respect of England and was the largest factor in bringing
the country to a policy of toleration.[58] The Toleration
Act passed in 1689, a few short years before Fox's death.

NOTES

[1]Herbert G. Wood, "George Fox and His Religious Background," New Appreciations of George Fox, A Tercentenary Collection of Studies (London: The Swarthmore Press Ltd., 1925), p. 53.

[2]Hugh Barbour, The Quakers in Puritan England (New Haven: Yale University Press, 1964), pp. 5-6, 16.

[3]Ibid., pp. 17-20.

[4]Ibid., pp. 212-13, 224-32.

[5]William Penn, "The Testimony of William Penn Concerning that Faithful Servant George Fox," The Journal of George Fox, ed. by Rufus M. Jones (New York: Capricorn Books, 1963), p. 50.

[6]Rufus M. Jones, The Life and Message of George Fox, 1624-1924, A Tercentenary Address Given at Haverford College, Haverford, Pennsylvania, May 17, 1924 (New York: The Macmillan Co., 1924), pp. 13-14.

[7]William C. Braithwaite, The Beginnings of Quakerism, 2nd. ed., revised (Cambridge: Cambridge University Press, 1955), pp. 41-42.

[8]Braithwaite, pp. 22-24, 40-41; Rufus M. Jones, Mysticism and Democracy in the English Commonwealth, Being the William Belden Noble Lectures Delivered in Harvard University, 1930-1931 (New York: Octagon Books Inc., 1965), pp. 136-38.

[9]Braithwaite, pp. 24-27, 130-31; R. Jones, Mysticism and Democracy, pp. 58-104.

[10]Geoffrey F. Nuttall, Christian Pacifism in History (Oxford: Basil Blackwell, 1958), p. 56.

[11]Ernst Troeltsch, The Social Teaching of the Christian Churches, trans. by Olive Wyon, Vol. II (New York: Macmillan, 1931), p. 781.

[12]Not all authors today place as much emphasis on Fox's mystical experience as did Rufus Jones and other earlier writers. T. Canby Jones speaks of it in terms of "conversion experience" in George Fox's Attitude Toward War (Annapolis, Maryland: Academic Fellowship, 1972), p. 6. Hugh Barbour in The Quakers in Puritan England, pp. x-xi, 1-2, 110-11, with few exceptions, denies that early Quakers were basically mystics. Yet these authors acknowledge that the ethics of early Quakers can only be understood by starting from and being related to their inner life. If as Louis Bouyer indicates, in "Mysticism," Dictionary of Theology, trans. by Charles U. Quinn (Paris: Desclée and Co., 1965), pp. 316-18, mysticism is understood, as originally,

in connection with the mystery of Christ in us, mysticism
is the Christian experience expressed in Gal 2:20: "It is
now no longer I that live, but Christ lives in me." In
this light it seems difficult to either deny or diminish
the mystical experience of George Fox.

[13]George Fox, The Works of George Fox, VIII volumes
reprinted from the 1831 edition published by M. T. C.
Gould, Philadelphia (New York: AMS Press, 1975), IV,
pp. 15, 219-20; V, p. 91.
    Titles of all eight volumes will be given now. Hence-
forth all references to Fox's writings will be cited by
volume and page numbers only.
I & II A Journal or Historical Account of the Life,
Travels, Sufferings, Christian Experiences, and Labour of
Love in the Work of the Ministry, of that Ancient, Eminent,
and Faithful Servant of Jesus Christ, George Fox, with an
Introduction by William Penn.
III The Great Mystery of the Great Whore Unfolded: and
AntiChrist's Kingdom Revealed unto Destruction.
IV, V & VI Gospel Truth Demonstrated, in a Collection of
Doctrinal Books, given forth by that Faithful Minister of
Jesus Christ, George Fox: containing Principles essential
to Christianity and Salvation, held among the People called
Quakers.
VII & VIII A Collection of Many Select and Christian Epis-
tles, Letters and Testimonies, written on Sundry Occasions,
by that Ancient, Eminent, Faithful Friend and Minister of
Christ Jesus, George Fox.
    [14]IV, pp. 61-62, 67, 151, 154-55.
    [15]IV, pp. 20-21, 23, 97.
    [16]IV, pp. 219, 288.
    [17]IV, p. 45.
    [18]IV, p. 357; V, pp. 434-35; VI, p. 85; VII, pp. 118,
179.
    [19]IV, pp. 16, 30-32, 132-33, 202-03.
    [20]Barbour, pp. 21, 24, 26-27.
    [21]Ibid., pp. 2-3, 28.
    [22]IV, pp. 17, 43, 200; V, p. 297.
    [23]IV, pp. 17-18: V, pp. 109, 224-25.
    [24]IV, p. 267; VII, p. 76; VIII, p. 43.
    [25]II, p. 382; V, p. 305; VI, pp. 433-34.
    [26]IV, pp. 45-46, 208-10, 214; V, pp. 217-21.
    [27]I, pp. 288-89; IV, p. 310; VII, p. 110.

[28]IV, p. 303; V, pp. 400-01, 403.

[29]IV, pp. 334-35, 339-41; VI, p. 414.

[30]VIII, p. 124.

[31]IV, pp. 364-65; VI, pp. 169-70.

[32]IV, p. 43.

[33]IV, p. 52.

[34]IV, pp. 88-89, 308.

[35]I, pp. 186, 396, 413; II, p. 28; IV, p. 342.

[36]I, p. 396; IV, p. 314.

[37]IV, p. 52.

[38]IV, pp. 163, 200.

[39]For a detailed analysis of this matter see James F. Childress, "Answering That of God in Every Man: An Interpretation of Fox's Ethics," Quaker Religious Thought, Vol. 15, no. 3 (Spring 1974).

[40]William Penn, "Introduction to Fox's Journal," I, p. xv.

[41]Barbour, p. 221.

[42]Ibid., pp. 4, 8, 11, 29.

[43]IV, pp. 331-32; V, pp. 147-48; VI, pp. 120-23.

[44]VII, pp. 240, 258-59.

[45]II, p. 291; IV, pp. 277-78; VI, pp. 257-58.

[46]IV, pp. 178-81.

[47]VI, p. 167; VII, pp. 295-96.

[48]VIII, p. 85.

[49]III, p. 6; VII, p. 20.

[50]T. Canby Jones, p. 94.

[51]Ibid., p. 97.

[52]Ibid., pp. 45, 61-62, 100, 103-04.

[53]I, p. 113.

[54]I, p. 116.

[55]I, pp. 208-09.

[56]I, pp. 387-90.

[57]I, pp. 420-25.

[58]Barbour, p. 223.

MARTIN LUTHER KING, JR.
(1929 - 1968)

by William D. Watley

*William D. Watley highlights the fact that Martin
Luther King Jr.'s non-violent ethic is an outgrowth of his theological foundation in evangelical liberalism and personalism. Non-violence is
the action of persons who are spiritually strong,
not that of cowards. Its goal is redemption and
reconciliation rather than the defeat of opponents. Creative suffering as a means of social
change has tremendous educational and redemptive
potential. Avoidance of both internal and external violence prepares the way for charity even
toward one's oppressors. King also maintains
that non-violence is supported by the universe
itself, which is on the side of justice.*

HISTORICAL BACKGROUND

Martin Luther King, Jr. was born January 15, 1929, in
Atlanta, Georgia. He came from strong roots. His father
was a powerful personality in his own right whose labors
had made the Ebenezer Baptist Church one of Atlanta's most
respected black congregations. Martin Jr.'s maternal
grandfather, the Reverend Alfred Daniel Williams had founded Ebenezer. Thus Martin Luther King, Jr. was born into a
stable, deeply religious, middle class household whose vocational tradition for at least two generations had been
the ordained ministry of the Baptist Church.

Although King became one of the third generation
preachers in his family, the decision to enter the ministry

was not as automatic as one might expect. When King entered Morehouse College in September, 1944, he was considering a career in either medicine or law. He had thought
about the ministry, but had been repelled by what he considered at that time to be the "emotionalism" that was
characteristic of much of the black Christian tradition of
worship and the lack of formal education among a number of
the black clergy. However, while at Morehouse he came under the influence of Dr. Benjamin Mays, the College President, and Dr. George Kelsey, Chairperson of the Religion
Department. Both of these men were seminary educated ministers who helped change King's perception of the ministry
as a vocation. Consequently, during his junior year, King
told his parents of his decision to enter the ministry. It
was also at Morehouse College that King discovered the
first intellectual source of his developing ethical consciousness when he read Henry David Thoreau's "Essay on
Civil Disobedience."

After graduating from Morehouse College, King entered
Crozer Theological Seminary in 1948. It was at Crozer that
he began a serious intellectual quest for a method to eliminate social evil. While at Crozer he was introduced to
Gandhian non-violence and to its potential as a method of
social protest, to the evangelical liberalism of George W.
Davis, the social gospel of Walter Rauschenbusch, and the
anthropology of Reinhold Niebuhr. The impact of these intellectual sources upon King's own non-violent ethic was
lasting. In 1951 he graduated from Crozer as the vale-
dictorian of his class and entered the School of Theology
at Boston University to begin his work on the Ph.D. degree
in Systematic Theology.

At Boston the two professors who had the greatest impact on him were Edgar Sheffield Brightman, who was noteworthy for his philosophy of personalism, and L. Harold

DeWolf, who was his major professor and adviser for this dissertation. King's study of personalism under Brightman, and the high spiritual value that it placed upon suffering, gave him his basic philosophical orientation and one of the major tenets of his non-violent ethic. It also helped him formulate his doctrine of God. King further refined his doctrine of God when he wrote his dissertation upon the God concepts of Paul Tillich and Henry Nelson Wieman. It was also during his Boston years that King met and married Coretta Scott of Marian, Alabama, a student at the New England Conservatory of Music.

In 1954 King ended his formal training with the acceptance of the pastorate of the Dexter Avenue Baptist Church in Montgomery, Alabama. On December 1, 1955, in Montgomery, an incident occurred which had a tremendous impact on the life and career of Martin Luther King, Jr. On that day, Mrs. Rosa Parks, a black seamstress, was arrested for refusing to give her seat (which was inside the designated area for persons of color) to a white male passenger. The arrest of Rosa Parks and the subsequent reaction of Montgomery's black community launched the career of Martin Luther King, Jr. as a civil rights fighter. In response to that historic arrest, the black community mobilized itself and organized a bus boycott that lead to the desegregation of Montgomery's transit system and King's emergence as a non-violent spokesman and practitioner.

When the Montgomery bus boycott began, King was essentially an exceptionally well-educated pastor in a Baptist Church, one who was engaged in those routines normally associated with shepherding the flock. He was a local leader who attempted to bring a certain perspective and to apply certain personally-held beliefs, that are fundamental to Christian faith, to the resolution of a local conflict. The Christian dimension was not meant to be exclu-

sive or accidental, but indicative of the source, the world
view and the theology that undergirded the exponent's point
of view. However, in the southern Bible belt that furnish-
ed the original arena for the application of King's non-
violent ethic, and among the church people who formed his
initial constituency, the Christian emphasis was more inclusive than exclusive. A Christian ethic in Montgomery,
Alabama, in the mid 1950's had broader mass appeal and commanded more respect than any other ethic. King attempted
to secure from his followers a commitment to non-violence
that was akin to religious conversion, one that was made
with the heart as well as the head. In doing so, he simply
reflected the basic style of the preacher that he was, a
man who Sunday after Sunday mounted his pulpit and called
"sinners to repentance."

Martin Luther King, Jr. held a Ph.D. in the theological tradition of evangelical liberalism. He was also an
activist and a Nobel Peace Prize winner (1964). Although
his perspective had been broadened by his exposure to a
number of ideas, persons and experiences throughout his
life, King remained fundamentally and essentially a black
Christian preacher. More than the thought of Gandhi or
Boston personalism or the evangelical liberalism of Crozer
Seminary, it was black religion that gave him his distinc-
tiveness among leaders. Nurtured in its bosom, he embraced
its "Songs of Zion" and shared much of its theology.

During the early days of the bus boycott when there
was no consciousness of Gandhi's influence on the part of
the leaders, there was an awareness of Christian princi-
ples--specifically the love ethic of Jesus, as understood
and articulated by the black preacher through the traditional, powerfully rooted, black church. The black Christian church perspective has its limitations, as does every
perspective. A perspective by its very nature limits and

defines its constituency. King's perspective not only defined his constituency, it also defined him. The personal
religious faith, the black church tradition, and the Christian theology that helped King understand and articulate
the meaning of his faith, may have at times seemed to limit
his appeal and the implications of some of his more mili-
tant views. However, these elements were also the source
of his inner strength. Without them he would not have been
the charismatic personality or the unique leader of humanity that he was.

MORAL THEORIST AND PRACTITIONER

Martin Luther King, Jr. was essentially a moral theo-
rist. The frame of reference from which he functioned,
from which he viewed life and the world in all of its many
facets, and from which he made his ethical decisions, was
not what was merely politically expedient; neither was it
totally dependent upon the exigencies of the situation. It
was what he considered to be morally right or wrong. King
viewed as moral that which is in accord with the eternal
and abiding principles of the Christian faith.

To understand King as person, leader, and thinker, and
to understand his non-violent ethic, one has to consider
him as a person of faith who subscribed to certain irrefut-
able and irrevocable moral laws. Hanes Walton has rightly
observed that "King's political philosophy and the technique he approved for implementing social change were a
direct outgrowth of his religious and moral principles, of
his methaphysical stand."[1] Social ethicist, John
Swomley, also recognized the relationship between King's
theology and his adoption of the non-violent method. He
considered the latter to be an outgrowth of the former. In
his book *Liberation Ethics* he wrote:

The fundamental basis for the use of nonviolence
in Martin Luther King's mind was pragmatic and at
the same time theological. He did not view his
practice as divorced from his theory about the
universe. He believed in "the ultimate morality
of the universe and . . . that all reality hinges
on moral foundations." Therefore any movement
that would be truly liberating had to have a moral base which he affirmed as "the sacredness of
all human life." Everyman is somebody because he
is a child of God.[2]

Martin Luther King, Jr.'s philosophy of non-violent
resistance, as it evolved out of the Montgomery struggle
and was developed by application and refined by experience,
consisted basically of six major principles. King delineated these principles in his book, *Stride Toward Freedom*.
Although this book was written in the early days of his en-
gagement with non-violence as a method of social change,
and although experience and an expanded ethical perspective
continued to redefine his priorities and reshape his thinking, these six principles remained the central integrating,
constituent elements of his non-violent ethic.

NON-VIOLENCE: THE WEAPON OF THE STRONG

The first principle listed by King is the assertion
that non-violence is the way of the strong and not a method
of cowards. Persons who use the non-violent method of protest, either because they are afraid or because they lack
the instruments of violence, are not truly non-violent.[3]

King asserted that only those are truly non-violent
who can choose an alternative method of protest or resistance. This idea was probably appropriated from Gandhi, who
also insisted that non-violence is the method of the
strong. Both King and Gandhi were referring to inner,

spiritual strength, rather than outward, physical force. Because one's natural inclination is to respond to violence with violence, a strong sense of purpose and commitment to the cause for which one is suffering, a great deal of discipline and self-restraint, and a strong self-image, are essential if a non-violent response to an act of aggression is not to be accompanied by feelings of defeat and powerlessness. Thus non-violence is a method of the strong. When one reflects upon the courage of an unarmed resister who faces an armed opponent, one recognizes that non-violence is a method for the brave, rather than the coward.

Gandhi's situation, however, was different from King's, as the Indian experience was different from the black experience. Gandhi's situation of numerical advantage made the assertion about non-violence and strength plausible for two reasons. First, numerical advantage in a struggle can fortify inner strength. Secondly, numerical advantage signifies that one has a realistic option of alternative methods and strategies of resistance. King's statement about non-violence and strength is plausible nonetheless because black Americans lack the numerical strength and the options which that advantage makes possible. When one considers all of the disadvantages that are a part of the existential situation of black Americans, to protest at all requires a great deal of courage, determination and inner resolve.

Since non-violence, in King's view, represents strength rather than weakness, it is not to be confused with "stagnant passivity," in that it does resist. King felt that the term passive resistance is a misnomer because it implies a "do-nothing method" which encourages acquiescence to evil and has led persons like Reinhold Niebuhr to misinterpret the pacifist position. Niebuhr, in King's opinion, interpreted pacifism as "a sort of passive non-resistance to evil expressing naive trust in the power of love." King felt that this was a serious distortion of pacifism. The non-violent resister is passive in the sense that he is neither physically aggressive nor violent toward his opponent. At the same time his emotions and mind are active as they seek to convince the opponent that he is wrong. The non-violent resister, consequently, is active spiritually. King's pacifism, then, is not a passive non-resistance to evil, but an active, non-violent resistance to evil. He insisted that Gandhi resisted evil with as much passion and conviction as the person who adheres to a violent methodology. Gandhi simply resisted with love instead of hate. In describing his position he wrote:

> True pacifism is not unrealistic submission to
> evil, as Niebuhr contends. It is rather a cour-
> ageous confrontation of evil by the power of
> love, in the faith that it is better to be the
> recipient of violence than the inflictor of it,
> since the latter only multiplies the existence of
> violence and bitterness in the universe, while
> the former may develop a sense of shame in the
> opponent, and thereby bring about a transforma-
> tion and change of heart.[4]

RECONCILIATION: THE GOAL OF NON-VIOLENCE

The second major principle of King's non-violent philosophy is that the goal of non-violent resistance is always redemption and reconciliation. The goal of non-violence is not the humiliation or defeat of the opponent but the winning of his friendship and understanding. Although the non-violent resister might protest through boycotts and non-cooperation, these are not ends in themselves but means to stir the conscience of the opponent or awaken in him a sense of moral shame. Bitterness, hatred and brokenness are

the aftermath of violence. Wholeness, healing and the creation of the beloved community are the fruits of non-violence.[5]

If the Montgomery bus boycott and the Birmingham and
Selma campaigns are to be credited as victories for King's
non-violent ethic, then one must understand that reconciliation, redemption and the creation of the beloved community
were long range ideals rather than immediately attainable
goals. After the Supreme Court issued the bus desegregation order, a number of churches and private homes were
bombed in Montgomery's black community. Birmingham's Sixteenth Street Baptist Church was bombed after the non-violent compaign there. A white woman from Detroit who was
working within the Selma voter registration drive was shot
to death on the very night that the mammoth march to Montgomery ended.

Although his rhetoric may have led his hearers or
readers to believe that he considered reconciliation to be
more immediate than distant in its realization--and at the
beginning he probably thought that if not imminent it was
not as distant as it turned out to be--King was aware that
the beloved community would not be an instantaneous creation.

> This method of nonviolence will not work miracles
> overnight. Men are not easily moved from their
> mental ruts, their prejudiced and irrational
> feelings. When the underprivileged demand free-
> dom, the privileged first react with bitterness
> and resistance. Even when the demands are couch-
> ed in nonviolent terms, the initial white reac-
> tion to Negro resistance has been bitter. . . .
> I do not predict that a similar happy ending will
> come to Montgomery in a few months, because inte-
> gration is more complicated than independence.[6]

Although one could debate which is more complicated, integration or independence, King's point here is that non-violence may facilitate the process, but the reconciliation of broken communities is a complex, difficult, time-consuming task, especially when there is resistance to change.

Ideally, reconciliation, like *agape* (love), is a process that is free of coercive elements. St. Paul in his declaration of the new being in Christ also expressed the essence of the theology of the crucifixion when he wrote: "All this is from God, who through Christ reconciled us to himself, not counting their trespasses against them, and entrusting to us the message of reconciliation" (2 Cor 5:18-19).[7] What Dietrich Bonhoeffer wrote about the costliness of grace can also be applied to reconciliation. Bonhoeffer wrote:

> Above all, it (grace) is costly because it cost God the life of his Son: 'ye were bought at a price,' and what has cost God much cannot be cheap for us. Above all, it is grace because God did not reckon His Son too dear a price to pay for our life, but delivered Him up for us.[8]

At Calvary God set the example of how costly reconciliation and redemption can be. While the price of God's only Son is a dear one to pay for the restoration of broken unions, it is not too great for divine *agape*. Yet with all of the pain involved in the reconciliation of creation with Creator, human beings are free to accept or reject God's "unspeakable gift." Human beings are still called or invited rather than conscripted into the kingdom. The kerygma, with all of its missionary intent, still ends with an invitation, rather than a demand, that essentially says, "whosoever will, let him or her come."

Those who work non-violently and in other ways, on be-

half of reconciliation and redemption, often find themselves in situations of conflict occasioned by those who
resist change. For a number of individuals, the pain that
change brings and the threat to security, that comes with
newness, are prices too dear to pay. Therefore the element
of pressure or coercion enters the process.

King was of the opinion that given the intransigence
that he often found in the opponents he faced, coercion was
a necessary element in the application of his non-violent
ethic. Although he continued to believe in the fundamental
decency of human nature, and although he continued to appeal to the consciences of those who opposed him, he soon
recognized that ethical appeals and moral suasion alone
would not bring about justice for America's oppressed minorities. This was a point that Niebuhr had made many years
earlier when he stated that "It is hopeless for the Negro
to expect complete emancipation from the menial, social and
economic position into which the white man has forced him,
merely by trusting in the moral sense of the white
race."[9] King insisted that ethical appeals must still be
made because morality and power must go together "implementing, fulfilling, and ennobling each other." As Walton
has pointed out: "The political philosophy of Martin
Luther King, Jr. is about the unity and continuum of morality, power and social change. His goal was simple enough:
social and economic justice necessary to the creation of
the beloved community."[10] While recognizing the legitimacy of ethical appeals, he also believed that "those appeals must be undergirded by some form of constructive coercive power."[11] Without the application of persistent
pressure the black American will end up "empty-handed."

King did not consider non-violent coercion to be anti-
reconciliatory. Although tensions increased in those communities when and where the non-violent method was used,

King felt that non-violence was not responsible for the estrangement and hostility between local blacks and whites.
Non-violence had simply unearthed the latent, long-standing
feeling of hostility which had been there all along. King
believed that latent tensions must first be unearthed, recognized and dealt with before true reconciliation can occur. Hence, he often used the term "creative tension" to
describe his method of bringing about healing, wholeness
and reconciliation by working through the tension created
by the demand for justice on the part of the oppressed.
Non-violent resistance, pressure and coercion simply help
to create the atmosphere in which the problem can not only
be identified and dramatized, but also one in which the
solution can be sought.

Although the black and white communities have remained
separate and largely unequal, some changes have occurred.
Both blacks and whites have learned to live with and accept
some of the changes that have occurred during their life-
times. These changes have heightened the sensitivities of
persons in both communities to the subject of race and the
existence of racism, and have increased the dialogue between blacks and whites on individual bases. These changes
have made it possible for blacks and whites to meet and
know each other in settings of social equality. As well,
the affirmative action programs, which should be looked
upon as by-products of the ferment of the 1960's have made
it possible for them to relate to each other as equals in
professional contexts and in work situations. These changes have also made it easier for some persons to cross the
social and cultural barriers that have historically separated black from white and white from black. They have also
made it easier in both communities to build relationships
and friendships based upon relative equality, mutual respect, trust and *agape*. Perhaps it will be these persons

and these relationships that will form the nucleus of King's beloved community.

OPPONENT AS SYMBOL OF A GREATER EVIL

Third, King depersonalized the goal of non-violence by defining it in terms of reconciliation rather than the defeat of one's opponent. He also depersonalized the target of the non-violent resister's attack. The opponent is only a symbol of a greater evil. Thus non-violence for King is directed against the forces of evil rather than the persons who do evil. The evildoer is as much a victim of evil as are the individuals and communities that evildoers oppress. According to King, the basic tension in Montgomery was not between whites and blacks, but between justice and injustice and between the forces of light and the forces of darkness. The victory would not merely be a victory for Montgomery's fifty thousand blacks, but a triumph for jus-. tice and the forces of light. King spoke of a defeat of injustice rather than a defeat of the white persons who may have been unjust.[12]

King's perception of the Movement as being one which is essentially "against principalities" rather than persons was to have profound implications for the future development of his non-violent ethic, particularly when it came to his inclusion of the controversial subject of the Vietnam War as a matter of ethical concern. Herbert Richardson has written:

The struggle against ideological conflict anywhere in the world is the struggle for the unity of men living together in the world. Conversely, because the struggle against racism is really a struggle against ideological conflict, Martin Luther King recognized that he had to oppose this kind of conflict wherever it appeared. He was,

so to say, under this obligation in principle.
Hence, King was the first of those who linked the
civil rights struggle to opposition to the Vietnam War.[13]

For King, the struggle "against principalities" also meant
an asymmetry between the manifestation of evil and the manner in which it is opposed. A symmetry between the response and the manifestation only perpetuates the existence
of evil. Thus King argued that violence must be met with
non-violence.[14]

Hanes Walton has pointed out the difficulty of deper-
sonalizing the struggle against oppression, by raising such
questions as:

How much of a person can actually be separated
from his actions? And who, if not that person,
is to be held responsible for those
actions. . . . How is the evil perpetrated by
one person to be distinguished from that bred by
social institutions and their conditioning effect?[15]

Both Niebuhr and Walton allude to the fact that although
one may intellectually, theoretically and theologically
make the distinction between the opponent as the source of
evil and the opponent as a symbol of an evil source, in the
realm of reality, it is almost impossible to do so. When
one is being beaten by a Jim Clark or hosed down by a Bull
Connor, it is hard to believe that either of them is just
as much a victim of an evil system as the one who is the
recipient of their brutality. King sought to depersonalize
his campaigns by concentrating on the issues rather than
the personalities involved. Nevertheless, his non-violent
method worked best in those situations in which there was a
person, who was a living embodiment of the evil system, a-
gainst whom sentiment could be molded. This was the role

of Bull Connor in Birmingham and Jim Clark in Selma, where King was successful. This was the role into which Laurie Pritchett and Richard Daley refused to be manipulated in Albany and Chicago where King failed.

REDEMPTIVE SUFFERING

The fourth principle of King's non-violent philosophy is redemptive suffering. Swomley has stated that non-violence as conceptualized and understood by both Gandhi and King is based upon certain assumptions about power. It assumes that there is social and economic power in non-cooperation, and that there is moral power in voluntary suffering for others. King's concept of redemptive or voluntary or creative suffering assumed:

> (1) that there is power in withdrawing support from an evil or exploiting structure; (2) that opponents are human beings . . . to be respected and not violated; and (3) that the acceptance of suffering rather than inflicting it on others, is itself a form of power, demoralizing to those who use violence without experiencing it in return and troublesome to the consciences of those who do not have an obvious vested interest in the maintenance of the system under attack.[16]

In King's view, the non-violent resister must be able to accept suffering without retaliating and accept blows without striking back. He continually stresses the educational possibilities of suffering and the redemptive potential of unearned suffering. In paraphrasing Gandhi, King said:

> We will match your capacity to inflict suffering with our capacity to endure suffering. We will meet your physical force with soul force. We will not hate you, but we cannot in all good con-

science obey your unjust laws. Do to us what you
will and we will still love you. Bomb our homes
and threaten our children; send your hooded per-
petrators of violence into our communities and
drag us out on some wayside road, beating us and
leaving us half dead, and we will still love
you. But we will soon wear you down by our capacity to suffer, and in winning our freedom we
will so appeal to your conscience that we will
win you in the process.[17]

King sought to answer those who maintain that an oppressor who causes the innocent to suffer ought to be stopped by any means necessary and that failure to do so makes
one an accomplice to injury. He argued that a symmetrical
response to a violent act has led to legitimating everything from maiming a would-be rapist to an apology for the
Vietnam War. Violence takes the form of altruism by claiming to prevent suffering. Its method is to inflict so much
more suffering that one must surrender unconditionally.
King rejected this type of altruism and insisted that suffering can only be stopped when it is endured, rather than
increased. In this way neither the personality of the oppressor nor that of the oppressed is violated. King insisted that his principle was applicable to the community,
the nation, and the sphere of international relations, as
well as to individuals.[18]

Bennie Goodwin has pointed out that King did not simply emphasize unmerited suffering. Blacks had already
experienced that for over 400 years. King called for creative suffering. He urged people to accept the suffering
that was meant for their degradation and wear it as a badge
of honor. When one has learned to use the suffering designed for his destruction as a means of his liberation,
then he has learned how to suffer creatively.[19] Reinhold

Niebuhr felt that although non-violence involved coercion, its willingness to endure more pain than it inflicts makes it a better method of producing moral good will than does violence. He wrote: "If non-violent resistance causes pain and suffering to the opposition, it mitigates the resentments which such suffering usually creates, by enduring more pain than it inflicts."[20]

A number of persons have had particular difficulty in accepting King's concept of creative suffering. John Oliver Killens, for example, has stated that "There is no dignity for me in allowing another man to spit on me with impunity. There is no dignity for him or me. There is only sickness, and it will beget an even greater sickness. It degrades me and brutalizes him. Moreover, it encourages him in his bestiality."[21] Hanes Walton has also observed that:

> Dehumanization can play more complex tricks with the psyche than a Christian ethic of love and redemptive suffering can perhaps adequately deal with. . . . Compassion from someone whom you consider beneath you or whom you have harmed is enraging. One can respond to humor, behave justly, and relate to compassion only in situations where justice, compassion and humor are valued. If this is so, then there are only certain circumstances under which people can respond at all, much less compassionately, to their fellow man's suffering.[22]

The attitudes of Laurie Prichett, Bull Connor and Jim Clark after their experiences with the non-violent resisters, validate the conclusions of Killens and Walton about King's concept of redemptive suffering. Pritchett, Connor and Clark still had the same contempt for blacks after their communities came under non-violent siege that they

had before. Their prejudice, their hatred, their resentments toward black Americans were neither lessened nor a-
bated. When one feels that one's way of life is being challenged, one does not visualize one's actions as brutal, but
sees them as the appropriate method of protecting and holding intact that which one regards as sacrosanct. In the
minds of the defenders of the status quo, those who were
injured in the process only received their just due for
"getting out of their place."

King, however, remained firmly convinced that unearned
suffering used creatively could effect social change. His
commitment was one which had evolved out of the crucible of
his own trials and sufferings. By the time that *Strength
To Love* was written, he had been imprisoned in Alabama and
Georgia twelve times. His home had been bombed twice and
he had been the victim of a near fatal stabbing. As his
suffering increased, he realized that he could respond to
it in one of two ways. He could react to it with bitterness or seek to transform it into a creative force. King
chose the latter course by attempting to make a virture out
of it. The approach personally convinced him of the value
of creative suffering.

> I have lived these last few years with the con-
> viction that unearned suffering is redemptive.
> There are some who still find the cross a stum-
> bling block, others consider it foolishness, but
> I am more convinced than ever before of the power
> of God unto social and individual salvation. So
> like the Apostle Paul I can now humbly, yet
> proudly, say, "I bear in my body the marks of the
> Lord Jesus."[23]

AGAPE

At the center of King's non-violent philosophy stands the principle of love. This fifth principle means that the non-violent resister must not only avoid external physical violence, but the internal violence of the spirit as well. He should not only refuse to shoot his adversary, he should refuse to hate him as well. This can only be done when the love ethic is projected to the center of one's life. When King spoke of love he did not mean sentimentality or affectionate emotion. He knew that it is neither feasible nor possible to expect the oppressed to love the oppressor in an affectionate sense. King identified the love ethic with the New Testament concept of *agape* and defined *agape* as "understanding, redeeming good will for all men." It is a purely spontaneous, unmotivated, groundless and creative, overflowing love. It is not set in motion by any quality or function of its objects, but is the love of God operating in the human heart.[24]

Agape for King is a disinterested love in which the individual seeks not his own good, but the good of the neighbor. It is entirely a "neighbor-regarding concern for others," which makes no distinctions between worthy and unworthy people, or between friend and enemy, but seeks the neighbor in every man it meets. King felt that the best way to assure oneself that love is disinterested is to love the enemy-neighbor from whom one can expect no good in return, but only hostility and persecution. *Agape* for King, also springs from the need of the other person. God demonstrated *agape* because the act of redemption occurred "while we were yet sinners," at the point of humanity's greatest need for love. The white man needs the love of the black man because of the way that segregation has distorted his personality and scarred his soul. Blacks examplify *agape* when they respond to that need by loving those whites who oppose them.

King conceptualized *agape* as an active love, which
not only seeks to preserve or create community, but will go
to any length to restore it. He understood the cross as
"the eternal expression of the length to which God will go
in order to restore broken community. The resurrection is
the symbol of God's triumph over those forces which sought
to block community. The Holy Spirit is the continuing community creating reality that moves through history."[25]
Therefore, to work against community is to work against the
whole of creation.

In agreement with the evangelical liberal tradition in
which he was trained, King concluded that in the final analysis *agape* means a recognition of the fact that all of
life is interrelated, and that all people are brothers to
the degree that one cannot harm another without hurting
oneself. To demonstrate his point King observed:

White men often refuse federal aid to education
in order to avoid giving the Negro his rights;
but because all men are brothers, they cannot
deny Negro children without harming their own.
They end, all efforts to the contrary, by hurting
themselves. Why is this? Because all men are
brothers. If you harm me, you harm yourself.[26]

Although King defined *agape* as a selfless and disinterested love, there are nevertheless self-interested
elements in his ethic. His love ethic is not entirely
selfless and disinterested. He did seek something in return: equality, freedom and personal dignity. The entire
non-violent ethic is a way of creating new terms for a
give-and-take between social groups, the result of which is
a mutually beneficial exchange.

The perfection of *agape*, as symbolized by the cross,
which transcended the particular and relative norms of justice as it conformed to love rather than human interests,
is not contained in history. Niebuhr wrote:

Whatever the possibilities of success for *agape*
in history (and there are possibilities of success because history cannot be at complete vari-
ance with its foundations) the final justification for the way of *agape* in the New Testament
is never found in history. The motive to which
Christ appeals is always the emulation of God or
gratitude for the *agape* of God.[27]

Hanes Walton has also questioned the capacity and the
capability of people to express *agape* as conceptualized
by King in their historical setting. He wrote:

It is questionable whether the ordinary person is
capable of achieving the *agape* level of love.
Can modern men, characteristically self-centered
and aggressive, overcome the qualities and attain
the transcendent love symbolized by Christ on the
cross? . . . How realistic is it to expect of
people united for basically political purposes a
standard of love normally out of reach of all but
the most singular among them?[28]

Walton argues further that experience has not validated
King's belief that love is necessary for the most effective use of the non-violent method. CORE and other groups
have used non-violence without emphasizing love as the
"regulating ideal" with excellent results. Non-violent
measures such as court injunctions, economic boycotts,
pickets, a strong and vocal press, sit-ins and similar tactics have succeeded quite independently of the presence or
absence of love.[29]

Gene Sharp has also concluded that it is desirable
that non-violent resisters minimize their hostility and
maximize their good will for their opponent for the sake of
effectiveness and beneficial long-term consequences. Yet
he maintains that the emphasis on love is still a "helpful

refinement" rather than a requirement for non-violent action. When love is interpreted as a requirement for non-
violence, persons who have been victimized and are unable
to love their oppressors, may turn toward violence as the
technique most consistent with their resentment and hostilities. Sharp has written:

> This confusion of secondary refinements with pri-
> mary requirements and alienation of many poten-
> tial users of the non-violent technique has some-
> times been aggravated by attempts of pacifists
> and believers in the principles of nonviolence to
> proselytize within nonviolent action movements,
> and blur the distinctions between their beliefs
> and the nonviolent technique. Such effort may in
> the long run impede rather than promote the sub-
> stitution of nonviolent for violent means.[30]

Eugene Bianchi has stated that King was acutely aware
of the need for political and legal power in the pursuit
and attainment of a liberating justice. However, King also
maintained that even when power was employed for the establishment of a more just order, it could still be misused
and result in debasing hatred by which both the victims and
the victimizers could lose their humanity. Thus love for
the self and the other, especially the enemy, became for
King the chief humanizing sentiment. Throughout his life,
King insisted that love was the only force capable of
transforming any enemy into a friend. He wrote: "We never
get rid of any enemy by meeting hate with hate; we get rid
of an enemy by getting rid of enmity. By its very nature,
hate destroys and tears down; by its very nature, love creates and builds up. Love transforms with redemptive
power."[31]

THE UNIVERSE AS AN ALLY OF JUSTICE

The sixth principle of King's non-violent philosophy also reflects the influence of evangelical liberalism upon his thinking. This principle expresses the conviction that the universe is on the side of justice. This conviction gives the non-violent resister faith in the future and strength to accept suffering without retaliation. King recognized that all non-violent practitioners may not ascribe to his belief in a personal God. He maintained, however, that even these persons believe in some kind of creative force which works for "universal wholeness." He stated that "Whether we call it unconscious process, an impersonal Brahma, or a Personal Being of matchless power and infinite love, there is a creative force in this universe that works to bring the disconnected aspects of reality into a harmonious whole."[32]

King's belief in non-violence was grounded in his faith in God. Although other significant non-violent theorists and practitioners have also affirmed the existence of a higher being or "creative force," it would be an error to conclude that non-violence presupposes theism. Although theism has been historically related to non-violence as well as to violence, there is no logical sequence of inevitability that requires a theistic premise for either the endorsement of violence or a commitment to non-violence. Humanists and atheists, as well as theists, may be committed to non-violence as both a method for social change and a way of life. A person's commitment to non-violence may be grounded in the social or political struggle in which one is engaged. Just as there is no inevitability between the adoption of non-violence as a strategy and its adoption as a way of life, there is no inevitability between non-violence and theism. Non-violence may or may not be grounded in theism as most people understand and live theism.

King's belief that the universe is on the side of justice cannot either be proven or disproven. King spoke and
wrote from the perspective of religious faith. The writer
of the Epistle to the Hebrews states that "Faith is the assurance of things hoped for, the conviction of things not
seen" (Heb 11:1). In the final analysis, matters of faith
cannot be proved or disproved--they are either believed or
they are not.

CONCLUSION

When King was killed by a bullet from a sniper's ri-
fle, some persons viewed his death as tragic. Others com-
mented that it was ironic that a person whose life was committed to non-violence died by violence. Still others felt
that King's violent death was a refutation of his philosophy and a demonstration of the failure of his non-violent
methodology. King, however, as a man of faith, viewed his
death as redemptive. In *Stride Toward Freedom*, he made a
statement that he repeated over and over again in later
years. "If physical death is the price that a man must pay
to free his children and his white brethren from a permanent death of the spirit, then nothing could be more redemptive."[33]

Martin Luther King, Jr., the man of faith, believed in
his God. And, on the night preceding his death, it was his
faith in this God that empowered him to declare, with renewed strength, his conviction that black people will inevitably and assuredly triumph.

We've got some difficult days ahead. But it
really doesn't matter to me now. Because I've
been to the mountain top. . . .

Like anybody else, I would like to live a
long life, longevity has its place. But I'm not
concerned about that now. I just want to do

God's will. And He's allowed me to go up to the
mountain. And I've looked over, and I've seen
the promised Land.

I may not get there with you, but I want you
to know tonight that we as a people will get to
the Promised land.

So I'm happy tonight. I'm not worried about
anything. I'm not fearing any man. Mine eyes
have seen the glory of the coming of the Lord.[34]

King's non-violent ethic evolved out of situations of
crisis. Although, as we have seen, King knew Gandhi's
thought and believed that non-violence had potential as a
viable strategy for the oppressed, he had not given serious
thought to the formulation of a Christian ethic of non-violence until he became involved in the Montgomery bus boycott. The organization, the codifying, and the pulling together of the various strands of evangelical liberalism and
personalism into the nucleus of a Christian, non-violent,
social ethic, was a process that happened subsequent to the
arrest of Rosa Parks.

King's non-violent ethic was undergirded by a distinct
theological perspective, and from its inception was intended to be practised in daily life. Its theological foundation provided it with its intellectual framework and ra-
tionale, as it attempted to respond to the various crises
and provide answers to the various ethical dilemmas en-
countered in black America's quest for freedom and equality. Its theological foundation gave a needed stability to
King's ethic, as well as room for growth, when those crisis
situations and dilemmas demanded flexibiiity, rethinking of
goals, and reordering of priorities. King's ethic was
subjected to one of the most rugged criterion for
validation. It was judged by its effectiveness in the
situation. Martin Luther King, then, was no armchair

Christian or ethicist. Much of his significance as an ethicist is to be found not in the originality of his thinking, but in his attempts to apply, in creative ways, the
central tenents of his faith and ethic in situations of social conflict.

One is hard pressed to identify either an American
leader or philosophy, in the last thirty years, that has
been able to mount and sustain a mass social movement that
appealed to as wide a constituency as did Martin Luther
King, Jr. and his non-violent ethic. He stands out as one
of history's most ardent adherents of non-violence. Even
more importantly, he ranks among the few heroic Christians
who have shown in word and deed that non-violence ought to
be recognized and lived as a central facet of Christian
ethics.

NOTES

[1]Hanes Walton, Jr., The Political Philosophy of Martin Luther King, Jr. (Westport: Greenwood Publishing Corporation, 1971), p. 45.

[2]John Swomley, Jr., Liberation Ethics (New York: The Macmillan Company, 1972), p. 172.

[3]Martin Luther King, Jr., Stride Toward Freedom (New York: Harper and Row, 1958), p. 102.

[4]"Playboy Interview with Martin Luther King," Playboy, XII (January, 1965), p. 78.

[5]King, Stride Toward Freedom, p. 102.

[6]Ibid., pp. 218-19.

[7]All Scripture passages are from the Revised Standard Version.

[8]Dietrich Bonhoeffer, The Cost of Discipleship (New York: The Macmillan Company, 1970), p. 48.

[9]Reinhold Niebuhr, Moral Man and Immoral Society (New York: Charles Scribner's Sons, 1932, 1960), p. 252.

[10]Walton, p. XXXIV.

[11]Martin Luther King, Jr., Where Do We Go From Here: Chaos or Community? (New York: Harper and Row, 1967), p. 152.

[12]King, Stride Toward Freedom, pp. 102-03.

[13]Herbert Richardson, "Martin Luther King--Unsung Theologian," New Theology No. 6, Martin Marty and Dean Peerman, eds. (London: Macmillan Company, 1969), p. 180.

[14]Ibid., p. 181.

[15]Walton, p. 80.

[16]John Swomley, Jr., p. 172.

[17]King, Stride Toward Freedom, p. 217.

[18]Warren E. Steinkraus, "Martin Luther King's Personalism and Nonviolence," Journal of the History of Icleos, XXXIV (January, 1973), p. 110.

[19]Bennie Goodwin, Dr. Martin Luther King, Jr.: God's Messenger of Love, Justice and Hope (Jersey City: Goodpatrick Publishers, 1976), p. 33.

[20]Niebuhr, Moral Man and Immoral Society, p. 247.

[21]John Oliver Killens, Black Man's Burden (New York: Pocket Books, 1965, 1969), p. 111.

[22]Walton, pp. 84-85.

[23]Martin Luther King, Jr., Strength to Love (New York: Harper and Row, 1963), p. 172.

[24]King, Stride Toward Freedom, p. 104.

[25]Ibid., pp. 105-06.

[26]Ibid., p. 106.

[27]Reinhold Niebuhr, The Nature and Destiny of Man (New York: Charles Scribner's Sons, 1941, 1943, 1949), Vol. 2, p. 88.

[28]Walton, pp. 79-80.

[29]Ibid., pp. 78, 81.

[30]Gene Sharp, The Politics of Nonviolent Action (Boston: Porter Sargent Publishers, 1973), p. 635.

[31]King, Strength to Love, p. 46.

[32]King, Stride Toward Freedom, p. 107.

[33]Ibid., p. 216.

[34]Coretta King, My Life with Martin Luther King, Jr. (New York: Holt, Rinehart, and Winston, 1969), p. 316.

THOMAS MERTON

(1915 - 1968)

by J. Norman King

*Thomas Merton's theology of non-violence is based
on his contemplative and mystical experience as
well as his social ethics. It confronts us with
the need for a renewed mentality open to the mystery of meaning and love at the heart of creation. N. King highlights aspects of Merton's
Christian vision of the person and shows why persons require a non-violent response. For Merton
non-violence involves an inner struggle to overcome evil in oneself and self-deception. Thus it
is closely associated with a search for truth.
It aims at dialogue and reconciliation, permits
active dissent and resistance, and is not to be
equated with passive acquiescence. After providing a vision, Merton suggests some strategies for
attaining peace non-violently.*

INTRODUCTION

In the present essay I shall set forth the main lines
of Thomas Merton's theology of non-violence and its roots
in his theory and practice of mysticism. As a fellow monk
puts it, "His social and political critique was the fruit
of a compassion learned through a life of monastic ascesis
and contemplation."[1]

A basic thread runs through all Merton's writings,
whether on prayer or on nuclear arms. The human person is
called to oneness with God in Christ, in truth and in love,
at the centre of his being. At this core he discovers a
solidarity with all men which unfolds into a deep compas-

sion. This, in turn, finds expression in sharing one's inner truth and love with others, both in interpersonal relationships and in social responsibility.[2] It is from and
towards this oneness with God and man that flows a non-
violence of strength.

Thomas Merton was born in 1915 in the small French
town of Prades, of an American mother and an itinerant
artist father from New Zealand. His early years were spent
between France, England and the United States, and marked
by the death of both his parents. This period was characterized by a nostalgic loneliness, a boundless physical and
mental energy, and a restless searching for a deep and
lasting truth and home of mind and heart. After pursuing a
master's degree in English and a brief teaching career, he
entered the Trappist monastery of Gethsemani, Kentucky, in
December 1941, three years after becoming a Roman Catholic. There he spent the rest of his life as monk, priest,
poet, spiritual writer and social critic. There too he was
buried after his untimely accidental death while attending
a conference on monasticism in Bangkok, Thailand in 1968.

Merton's own inward pilgrimage, glimpsed in his various journals,[3] parallels the development of his central
vision. After his youthful explorations of the secular
world, he enters the path of rigorous discipline and interior silence. In this solitude he becomes enmeshed in a
painful inner struggle, in which smugness and illusions are
shed, a truer self discovered, and the divine presence in
the depths of his being touched more deeply. He discovers
too his oneness with all others. From his own silent
place, he then speaks, with clarity and compassion, the
truth he has experienced. He addresses himself to the key
issues of the day in which this truth is threatened or
undermined; especially war, the arms race, racism, and
other forms of violence. In doing so he fashions his own
unique theology of non-violence.

The sources of this theology include his own monastic experience and, as he insists, his inescapable experience as a man of the twentieth century. It is rooted as well in the whole tradition of Christian monastic literature and mystical writings, as enriched, especially in his later years, by the contemplative tradition of the East.[4] His specifically social writings also display the marked influence of the papal social encyclicals of recent decades to which he frequently refers.

MERTON'S CENTRAL VISION

Much of Merton's central vision is concisely presented within its historical context in *Contemplative Prayer*, completed shortly before his death. It is difficult today, he observes, not to live an alienated existence, out of touch with our own inner self, and buffeted from without by the many and constant pressures of a mass technological society. People readily fall into a busy, compulsive, superficial life, filled with activity and diversions. This life is devoid of really creative work and dedicated love, and permeated with a gnawing sense of emptiness and anxiety.[5]

To clear away such obstacles which blind us to our true identity and enslave our authentic freedom, we must put some order and discipline into our lives and introduce a dimension of silent contemplation. On the one hand, we must overcome domination by our own unfree impulses and the inducements of a consumer society. On the other hand, we must begin to wrestle in silence with the question of who we are and what is the ultimate meaning of our life.

This reflection must be neither a morbid introspective analysis nor a sterile spinning out of our private little world of thoughts and feelings, walled up and sealed off from real life. Meditation remains pointless, and even destructive, unless it is rooted in the concrete realities of everyday life. It depends upon and must find expression in an openness to and concern for other persons, and ordinarily needs some communal support. A genuine inner awareness must be grounded in real experience and is the dawning of the latter's fullest meaning.[6]

If a person persists in this inner journey, his interior silence deepens and he gradually passes from the outer surface to the very centre of himself. His prayer becomes less reflective and more of a silent, attentive listening in solitude. He becomes more attuned to the deepest voices of the world which echo in him, to his own deepest self, and to the infinite Presence to which that self opens.

The passage from the surface self to the inmost self involves much risk, struggle and dread. The former is the empirical self which can be observed and measured. It is the individualistic self, viewed as an isolated, self-contained unit, struggling and competing for survival, worldly goods and gratification. It is the societal self, caught up in routine, conformity and prejudice. A person is strongly tempted to cling to the external self for identity, rather than let it fall or be peeled away in the crucible of contemplation.[7]

In meditative and contemplative silence, we are gradually drawn to let go of these masks and defences and are brought, naked and defenceless, as it were, to the centre of our being. At first we experience a profound dread, which springs from a vivid realization of our finiteness and guilt. Our very self appears as engulfed in a dark void of nothingness. In this experience of our contingency we realize that we have neither created ourselves nor can we avert our dissolution in death. Our very existence between birth and death lies suspended, so to speak, over an endless abyss. Beyond our finitude, we also have an at least dim awareness of guilt. This entails much more than a mere surface knowledge of going against moral laws or social taboos. We sense rather that we have somehow been untrue to our own inmost truth. We have in some degree betrayed or missed our true vocation.[8]

Yet just where this void seems to open out into dark despair, a new hope is born. From the darkness comes light, from death comes life. We come to experience that we are enveloped not by total darkness, but by incredible and overwhelming light that enlightens, sears and purifies our minds and hearts. We experience our true self without illusions, as somehow known and loved at the very core of our being. We awaken to our own reality as received, as a free gift of love, endowed with meaning. In Christian terms, we experience the indwelling Spirit of Jesus Christ sent by the Father.

This awareness of God is not like seeing or knowing an outside object by our conscious mind. It is not like the subject-object relationship that characterizes our familiar acts of knowing.

> We know him insofar as we become aware of ourselves as known through and through by him. . . .
> We know him in and through ourselves insofar as his truth is the source of our being and his merciful love is the very heart of our life and existence.[9]

We likewise experience our true self as called from within to accept that self and to create our meaning by echoing in our lives the Voice which utters us, reflecting its truth and love. We do so by responding to the personal reality of our human brothers within the demands of our specific life-situation.

Moreover, once a person has come in touch with his deepest self as a sustained gift, an important consequence

follows. He no longer needs to cling to his superficial,
false self for identity nor protect it against others at
all costs. And because it is this illusory self set over
against others which is the occasion of defensiveness, hostility and aggressive action, the discovery of one's true
self in contemplative prayer removes a very central cause
of violence.

Even as a young man Merton discerned something of this
truth in reflecting on the second world war. He expresses
the fear that his ownership of anything may lead him to at
least a complicity in the killing of others. If we see our
identity as bound up with our possessions, our occupation,
our societal role, or our nationality, such that without
these our very self would be destroyed, then we will fight
to the teeth to defend and even extend them.[10]

If, however, we come to realize in contemplation the
void of contingency and of sin that pervades our being, we
shall see that we do have literally nothing to defend. At
the same time in experiencing our true self as gift rooted
in divine meaning and love, we become aware of an identity
that cannot be taken away, and thus need not be defended.
"Only the man who has attained his own spiritual identity
can live without the need to kill and without the need of a
doctrine that permits him to do so with a good conscience."[11]

Far from being an escape which blinds us to reality,
contemplative prayer also tranforms our vision into one
that is more truthful. We begin to see all human persons,
all the history of mankind in the light of God. We come to
recognize that the inexhaustible truth and inscrutable
love, of which our own deep self is a word and gift, is the
ultimate Ground of all that is. This infinite Source is a
creative, forgiving, and challenging Presence, active and
at work at the core of every human person, behind all the
complexities and intricacies of human existence.

This means, in effect, that we are enabled to see our true identity and that of others in the deep self which opens onto and is an echo or image of God. We no longer identify the other with his external or superficial self. We penetrate beneath the surface distinctions and oppositions to a more fundamental unity. We acknowledge in the other a unique person who is contingent, yet a precious gift; wounded, yet able to be forgiven; tempted to identify with his surface self, yet summoned to live out the meaning of his true self. As a result there is a stable basis of community and solidarity. "In this inmost 'I' my own solitude meets the solitude of every other man and the solitude of God. Hence it is beyond division, beyond limitation, beyond selfish affirmation."[12]

To the extent that we are in touch with our true self as word of God, we can embody that truth in our actions without resorting to illusion or falsehood. To the extent that we acknowledge the true self of others, we can express that truth with compassion; not with a view to antagonizing or provoking, but as an invitation to unity.

We noted above that contemplation must itself be rooted in concrete human life. Conversely, only if a person comes to grips with himself in quiet solitude is he in a position to do anything for others.

> He who attempts to act and do things for the world without deepening his own self-understanding, freedom, integrity and capacity to love, will not have anything to give others. He will communicate to them nothing but the contagion of his own obsessions, his aggressiveness, his egocentred ambitions, his delusions about ends and means, his doctrinaire prejudices and ideas.[13]

For Merton, then, the human person, grasped in contemplative experience, is one who has a divinely endowed dignity and vocation, despite finitude and guilt. His theology of non-violence is essentially the elaboration of this vision in confrontation with the major social problems of the day. It is an exploration of these issues in the light of his underlying mystical or contemplative awareness.

In large part, the difference between an essentially non-violent and violent thought and action on social issues will depend upon whether these are seen in the light of one's true or false self. To the extent that a person lives in terms of his false self, his view of social issues will be formed in a context of fear, anxiety, defensiveness, hostility, and aggression. He who has struggled through to an awareness of the deeper self which is in solidarity with all others, must witness to that solidarity in his concrete life.

Nevertheless, where persons have been victims of maltreatment, abuse or discrimination, they may be estranged from their true selves, and left with neither the insight nor strength for such non-violence. Yet people must be encouraged not to acquiesce, but to resist all that violates the true self of man. Certain limit-situations may arise where non-violent resistance is impossible. These situations must be seen, however, in the context of an overall theology of non-violence, and not used as a pretext to cast it aside.

PRESUPPOSITIONS AND AIMS OF NON-VIOLENCE

We shall develop Merton's theology of non-violence by contrasting its presuppositions and aims with those that pursue a more violent understanding of and orientation to life. At the outset, we must insist that for Merton the central issue is one of vision and way of life. The matter of political or social tactic is a secondary and derivative consequence.[14]

In his extensive social writings, Merton maintains
that the basic presuppositions of non-violence are the inherent unity, dignity, trustworthiness and forgiveability
of human beings. There is a common humanity shared by
all. Its deepest orientation is towards truth and love,
which provides a ground for hope. Even the moral evils
which afflict everyone may be regarded as the violation of
a deep inner dignity which cannot be erased. Such evils
may be forgiven and ultimately overcome. The existential
understanding of these truths dawns upon a person only in
contemplative prayer.

The opposing vision of life, which invariably flows
into violence, regards human beings as essentially divided
among themselves and, in the last analysis, hopelessly corrupt. Opposition, rivalry and enmity comprise the deepest
truth about men. They are inescapably aggressive. At the
very least each side proclaims its own innocence and goodness and considers its declared enemy as totally evil.
Evil may be repulsed or destroyed, but never forgiven or
overcome by good.

Merton presents an explicitly Christian articulation
of the unity of mankind discerned in contemplation. All
persons spring ultimately from the same creative Source and
are gifted with a common nature shared by Jesus. He has
died for all in order to live in all by the gift of his
Spirit. The Spirit is the divine Presence acting in us to
unite us to one another, and urging us towards the healing
and reconciliation of all conflicts, hatred, and wars which
betray this unity. The final goal of this impetus is the
eschatological kingdom of God, a kingdom of truth and justice, of peace and love. The coming of this kingdom is
proclaimed and made actual in the openness, simplicity, humility and loving self-sacrifice of Christians and others,
lived in the circumstances of their own time and place, and
applied to the human problems of their age.[15]

At the same time, Merton also adopts as his own the
non-violent perspective of Mahatma Gandhi, whom he sees as
embodying a universal human tradition. Gandhi, who was a
man of the East, yet totally conversant with the West,
united the two in his own person. Like Merton, Gandhi also
underlines the religious and philosophical foundations of
non-violence. The spirit of non-violence bears witness to
the truth that all life is one because it comes from the
one universal Source. All political action must strive to
express and realize this oneness with all life, and must
therefore be non-violent. To realize this goal, a person
must first achieve a spiritual unity within himself. By
discipline and silence, he must overcome and heal inner division and acquire an inner spiritual and personal
freedom. Only then can his activity reflect and promote
unity and be non-violent.[16]

Behind Gandhi's view of the possibility and necessity
of non-violence lies a threefold conviction: that in the
hidden depths of our being we are more truly peaceful than
destructively aggressive, that love is more natural to us
than hatred, and that truth is the law of our being. This,
adds Merton, is a reflection of the traditional Christian
doctrine of original sin, which, properly understood, is
optimistic. This doctrine does not teach that man is by
nature evil, but rather that evil and hatred are an unnat-
ural disorder. For this reason they leave man disturbed
and unhappy. They belong to the false self which betrays
but cannot eradicate the true self.[17]

If this is so, then man has an essential trustworthiness and a potentiality for peace and order, given the
right conditions. The Christian is called to create these
conditions by opting for love and trust rather than hatred
and suspicion. Indeed, unless the human heart craves and
tends to peace more deeply than destruction, no real harmo-

ny and unity among people is possible. If man defines himself as a "gorilla with a gun," then he commits himself to a world view in which violence and every form of depravity are bound to prevail. The only alternatives are either to undermine and attack those we define as enemies before they ambush us, or to arm to the teeth in order to keep them at bay, or simply to give up in self-pitying despair. In this event the ultimate truth about reality is not oneness or meaning. Reality is finally harsh, cruel, and pointless.[18]

Still, even if we are oriented to peace, truth and union with each other in God, many manifestations of fear, greed, hatred, lies, and injustice remain. We must not pretend that these do not exist or can be wished away with pious slogans. But if such moral evil is the violation of an intrinsic dignity which cannot be lost, then forgiveness must be possible. In fact, it is only if we have the assurance of a power of love and forgiveness deeper than any unworthiness or wrong, that we can even admit such offences to ourselves and struggle against them. Otherwise we refuse to acknowledge them, seek to justify them, or project the evil exclusively on to others.

In the latter case, the presumption is made that evil is clearcut and definite, that it is in the other and not in oneself, and that it is irreversible and cannot be forgiven. In its most tyrannical form, this view presupposes that such a moral blemish can and must be punished and eliminated once and for all by the use of force. But the seeds of massive violence, such as Auschwitz, are present wherever a person or group persuades itself that at least one sector of humanity is to be defined as totally and irremediably evil or corrupt.

It is enough to affirm one basic principle: Anyone belonging to class X or nation Y or race Z is

to be regarded as subhuman and worthless, and
consequently has no right to exist. All the rest
will follow without difficulty.[19]

Behind this outlook, says Merton, lies a hatred of self
that is rooted in the loneliness, unworthiness, and insuf-
ficiency experienced by every human being. When this hate
is too deep and powerful to be consciously faced, it is
projected on to another. We then try to correct it by destroying that individual or group.[20]

The beginning of the conquest of hatred lies in the
conviction that we are loved despite our unworthiness.
This experience may be reached through contemplation and is
articulated in the assurance of forgiveness proclaimed by
Christ. We are then able to recognize destructive elements
in ourselves, because as forgiveable, they do not utterly
define us and deprive us of every shred of dignity. We can
acknowledge the greed, the self-deception, the injustice,
and the tendency to aggression in ourselves as well as in
others. We are then able to struggle to overcome this sin
in ourselves. And we must do so not once and for all, but
daily.

If we come to recognize moral evil as a violation of
our true self, we grasp it as self-destructive, and so as
carrying its own intrinsic punishment. We may then find in
the sins of others not a pretext for hatred, but a motive
of compassion and forgiveness. To recognize the reality of
forgiveness for oneself and others, and to accept and con-
vey that forgiveness is, for a Christian, to enter into the
healing mystery of the death and resurrection of Christ.[21]

If the evils we suffer are common, so too must be the
solution. It cannot consist of one part of humanity oblit-
erating, or reducing another part to servitude. The only
real liberation from evil is one which liberates both the
oppressor and oppressed from the tyrannical cycle of vio-

lence. Violence never produces any real change. To punish
and destroy an oppressor is to initiate a new process of
violence and oppression. The only change is in the names
of the oppressors. It is necessary, rather, to assume the
common burden of evils which weigh upon both ourselves and
our adversaries, and to overcome the enemy by helping him
to become other than an enemy. To do so requires tremendous spiritual maturity and inner strength, the fruit of
discipline and contemplation.[22]

The non-violent vision, therefore, is built upon the
presuppositions of the intrinsic dignity, unity, and forgiveableness of the human being. In contrast to these
truths, the opposite view affirms the incorrigible corrupt-
ness and internecine conflict and aggression of man. Out
of these different perspectives come opposing aims and approaches. Or perhaps it is more accurate to say that beneath the divergent goals and methods we can detect diverse
visions of the human person.

To the extent that it is faithful to its vision, a
genuine non-violence will seek truth, communication, and
reconciliation rather than self-justification, propaganda
or domination. In the light of its awareness of the true
inner self, it seeks truth and right; in the light of its
awareness of the oneness of all persons, it seeks communication and dialogue; in the light of its hope for forgiveness, it seeks reconciliation.

An authentic non-violence must struggle for the truth
contained in the previously delineated vision. Truth here
is much more than mere conformity of our outer words to our
inner thoughts. Our aims, outlooks, attitudes and habitual
responses to the problems and challenges of life also reveal our fidelity or infidelity to our inner being. Nor is
it a matter of some abstract idealistic truth, but of truth
that is incarnate in a concrete human situation, involving

living human beings, whose rights may be denied or whose
lives may be threatened.[23]

This is a question, moreover, of a struggle for what
is objectively and universally true for all men. It cannot
be an attempt to defend one's own shallow interests at the
expense of others. We are tempted to care more about
money, possessions and pleasure than our fellow men. If
anyone comes between us and our material interests we are
led to hate him. Rather than see things as they truly are,
our view tends to be distorted by fear, greed, ambition and
pleasure. Non-violence therefore involves the struggle to
get beyond the self-deception and illusions of our outer
self and to discover the real truth about a situation.[24]

This aim also excludes the effort to prove oneself
right and one's adversary wrong, to vindicate oneself at
the expense of others. Public dissent for example, should
not be merely a dramatic and superficial bid for instant
publicity, nor just an outlet for indignation, frustration
or anxiety. It should be constructive and educative, re-
calling people to their senses, leading them to think deeply, and awakening their deeper need for truth, reason, and
peace. Error can only be silenced by truth, Merton maintains, not by blatant or even subtle forms of aggression.[25]

A test of sincerity here is the willingness to learn
something from an adversary, and to admit that he is not
totally unreasonable and wrong. An unwillingness to learn
a new truth from him shows that we are more interested in
self-righteousness than in truth. It displays as well an
uncertainty about our own convictions, because we are
afraid to risk seeing them in a new light. Nor will we
ever be able to show another his error unless he is convinced that we see and appreciate the good and truth that
is in him as well.[26]

Such a quest for truth must prevail over the desire for immediate visible results. Otherwise we never see beyond the next automatic response; we rely chiefly on political technique backed by force, and are, in fact, basically interested in power rather than truth. But power never fosters the rights, justice or good of mankind. It only protects the narrow interest of some at the expense of others. Non-violence seeks to carefully choose what one believes to be truly good, and allows the good itself to produce its own good consequences in its own time. The strength to do so is rooted in the conviction that truth rather than pragmatic expediency is the more fundamental law of our being.[27]

Because the non-violent vision holds to the underlying unity of human beings, it seeks openness and dialogue with one's opponent or adversary. It does not encourage, excuse, or seek to justify the hatred of a special class, nation, or social group. It avoids the extreme of seeing all goodness on one side and all evil on the other, but recognizes the two on both sides. This recognition involves the arduous challenge of operating without hostility, resentment or aggression, and of aligning ouselves with the good we are able to find already present in the adversary.[28]

A policy of blind hatred and narrow nationalism eliminates all alternatives, and seeks by the threat of total destruction to force the other side to unconditionally accept its own one-sided position. In this instance, sheer arbitrary will and brute force simply eliminate any meaningful communication. On the other hand, dialogue does not seek to force a decision upon another from outside. It respects the personal conscience of the other. Even while insisting on one's own rights, it is crucial, observes Merton, to respect the moral and legal rights of everyone else, even an unjust oppressor. In this vein, we must also acknowledge the rights of other nations, races, and societies to be and remain different, and to open up new horizons.[29]

To the extent that we are more interested in being right than in truth, we seek to provoke and antagonize the other more than to communicate with him. The goal of non-violence, however, is not to destroy or humiliate an opponent, so that he wishes to respond with nothing but bullets or missiles. On the contrary, its goal is frank, open-minded negotiation and arbitration which will bring about more lasting and harmonious solutions to problems.

Since it does not dismiss an opponent as utterly corrupt, non-violence enters into dialogue with some positive and reasonable, although not naive expectations, addresses his intelligence and freedom, and invites him to arrive co-operatively at a decision of his own. The purpose is to work logically, patiently, and humanely for interests which transcend the limits of any national or ideological group and concern the common good of the human community.[30]

In this regard Merton emphasizes that violence is essentially wordless and inarticulate. It can only begin where thought and rational communication have broken down. The cascade of words in advertising, political statements and military reports is a language of propaganda, pseudo-scientific jargon and doubletalk. It is merely organized noise destined to arrest thought, block communication, and silence dialogue. "The incoherence of language that cannot be trusted and the coherence of weapons that are infallible, or thought to be: this is the dialectics of politics and war, the prose of the twentieth century."[31] The adversary is regarded as an evil being who understands no language but that of force.

The striving for dialogue is an expression of the love

of neighbour, including our enemies, which the Christian Gospel sees as the deepest law of our being, fidelity to which alone leads to human fulfillment. Such love is not mere sentimentality or condescension or abstract benevolence, but the arduous struggle to treat others with dignity and to further their good. Its opportunities and limits are bounded by the concrete realities of our time, place, society, and state in life.[32]

The aim of truth and of dialogue flows into that of forgiveness and reconciliation, for our basic dignity and orientation is wounded by destructive tendencies to lie and hate. We are, says Merton, a body of broken bones. There remains invariably a degree of conflict and division within and among us which is painful. Yet the path to healing and reconciliation lies in accepting oneself and loving the other in spite of our unworthiness, as well as in struggling against the evils in self and other. It does not lie in attacking the other on whom we project our own evils.

The basic demand here is not to resist evil with evil by hating those who hate us and trying to destroy them. To do so is not to resist evil but to become its deliberate and active collaborator. The only way to conquer evil is to refuse to render evil for evil, and to counter it with good. Once again, the only way to effectively overcome one's enemy is to help him to become no longer an enemy but a cooperator in a common cause.

The need for forgiveness and reconciliation applies to nations and collectivities as well as individuals. People sanction brutal actions by a nation which they would never tolerate in private individuals. At the same time, in recognizing the possibility of healing, a genuine non-violence refuses to despair of the world and abandon it to its supposedly evil fate. This is a reasonable optimism sustained by the eschatological hope revealed in Christ.[33]

APPROACHES TO NON-VIOLENCE

For Merton, then, a genuine theology of non-violence is grounded in the firm conviction of the dignity, unity, and forgiveableness of human beings, and aims at dialogue, truth, and reconciliation among men. It is time now to consider what approaches Merton deems necessary in order to be faithful to this vision and realize this goal.

Many of these means have already been stated or implied in the preceding development, and it is not necessary to repeat them here. In general, it can be said that non-violence will address people's understanding and freedom and will employ spiritual rather than material weapons.

Merton distinguishes here between what he calls a nature-oriented and a person-oriented approach. The former considers man in general as an abstract nature governed by certain laws. It is concerned with man insofar as he is subject to necessity and seeks out areas in which he is consistently vulnerable in order to coerce him physically and psychologically. This coercive perspective treats people as objects to be manipulated, in order to control the course of events and make the future conform to certain rigidly preconceived expectations and ends.

A non-violent approach, on the other hand, is person-centred. It is based upon respect for the concrete human person insofar as he is endowed with intelligence, freedom and strength, which transcend natural necessity. Instead of attempting to compel another from without, it speaks to him as a unique person and endeavours to awaken his understanding and invite his own free decision through dialogue and cooperation. Rather than demanding that persons and events conform to a preestablished ideal or ideology, non-violence seeks only the openness of free exchange in which reason and love or respect have scope to operate. In such a situation, the future can be left to take care of it-

self. Certainly, Merton recognizes, conflict will never be
fully abolished on earth. But a new way of solving it can
become habitual--by reason and arbitration instead of by
deceit, slaughter and destruction.[34]

Such an approach to persons and social issues will
necessarily refuse any dishonest, unreasonable or inhuman
tactics. It will certainly not place its sole trust in
political manoeuvres and external compulsion backed by
brute force. Non-violence is convinced that spiritual arms
are more effective than material ones, and that they alone
have had and continue to have any lasting effect on society. Unless the mind and heart of human beings are changed,
so that insight is deepened and consciences are refined,
mere force will not bring about anything of permanence. In
effect, if the sole way to overcome hatred, violence and
destruction is by more hatred, violence and destruction,
these are not overcome but merely prolonged. Only those
means that transform man himself will have any durable impact upon society.

> The only way to change such a world is to change
> the thoughts and desires of the men who live in
> it. The conditions of our world are simply an
> outward expression of our own thoughts and de-
> sires.[35]

It should be clear at this point that the non-violence
of which we are speaking, in the contemplative depth out of
which it arises, and in the uncompromising presuppositions,
aims and approaches in which it consists, is a matter of
profound inner strength. It has nothing to do with a non-
violence of weakness which cringes in fear before every
difficulty, obstacle or threat, and is willing to com-
promise in any way in order to be left in peace.[36]

The non-violence of strength entails all the positive
efforts outlined above, and also involves active dissent,

protest and resistance, rather than passive acquiescence in
the case of social injustice. But it does so in a manner
that is in keeping with its basic principles. The very
idea of the affluent society, for example, is one which to
some extent lives by organized greed and systematic oppression, and therefore always tends to foster injustice and
violence. The first principle of valid political action
in such a society becomes non-cooperation in its injustices. But this response must be carried out in such a way
as to reveal the untruth of the situation to others, appeal
to their deepest moral instinct, and awaken them to a new
social consciousness. It must not merely antagonize them
and confirm them in an illusory self-righteousness.[37]

A good example of the above is found in an acceptable
form of civil disobedience. A careful distinction must be
made between a specific unjust law itself and a fundamental
respect for social order and the essential legality of
structures. Genuine non-violent resistance permits only
clear and unambiguous disobedience to a law that has been
shown to be unjust. At the same time it affirms its respect for law and order itself, for just laws, by accepting
punishment for this act of disobedience.[38]

In advocating tactics that are themselves non-violent
and that are compatible with the non-violent vision and
aims delineated above, there is no question of affirming,
for example, that a person has no right to defend his life
or his family if they are attacked. He must not stand by
and let his helpless dependents be killed or overrun. In
certain extreme or limit situations, where non-violent resistance may no longer be possible, then violent resistance
must be used rather than passive submission. Non-violence
is not cowardly acquiescence, but positive and active resistance to evil.

Yet the individual overt cases of violence so often

cited are frequently not considered as a last resort when all else has failed. They are readily taken as a starting point to justify amassing arms and an underlying, pervasive hostility which looks for any pretext to assert itself. This is far removed from the non-violent resistance which seeks true dialogue and reconciliation, the model of which is Jesus Christ who overcame evil by suffering rather than by retaliation.[39]

Moreover, we must not let ourselves be deceived by focusing upon individual instances taken in isolation. In Merton's eyes, the real violence today is the much more covert, abstract and organized violence exercised on a massive and corporate scale, where the individual's role is easily lost from sight. "Violence today is white-collar violence, the systematically organized, bureaucratic, and technological destruction of man."[40] The real problem is not so much the individual with the revolver as that of death and even genocide as big business.

In this issue, courageous resistance may involve a self-sacrifice for the sake of truth which can amount to heroic proportions. Merton presents the examples of the Austrian peasant, Franz Jagerstatter, the German Jesuit, Alfred Delp, and the German priest, Max Joseph Metzger, all of whom were executed for refusal to comply with the Nazi regime.[41]

Finally, we may bring our study of non-violent approaches to a close with a quotation which sums up the position of non-violence of strength in contrast to passive acquiescence. Since it deals also with the struggle for peace, it may serve as an introduction to our final brief discussion of the problem of war.

The duty of the Christian as a peacemaker is not to be confused with a kind of quietistic inertia which is indifferent to injustice, accepts any

kind of disorder, compromises with error and with
evil, and gives in to every pressure in order to
maintain 'peace at any price'. The Christian
knows well, or should know well, that peace is
not possible on such terms. Peace demands the
most heroic labour and the most difficult sacrifice. It demands greater heroism than war. It
demands greater fidelity to truth and a much more
perfect purity of conscience.[42]

THE PROBLEM OF WAR

Merton is clear and unequivocal in his condemnation of
nuclear war. "The massive and uninhibited use of nuclear
weapons either in attack or in retaliation is contrary to
Christian morality." "Nuclear war is totally unaccept-
able. It is immoral, inhuman, and absurd. It can lead nowhere but to the suicide of nations and cultures, indeed
the destruction of human society."[43] The horrendous results of such a war preclude any justification whatsover,
no matter what the values to which appeal is made. Far too
frequently nations are merely engaged in a struggle for
power, which they often disguise as a spiritual and ideological conflict.

Yet the presence of nuclear arms is simply taken for
granted by the leaders and the majority of the populations
of nuclear powers. They also assume that the threat of using these weapons is a way of preserving peace, and alleg-
edly, in the name of peace, engage in a global arms race,
although existing weapons could destroy the world many
times over. This situation Merton describes as one of
moral paralysis on the part of military, political, and
even religious leaders, and of passivity, confusion, and
unresisting compliance and fatalism on the part of members
of the mass society.[44]

The traditional just war theory of Christian morality no longer applies in the case of nuclear conflict. According to this teaching, war may be sanctioned as a last resort if it is purely defensive, if all measures are taken to avoid the death of innocent people (and even combatants as much as possible), and if the destructiveness which results is not greater than the injustice involved. Merton does not dispute this theory as theory, but states that there is no adequate defence against nuclear arms and that the massive annihilation it unleashes can in no way be condoned. Yet there are some Christians who, in what Merton terms a corruption of Christian ethics, envision nuclear war as a possiblity and even as a possible Christian response against the threat of atheistic communism. Aside from the fact that the West is no longer really Christian, "it is absurd and immoral to pretend that Christianity can be defended by the H-bomb."[45]

Many persons also assume that a limited war with conventional forces is a realistic way to avoid a full-scale nuclear war. The underlying pessimism here tacitly takes for granted that man cannot get along without some kind of war, and that it is therefore better to keep the slaughter in the thousands rather than in the millions. Modern conventional war, however, is no longer just combat between opposing armies. It is always total war, a systematic terrorism that invariably engulfs the civilian populations of whole areas. Merton feared in this instance as well a further escalation into nuclear confrontation which might destroy the world. The persistence of the cold war and the mounting stockpile of weapons, against which there is no defence, push people toward fanaticism on the one hand or despairing pessimism on the other.[46]

Behind the policies of hatred and destruction, which already produced two world wars this century and presently

thrust the world to the brink of nuclear war, lie "the ra-
bid, shortsighted, irrational and stubborn forces which
come to a head in nationalism."[47] Such narrow nationalism is distinct from and a perversion of the combination of
positive values which characterize a particular social
group. It is rather the setting up of the nation state as
the final object of man's allegiance, overriding all other
human truth and values.

Each nation considers itself the sole judge in it own
case and decides for itself what is right and wrong with no
appeal except to the power of the bomb. No political system at present seriously considers abolishing war. All
still assume that the only way to peace is to abolish the
enemy or at least reduce him to helplessness. Such narrow
nationalism cannot acknowledge any wrong in itself, but
projects all fault onto the enemy whom it regards as totally evil. If human nature is evil as such a view implies,
then the struggle for power is indeed inescapable and war
remains inevitable.[48]

As we have seen, however, Merton's whole vision runs
counter to this despairing outlook. We must shoulder our
moral responsibility and struggle against war and the presuppositions, aims, and approaches that invariably lead to
it. We must work unrelentingly for peace with spiritual
weapons directed towards changing the mind and heart of
human beings.

What faces us all, Christians and non-Christians
alike, is the titanic labour of trying to change
the world from a camp of warring barbarians into
a peaceful international community from which war
has been perpetually banned.[49]

We must cease regarding war as a fatality to which we
must submit, whether with bravery or with desperation, and
begin to consider it as a problem to be solved with rational

analysis and moral will. We must come to see that the only
winner in war is war itself. It is not truth or justice or
liberty or morality, for these are all vanquished by war.
We must recognize too that the real enemy is not to be
found on one side or the other, but is in all of us. The
real enemy is war and its roots: fear, hatred, lies, injustice, selfishness, greed, and their countless destructive manifestations. We must struggle, therefore, with
these factors in ourselves. We have also to repect the
rights and life of our opponents, their highest spiritual
interest as well as our own, even in the face of apparent
injustice and malice. Outright belligerence seems ill-
suited to the imitation of one who allowed himself to be
nailed to a cross and who died praying for his execution-
ers.[50]

Speaking a little more specifically, Merton stresses
that we must examine and question rather than passively
comply with the policies and actions of military and political leaders and their bureaucracies. We must especially
beware of seeing in our civic duties, a sweeping justification for every kind of cruelty, cowardice and moral aberration. This is difficult because in matters of defence policy we so often seem to be at the mercy of the anonymous
power of managers and generals who stand behind the facade
of government.[51] In this vein, Merton stresses the importance of working for interests which transcend the limits of any ideological or national community, and especially of striving for the establishment of a truly effective
international authority, as a means of solving disputes.[52]

He advocates as well achieving some degree of control
over the production and stockpiling of weapons. These become obsolete almost overnight and result in massive spending on armaments while the majority of mankind still lives
in subhuman conditions. Certainly, unilateral disarmament

would be naive, and might simply precipitate an attack. At
the same time, unilateral initiatives involving gradual
steps toward disarmament are imperative. It would, of
course, do little or no good to disarm, even on both sides,
if men continue to live in the same state of confusion,
suspicion, hostility and aggressiveness. The task is to
create a climate in which matters can be dealt with sanely,
and finally to change the minds and hearts of people.[53]

In all these efforts towards peace, the Christian may
be sustained by the hope that in Jesus, crucified and
risen, there is assured the final eschatological victory of
truth and love over falsehood and hatred.

CONCLUSION

The roots of Merton's theology of non-violence, as indeed of his whole social commentary, lie in his underlying
contemplative experience and vision. Herein lies the
source of its strength, clarity, and incisiveness.[54] It
is a vision of great depth which enables him to see social
questions in the light of man's relationship to the silent,
infinite Mystery of meaning and love, present and active at
the heart of all creation. As a result, he is able to
raise the right and provocative questions, and to lay bare
the real issues at play in any social problem. These involve the titanic struggle between anxiety, fear, greed,
deception, hatred and the like, on the one hand, and trust,
peace, generosity, truth, and love, on the other: the
struggle, in brief, between the true and the false self.

Merton questions, for example, defending by nuclear
weapons the ideal of a way of life based on greedy, waste-
ful, and over-indulgent consumption. His writings challenge people to recognize their own hidden motivations, to
discern and discard their self-deceptive illusions, and to
enlighten and purify their consciences. He cautions

against a naive and superficial optimism which refuses to
confront destructive forces in oneself and in the world.
At the same time, he rejects any despairing pessimism which
fails to acknowledge the intrinsic dignity and basic orientation to truth and love at the heart of every person. Despite our fragility and wounds, this dignity and orientation is what is deepest in each of us as beings who flow
from and are summoned to oneness with the God revealed in
Christ.

Merton insists that it is in such oneness with God,
experienced in contemplation, that a person finds his true
self and his solidarity with others. In his view, no purely
external change really effects anything of lasting significance. True and lasting social reform occurs only if the
mind and heart have been transformed. A valid test of such
inward change, however, is its expression in all dimensions
of one's self and in a respect for others which works, in
its own life-situation, for social justice.

It could perhaps be objected that Merton's writings
lack specific suggestions for dealing with particular problems. He does not provide explicit guidelines and practical answers for tackling the enormously complex issues facing the human community today. Here, Merton might respond
that, while important, this is not his task. He would certainly observe that unless one's angle of vision and direction of will are refined and deepened, any such practicali-
ties are a mere tinkering with details which leave the central problems untouched.

It could also be argued that there are possibly more
limit-situations (or indeed that we are living in a general
limit-situation) in which the use of violence is inevitable
in order to resist large-scale, covert, exploitative, institutional violence. To this point, Merton might counter
that here above all we must guard against illusion and un-

acknowledged fears and hostilities. We must also be careful not to project all evil unto the other side while cam-
ouflaging this move behind high-sounding rhetoric. While
not succumbing to cowardly acquiescence, it is important to
continually assess the extent to which violently introduced
external change does in fact bring about lasting and positive results.

It remains true that Merton's basic contribution to
social issues in general and to that of non-violence in
particular lies in his contemplative vision, his posing of
crucial questions, and his uncovering of the deep human
values and disvalues at stake in any social issue. Yet
precisely because of this factor, his theology of non-
violence poses a challenge to all who would canonize or
tolerate the status quo or resort to violence either to defend or alter the prevailing situation.

Merton's social and more mystical writings together
form both a challenge and an invitation to honestly come to
grips with where we stand in our inmost hearts and in our
relationships with others. His thought on non-violence is
perhaps not the final word on this topic. But no future
word on it can neglect his lasting contribution with its
unique blend of realism and hope.

NOTES

[1]John Eudes Bamberger, Preface to Henri Nouwen, Pray
to Live: Thomas Merton, Contemplative Critic (Notre Dame:
Fides/Claretian, 1972), p. ix.

[2]A frequently cited statement of Merton's basic focus is the following: "Whatever I have written, I think it
all can be reduced in the end to this one root truth: that
God calls human persons to union with himself and with one
another in Christ. . . . It is certainly true that I have
written about more than the contemplative life. I have ar-
ticulately resisted attempts to have myself classififed as
an 'inspirational writer'. But if I have written about in-
terracial justice or thermonuclear weapons, it is because
these issues are terribly relevant to one great truth:
that man is called to live as a son of God. Man must respond to this call to live in peace with all his brothers
in the one Christ." "Concerning the Collection in the
Bellarmine College Library," The Thomas Merton Studies
Centre (Santa Barbara, Cal.: The Unicorn Press, 1971).

[3]Both Merton's outer and inward life journeys are
reflected in his successive journals. These include, in
chronological order, The Secular Journal of Thomas Merton
(New York: Farrar, Straus, and Giroux, 1977); The Seven
Storey Mountain (New York: New American Library, 1963);
The Sign of Jonas (Garden City, N.Y.: Doubleday Image,
1956); Conjectures of a Guilty Bystander (Garden City,
N.Y.: Doubleday Image, 1966); The Asian Journal of Thomas
Merton (New York: New Directions, 1973).
     While The Seven Storey Mountain is an autobiographical
work rather than a journal, it is included in this list be-
cause of the vast information it contains on his life and
development.
     A good brief presentation of Merton's life and thought
is the work of Nouwen, cited above n. 1. An interesting
portrayal is also given by Edward Rice, The Man in the Syc-
amore Tree (Garden City, N.Y.: Doubleday Image, 1972).
Further appreciations are given in Patrick Hart (ed.).
Thomas Merton Monk: A Monastic Tribute (Garden City,
N.Y.: Doubleday Image, 1976) and Gerald Twomney (ed.),
Thomas Merton: Prophet in the Belly of a Paradox (New York:
Paulist Press, 1978).

[4]On the historical background of his thought in the
Western tradition, see The Waters of Siloe (New York: Har-
court, Brace, and Co., 1949); The Silent Life (New York:
Dell, 1959); The Wisdom of the Desert (New York: New Di-
rections, 1960); Contemplation in a World of Action (Garden
City, N.Y.: Doubleday Image, 1973); Contemplative Prayer
(Garden City, N.Y., 1971).
     A collection of writings comprising Merton's mature

thought on the monastic life and tradition is found in
Patrick Hart, ed., The Monastic Journey (Garden City,
N.Y.: Doubleday Image, 1978).
For Eastern influence on his thought, see The Way of
Chuang Tzu (New York: New Directions, 1965); Mystics and
Zen Masters (New York: New Directions, 1968); and The
Asian Journal of Thomas Merton.
The clearest expression of his involvement in the
twentieth century is found in "Is the World a Problem?,"
Contemplation in a World of Action, pp. 159-71.

[5]Contemplative Prayer, pp. 19-26. See also the
title essay in Contemplation in a World of Action, pp. 172-
79.

[6]Contemplative Prayer, pp. 24f, 38-41, 72-74. See
also New Seeds of Contemplation (New York: New Directions,
1972), pp. 84-89.

[7]Contemplative Prayer, pp. 42-45, 89-95. On the
distinction between the true and false self, see especially
New Seeds of Contemplation, pp. 29-46; Disputed Questions
(New York: New American Library, 1965), pp. ix-xi; Faith
and Violence (South Bend, Ind.: University of Notre Dame
Press, 1968), pp. 111-18; Zen and the Birds of Appetite,
pp. 71-78.

[8]Contemplative Prayer, pp. 24, 67-71, 96-102, 105-11.

[9]Ibid., p. 83. On this mode of awareness of God,
see also ibid., pp. 67-71, 75-78, 82-88; New Seeds of Contemplation, pp. 1-13; Zen and the Birds of Appetite,
pp. 22-32, 71-78. Two helpful studies on Merton's theology
of prayer and mysticism are: John Higgins, Thomas Merton
on Prayer (Garden City, N.Y.: Doubleday Image, 1975) and
Raymond Bailey, Thomas Merton on Mysticism (Garden City,
N.Y.: Doubleday, 1975).

[10]The Secular Journal of Thomas Merton, entry of
June 16, 1940, pp. 109-12.

[11]"Rain and the Rhinoceros," Raids on the Unspeakable (New York: New Directions, 1964), p. 22. See also
Contemplative Prayer, pp. 109-10.

[12]"Notes for a Philosophy of Solitude," Disputed
Questions, p. 160. On this sense of oneness with others
rooted in contemplation, see the entire article, pp. 139-
60; and also Contemplative Prayer, pp. 112-16; New Seeds of
Contemplation, pp. 46-79; No Man is an Island (Garden City,
New York: Doubleday Image, 1967), pp. 152-56, 183-89. A
concise statement is given in New Seeds of Contemplation,
p. 64: "One of the paradoxes of the mystical life is
this: that a man cannot enter into the deepest centre of
himself and pass through that centre into God, unless he is

able to pass entirely out of himself and empty himself and
give himself to other people in the purity of a selfless
love."

[13]"Contemplation in a World of Action," pp. 178-79.
For Merton, this statement applies also to religion which
remains on a surface level, out of touch with this inner
ground of meaning and love. Such superficial religion is
untrue to itself and to God, an artifical facade used to
justify a particular social and economic system, and a
front for greed, injustice, sensuality, selfishness, and
violence. See Contemplative Prayer, pp. 111-15.

[14]"Blessed are the Meek," Faith and Violence,
pp. 15-16. Almost all of Merton's writings on non-violence
are contained in the collection: Gordon C. Zahn (ed.),
Thomas Merton on Peace (New York: McCall, 1971). The
present reference is found in Zahn, p. 209.

[15]"Blessed are the Meek," pp. 16-18, (Zahn, pp. 209-
10); "The Christian in World Crisis: Reflections on the
Moral Climate of the 1960's," Seeds of Destruction (New
York: Farrar, Straus, and Giroux, 1964), pp. 125-30, (Zahn,
pp. 35-37).

[16]"Gandhi and the One-Eyed Giant," introduction to
Gandhi on Non-Violence (New York: New Directions, 1965),
pp. 3-10.

[17]Ibid., pp. 10-11; Conjectures of a Guilty Bystander, pp. 85-86, 121-22.

[18]"Is Man a Gorilla With a Gun?," Faith and Violence, pp. 96-105, (Zahn, 168-71); "Blessed are the Meek,"
pp. 25-27, (Zahn, pp. 215-16); "The Christian in World
Crisis," pp. 172-83, (Zahn, pp. 56-62).

[19]"Auschwitz: A family Camp," (Zahn, p. 159). On
the question of the forgiveableness of evil, see "Gandhi
and the One-eyed Giant," pp. 11-18; "Preface to Vietnamese
Translation of No Man is an Island," (Zahn, pp. 63-66).

[20]"A Body of Broken Bones" and "The Root of War is
Fear," New Seeds of Contemplation, pp. 71-79, 112-22.

[21]Ibid., See also "Gandhi and the One-Eyed Giant,"
pp. 12-18; No Man Is an Island, pp. 153-56.

[22]"Gandhi and the One-Eyed Giant," pp. 14-15; "Preface . . .," (Zahn 64-65); "Peace: A Religious Responsibility," (Zahn, pp. 114-15).

[23]"A Tribute to Gandhi," Seeds of Destruction,
pp. 230-21, (Zahn, p. 182); No Man Is an Island, 145-52.
On p. 146 of this latter work Merton gives a definition of
truth: "Truth, in things, is their reality. In our minds,
it is the conformity of our knowledge with the things

known. In our words, it is the conformity of our words to
what we think. In our conduct, it is the conformity of our
acts to what we are supposed to be."

24"Blessed are the Meek," p. 15, (Zahn, p. 209); No
Man Is an Island, p. 147; Conjectures of a Guilty Bystand-
er, pp. 68-69; "St. Maximus the Confessor of Non-violence,"
(Zahn, p. 174).

25"Blessed are the Meek," pp. 14-15, (Zahn, pp. 208-
09); "Peace and Protest," Faith and Violence, pp. 43-45,
(Zahn, p. 68); Conjectures of a Guilty Bystander, pp. 84-
85. In this last reference, Merton makes the corresponding
point that lying is the mother of violence, just as a truthful man cannot long remain violent.

26"Blessed Are the Meek," pp. 23-24, (Zahn, 214-15);
No Man Is an Island, pp. 149-50; Conjectures of a Guilty Bystander, pp. 68-69.

27"Blessed are the Meek," p. 22, (Zahn, p. 213);
"Peace and Revolution: A Footnote from Ulysses," (Zahn,
p. 75).

28"Blessed are the Meek," pp. 19-20, (Zahn, p. 211);
Conjectures of a Guilty Bystander, pp. 84-85; "Christian
Action in World Crisis," (Zahn, pp. 220-21).

29"Blessed Are the Meek," p. 24, (Zahn, p. 214-15);
Conjectures of a Guilty Bystander, pp. 87-88; "Non-violence
and the Christian Conscience," Faith and Violence, p. 37.

30"Blessed Are the Meek," pp. 19-22, (Zahn pp. 211-
13); "The Christian in World Crisis," pp. 112-13, (Zahn,
p. 29); "Gandhi and the One-Eyed Giant," p. 11; "Peace: A
Religious Responsibility," p. 111.

31"War and the Crisis of Language," (Zahn, p. 235).
On the question of violence and the use of language, see
the rest of this article, pp. 234-47; and "Gandhi and the
One-Eyed Giant," pp. 7-8.

32Conjectures of a Guilty Bystander, pp. 120-22.
See also Life and Holiness (Garden City, N.Y.,: Doubleday
Image, 1964), pp. 86-92; and his longer essay, "The Power
and Meaning of Love," Disputed Questions, pp. 81-101.

33"A Body of Broken Bones," New Seeds of Contemplation, pp. 70-79; "Blessed Are the Meek," p. 15, (Zahn,
p. 209); "Christian Action in World Crisis," p. 224; "Gandhi
and the One-Eyed Giant," p. 15.

34"Blessed Are the Meek," pp. 27-29, (Zahn, pp. 216-
18). The position of Karl Rahner bears a number of simi-
larities to that of Thomas Merton. He stresses that one
must always address the understanding and freedom of another person, and may only resort to any form of coercion

as a very last resort, and that this must always aim at its
own abolition. See "On the Theology of Power," Theological
Investigations, vol. 4 (Baltimore: Helicon, 1966),
pp. 391-410; "Peace of God and Peace of the World," Theological Investigations, Vol. 10 (New York: Herder, 1973),
pp. 371-88; "On the Theology of Revolution," Theological Investigations, Vol. 14 (New York: Seabury, 1976), pp.
314-30.

[35]"Preface . . .," (Zahn, p. 65). On this question
of spiritual 'weapons' and inner transformation see also
"Blessed Are the Meek," p. 22, (Zahn, p. 213); "Peace: A
Religious Responsibility," pp. 114-15; Conjectures of a
Guilty Bystander, pp. 117-18; "The Christian in World
Crisis," pp. 164-65, (Zahn, pp. 52-53).

[36]"Peace and Revolution: A Footnote from Ulysses,"
pp. 70-75; "Peace: A Religious Responsibility," pp. 112-13.

[37]"Gandhi and the One-Eyed Giant," pp. 10, 19-20;
"Passivity and Abuse of Authority," (Zahn, pp. 129-31);
"Peace and Protest," pp. 43-44 (Zahn, p. 68).

[38]"Note on Civil Disobedience and Nonviolent Revolution," (Zahn, pp. 227-28); "Note for Ave Maria," (Zahn,
pp. 232-33); "Is the World A Problem?," pp. 164-71.

[39]"Toward a Theology of Resistance," Faith and Violence, pp. 3-13, (Zahn, pp. 186-92); "The Machine Gun in
the Fallout Shelter," (Zahn, pp. 103-06).

[40]"Toward a Theology of Resistance," p. 6, (Zahn,
p. 188).

[41]"An Enemy of the State," Faith and Violence,
pp. 69-75, (Zahn, pp. 134-38); "The Prison Meditations of
Father Delp," Faith and Violence, pp. 47-68; "A Martyr for
Peace and Unity," (Zahn, pp. 139-43).

[42]"Peace: A Religious Responsibility," pp. 112-13.

[43]Ibid., pp. 108, 109. See also "Christian Ethics
and Nuclear War," (Zahn, p. 83).

[44]"Passivity and Abuse of Authority," pp. 129-33;
"Christianity and Defence in the Nuclear Age," (Zahn,
pp. 88-89, 92-93); "Peace: A Religious Responsibility,"
pp. 108, 111, 117-18; "Christian Action in World Crisis,"
pp. 219-20.

[45]"Christian Ethics and Nuclear War," p. 86. See
also pp. 85-87; "Peace: A Religious Responsibility,"
pp. 114- 15.

[46]"Target Equals City," (Zahn. pp. 100-01); "Peace:
A Religious Responsibility," pp. 108-09, 115; "Peace and
Protest," pp. 40-41; "The Christian in World Crisis,"
pp. 172-83, (Zahn, pp. 56-62); "Christianity and Defence

in a Nuclear Age," pp. 88-89; "Breakthrough to Peace," (Zahn, pp. 77-78).

[47]"Peace: A Religious Responsibility," p. 126.

[48]Ibid., pp. 126-27; "Peace and Protest," pp. 43-44, (Zahn, p. 68); "The Christian in World Crisis," pp. 174-81, (Zahn, pp. 57-61).

[49]"Christian Ethics and Nuclear War," p. 87.

[50]"Pacifism and Resistance in Simone Weil," Faith and Violence, pp. 80-82, (Zahn, pp. 146-48); "Christian Action in World Crisis," p. 220; "Peace: A Religious Responsibility," p. 112; "Target Equals City," p. 84.

[51]"Passivity and Abuse of Authority," pp. 130-31; "A Devout Mediation in Memory of Adolf Eichmann," Raids on the Unspeakable, pp. 45-49, (Zahn 160-62); "Peace: A Religious Responsibility," pp. 119-123. See also his very powerful criticism of the use of nuclear arms on Japan during the second world war in Original Child Bomb (New York: New Directions, 1962), (Zahn, pp. 3-11).

[52]"The Christian in World Crisis," pp. 170-71, (Zahn, pp. 55-56); "Peace: A Religious Responsibility," pp. 111, 118-20.

[53]"Peace: A Religious Responsibility," p. 125; "Christianity and Defence in the Nuclear Age," p. 90; "The Christian in World Crisis," pp. 116-18, (Zahn, pp. 31-32).

[54]For evaluations of Merton's social thought, see: Frederic J. Kelly, Man Before God: Thomas Merton on Social Responsibility (Garden City, N.Y.: Doubleday, 1974), esp. pp. 252-74; Gordon C. Zahn, "Original Child Monk: An Appreciation," Introduction to Thomas Merton on Peace, pp. ix-xii, and "Thomas Merton: Reluctant Pacifist," in Twomney, pp. 55-79; James Forest, "Thomas Merton's Struggle with Peacemaking," in Twomney, pp. 15-54; James Baker, Thomas Merton Social Critic, (Lexington: University of Kentucky Press, 1971), esp. pp. 145-48; John Higgins, pp. 114-24.

REINHOLD NIEBUHR

(1892 - 1971)

by John C. Hoffman

*Although the early Niebuhr was a pacifist, he
finally rejected this stance. While always recognizing the place of religious pacifism as an
eschatological sign, he rejected pacifism as an
historical strategy. Niebuhr's position, J.
Hoffman demostrates, is anchored in his theology,
especially in his images of Christ's suffering
love and the power of sin. These, coupled with
his pragmatism, led to a position which recognized the witness of religious pacifism while
making no claim for its historical efficacy. Unlike St. Francis and others, however, Niebuhr,
again from within his theological understanding,
abjured pacifism, opting for responsible action
rather than eschatological witness.*

Born in 1892, the son of an Evangelical Church pastor,
Reinhold Niebuhr became one of the dominant voices of twentieth century American theology. After completing his formal education at Yale Divinity School in 1915, he served
thirteen years in a Detroit parish. Those years, he re-
marked, "determined [my] development more than any books I
may have read."[1] He came as a liberal. Indeed his first
book written in 1927 reflects many of his liberal assumptions. But "the brutal facts of life in a great industrial
center" profoundly shook what he later regarded as the too
easy optimism of liberal Protestantism.[2] Thus in the
late 1920's he helped organize the Fellowship of Christian

Socialists, a group with a strong Marxist bias, Niebuhr regarding himself as a Christian Marxist. (Later he was as
critical of Marxism as of liberalism.) During this same
period he was a pacifist, a member of the Fellowship of
Reconciliation. He became professor of Christian Ethics at
Union Theological Seminary in New York in 1928, a post he
held for over thirty years. The seminary made possible a
careful and systematic development of his basic thought,
leading to a dozen major works.

Broadly speaking, he belongs among the neo-orthodox, a
group which includes such figures as Karl Barth and Emil
Brunner. He shared their rejection of the optimism of liberal theology and their reassertion of the biblical doctrine of sin. Like them, he also attempted to come to
terms with modern culture, rejecting traditional appeals to
the supernatural. He was, however, less orthodox than many
in his views of biblical authority and in his attitude towards the classical Christological doctrines.

Niebuhr never thought of himself as a theologian.
That honour for the family he left to his brother,
H. Richard. He produced no theological system. He never
developed, for instance, a full doctrine of God. Yet
clearly he was a man who sought to interpret some of the
most painful and pressing dilemmas of his time in the light
of the Christian faith, looking both to the biblical witness and to the writings of major theologians. In a sense
he always began as the pastor with a concrete problem, pro-
ceeding to the seminary professor who sought to understand
that problem theologically. Assuredly his was a theological ethic, and Morton White is correct in his claim that to
reject Niebuhr's doctrine of original sin leaves one with
no way to justify his ethics. (Certainly this was no blind
biblical faith. Rather, that difficult doctrine became for
Niebuhr a powerful expression of what he had experienced to

be true of human nature.) I would add that attention need
be given also to his Christology and his doctrine of grace.

Niebuhr's stance on pacifism also followed the "pas-
tor-professor" pattern. It arose during his pastorate in
response to practical choices facing the Christian but it
was only at Union in four major works, *Moral Man and Immoral Society*, *An Interpretation of Christian Ethics*,
Christianity and Power Politics, and *The Nature and Destiny of Man* that he fully articulated the theological justification for his posture. It would be false, however, to
conclude that he was merely developing a theological rationalization for a position based upon other considerations. More accurately, he was slowly clarifying the faith
that was in him--whether or not one agrees with his final
vision. In keeping with this pattern, I shall begin by
outlining the historical development of Niebuhr's stance on
pacifism and then indicate the theological basis he offered
in defense of that stance.

THE HISTORY OF NIEBUHR'S STANCE ON PACIFISM

Pacifism is usually identified basically with the rejection of war. In this sense Niebuhr once qualified as a
pacifist. Indeed, he regarded his own role as chairman of
his denomination's wartime commission (including visits to
training camps to speak in favour of "Wilson's War") as a-
postasy from his pacifist principle.[3] His experience of
the residual hatred in Europe during a 1921 visit again
convinced him of the folly of war. As late as 1928 he
could still write that "the use of physical violence in international life has impressed itself upon [my] mind as an
unmitigated and unjustified evil."[4]

The issue of pacifism for Niebuhr, however, was never
one to be faced only in relation to international
conflict. His parish experience in Detroit with the suffer-

ing and injustice of industrial society and his involvement
in the Marxist analysis inevitably raised for him the question of class conflict in the struggle for social justice.
Thus while renouncing war, he could write in the same article that "some form of social compulsion seems necessary
and justified on occasion in all but the most ideal human
societies."[5] This conviction, together with his renunciation of war, were basic assumptions as he came to Union.
His posture then was not absolutist. ". . . pacifists may
be defined as social idealists who are profoundly critical
and skeptical of the use of physical force in the solution
of social problems."[6]

Clearly this view of pacifism does not totally rule
out the use of force in all circumstances, though Niebuhr,
the pacifist, believed at this time that love could achieve
greater victories than the cynical would credit. One could
say that he was in transition between his liberalism and
his neo-orthodoxy. Like his liberal past, he was an absolute pacifist concerning war, but in keeping with his neo-
orthodox future, he was skeptical about the achievement of
social justice through absolute pacifism. In practical
terms, this became for him a tension between his allegiance
to pacifism and to the Marxist social analysis, between his
renunciation of violence, especially in relation to international disputes, and his belief in the inevitability of
class struggle in the pursuit of social justice. Such was
his internal struggle during the period from 1928 to 1934.
By 1932 he could write that "the relation of *nations* and
of economic groups requires the use of coercion in the pursuit of justice."[7] Obviously he could no longer draw a
sharp line between class struggle within a nation and the
conflicts between nations. Later in the same year he wrote
that "pure pacifism is an impossible goal for political
life, if by pure pacifism we mean the use of nothing but
moral suasion to resist injustice."[8]

The Marxist-pacifist tension came to a head in 1934
when certain Marxist members of the Fellowship of Reconciliation were expelled. Niebuhr felt compelled to join them,
no longer being able to hold an absolute position even as
pertains to war. Once we acknowledge the necessity of coercion in the pursuit of justice, he asserted, then the
limits of such coercion, the question of violence, becomes
a pragmatic issue.[9] In the late 1930's this rejection of
pacifism was heightened by the rise of European Fascism.
With the hostilities about to erupt he declared in his Gifford Lectures that the fact that all nations manifest sinful pride "does not mean that men may not have to make
fateful decisions between types of civilizations in mortal
combat."[10]

At this time he was instrumental in founding a new
journal, *Christianity and Crisis*. Commenting upon the
period and the motives of the founders, he wrote in 1962
that "they disavowed their earlier pacifism when they recognized that our neutrality in the face of the Nazi threat
posed the problem of guarding our virtue by irresponsibly
ignoring the dangers facing other nations."[11] Whether
one defines pacifism broadly as the rejection of coercion
in the pursuit of social justice or narrowly as the rejection of war, one sees that Niebuhr had made a major shift
between 1921 and 1934. It was a shift beginning from a
deeply felt, intuitive sense of the moral realities of the
human situation, but it was not until the development of
his more mature thought, starting with the publication of
Moral Man and Immoral Society, that Niebuhr fully articulated this position theologically. To this let us now turn.

BASIC ELEMENTS OF NIEBUHR'S THEOLOGY

While Niebuhr really developed no full doctrine of
God, all his thought was anchored in his Christology. The

redemptive power of Christ's suffering love on Calvary became the clue not only to the saving work of Christ but also to the nature of God and of the fullest humannness. His
Christology, in this sense, was revelational rather than
metaphysical.

What is the work of Christ? It is God's dealing with
human sin. (Here Niebuhr quite specifically discarded the
views of some early Greek fathers who tended to see Christ
less as an answer to the problem of sin than to the problem
of death.) But how does the suffering of the Son of Man
overcome sin? Niebuhr rejected the liberal optimism which
claimed "that vicarious love is a force in history which
gradually gains the triumph over evil and therefore ceases
to be tragic." "The New Testament," he countered, "never
guarantees the historical success of the 'strategy' of the
Cross."[12] Yet it is a triumphant love for, in Jesus, God
takes upon himself the consequences of sin. This means no
sentimental setting aside of the reality of sin. Rather,
it points to God's freedom and power over sin for God "has
a resource of mercy beyond His law and judgment but He can
make it effective only as He takes the consequences of His
wrath and judgment upon and into Himself."[13] Suffering
or sacrificial love is the supreme form in which God in his
very divinity is revealed to us in the saving work of
Christ.

What would it mean for such a God to enter history, to
become incarnate? "The final majesty, the ultimate freedom
and the perfect disinterestedness of the divine love can
have a counterpart in history only in a life which ends
tragically, because it refuses to participate in the claims
and counterclaims of historical existence."[14] For Niebuhr this image made far greater sense of the Incarnation,
both religiously and morally, than either the metaphysical
speculations of the early Christological debates or the at-

tempts to speak in terms of the sinlessness of the historical Jesus in liberal Protestantism.

Furthermore, in Christian tradition the God-man reveals not only the character of God but also the deepest
nature of man. Thus Niebuhr saw the suffering love of
Jesus as the ultimate norm for true humanness as well, albeit a paradoxical norm. It points to a human perfection
which will always transcend the possibilities of historical
existence while remaining relevant to history and acting as
a valid measure for human life. In Niebuhr's famous
phrase, it is the "impossible possibility." Specifically
he claimed that such love has a threefold relationship to
historically possible mutual love. Mutual love can survive
only when there is within it a willingness to express something of the quality of sacrificial love, to risk oneself
beyond a carefully calculated balance. Such love also
clarifies our human situation in the very fact that it always remains suffering love, thereby proclaiming the truth
that "sin is overcome in principle but not in fact."[15]
Finally, the sacrificial love of Christ corrects the false
understanding of ourselves by revealing the imperfections
in all our righteousness, the pride and pretension in all
our actions.

Niebuhr's greatest contribution to contemporary theology has undoubtedly been in the development of his theological anthropology, particularly in his careful and in-
sightful articulation of the dynamics of sin. Central to
his understanding of the issues involved in pacifism was
his conviction concerning the universality and power of sin.

Christianity is a religion which measures the total dimension of human existence not only in
terms of the final norm of human conduct, which
is expressed in the law of love, but also in
terms of the fact of sin. It recognizes that the

same man who can become his true self only by
striving for self-realization beyond himself is
also inevitably involved in the sin of infinitely
making his partial and narrow self the true end
of existence.[16]

We note here not only Niebuhr's emphasis upon the universality of sin but also its relation to human dignity, to
our highest capacities. It is only one made in the image
of God who is able to sin. Niebuhr understood the *imago*
as a dramatic picture of the human capacity for self-tran-
scendence which makes possible creativity, rationality and
the deepest human relationships, including one's relationship to God. But people remain creatures made in the image
of God. Though able to transcend it, they are inescapably
part of the natural order. Possessing freedom, they sense
that it is a finite freedom. This very ambiguous posture
means that the individual lives with anxiety, and this
anxiety is the occasion--though not the cause--of sin. If
we could trace sin to some cause, then we would no longer
be guilty. The possibility is always there to overcome
anxiety through faith. The human failing is to seek in the
self the remedy for anxiety either by denying one's finitude in arrogant self-assertion, which is pride, or in the
flight from freedom and responsibility into sensuousness.
(It is interesting to note that Niebuhr was far more sensitive to the sin of pride than to the sin of sensuousness
or, as I would prefer, more sensitive to pride than to
sloth and the sins of weakness.) Lying thus at the very
core of human nature, sin infects all accomplishments, even
those we regard as our highest achievements of virtue and
creativity. Even religion for Niebuhr could be merely "the
final battle ground between God and man's self-esteem."[17]

Here was a posture which rejected easy or unambiguous
solutions to social problems. "To the end of history," he

wrote, "the peace of the world, as Augustine observed, must be gained by strife. It will therefore not be a perfect peace."[18] One must not expect historical victories for love, if by that we mean victories which will totally overcome the power of sin. Sin will always be present and will undermine the highest victories that appear to have been achieved by love. The ultimate triumph of divine love in the world comes at the end of history through the intervention of God. "The moral resources of men would not be sufficient to guarantee [such triumphs]."[19] Such was Niebuhr's realistic appraisal of the human condition. One notes a major shift from the Niebuhr of 1928 who held greater hopes for the victories of love.

Left with only this doctrine, one would have an extremely gloomy view of humanity but this would not be true of Niebuhr's total anthropology. We must not fail to appreciate his understanding of original righteousness. Analogous to his treatment of original sin, Niebuhr did not regard original righteousness as a virtue once possessed in Adam and lost in the Fall. Rather he saw it as a symbol of mankind's residual capacity for righteousness which leads to a disquieting awareness of sin, proving, ironically, that we are not merely sinners. "Though Christian theology has frequently expressed the idea of the total depravity of man in extravagant terms," Niebuhr wrote in the Gifford Lectures, "it has never been without witnesses to the fact that human sin cannot destroy the essential character of man to such a degree that it would cease being implied in, and furnishing a contrast to, what he had become."[20] The moral character of mankind can only be understood by recognizing the presence of both original sin and original righteousness. In this same anthropology Niebuhr saw the ultimate justification for democracy. "Man's capacity for justice makes democracy possible; but man's inclination to injustice makes democracy necessary."[21]

Finally, we turn to Niebuhr's doctrine of grace. Many
have charged him with believing in justification but not
really in sanctification. To be sure, one can find passages supportive of this evaluation. Witness his assertion, already quoted, that sin is "overcome in principle
but not in fact." (Niebuhr himself later rejected this
phrase as inadequate.[22]) Paul Lehmann suggests that
there is at least a tendency in Niebuhr to neglect grace as
working effectively in mankind, a failure to appreciate
fully the Reformers' sense of the Holy Spirit as the energizing and enlightening power by which the work of Christ
is made effective in the individual believer.[23] Nevertheless, Niebuhr, I suggest, was not unmindful of the reality of sanctification. His theology at this point stands
in close relation to the Reformers with their tension between justification and sanctification. Luther might well
have written what follows.

> The question is whether the grace of Christ is
> primarily a power of righteousness which so heals
> the sinful heart that henceforth it is able to
> fulfil the law of love; or whether it is primari-
> ly the assurance of divine mercy for a persistent
> sinfulness which can never be completely over-
> come.[24]

Clearly, for Niebuhr, grace is both. The Christian
knows the experience of the sanctifying power of God and
yet is aware at every moment of the necessity for forgiveness. Like Calvin and Luther, Niebuhr affirmed the organic
wholeness of justification and sanctification in the experience of faith but continued to grant priority to justification. In keeping with that tradition, however, the affirmation of mankind's free right to be does not mean the
end of moral striving. Rather, it affirms the freedom to
risk oneself in moral decision, knowing that one's motives

can never be pure. For that very reason one is free to dare the imperfect and failure in the struggle for social justice. Such awareness is "the only way of preventing premature completions of life, of arresting the new and more terrible pride which may find its roots in the soil of humility, and of saving the Christian life from the intolerable pretension of saints who have forgotten that they are sinners."[25]

Before applying these central elements to Niebuhr's understanding of pacifism, let me draw attention to a last significant factor in his thought, namely his pragmatism. Niebuhr was very conscious of this dimension. "We have previously insisted," he wrote, "that if the purpose of a social policy is morally and rationally approved, the choice of means in fulfilling the purpose raises pragmatic issues which are more political than they are ethical."[26] Atomic war presented a particularly difficult problem. Obviously all-out nuclear conflict represented a degree of violence and destruction which could never be justified. Yet the absolute pacifist's rejection of the use of atomic weapons might in fact encourage an aggressor to make excessive claims, leading to cruel tyranny and possibly triggering a nuclear conflict in retaliation. All such decisions, while guided by Christian moral principles, involve a careful balancing of many factors in the attempt to discern a morally correct and pragmatically sound policy.

PACIFISM IN THE LIGHT OF NIEBUHR'S THEOLOGY

We have seen that by the mid 30's Niebuhr was no longer a pacifist. We are now in a position to see how this stance was justified in terms of his understanding of the Christian faith. To begin with, while no longer a pacifist himself, Niebuhr continued to recognize the validity of such a posture. In *An Interpretation of Christian Ethics,*

which is probably his first book actually written following his break with the Fellowship of Reconciliation, Niebuhr differentiated between pragmatic and religious pacifism, at that time granting validity to each. He warned,
however, that arguments against the use of violence often
indiscriminately employ pragmatic and religious reasoning,
thereby confusing the nature and validity of each. As the
name would imply, the pragmatic pacifist makes all attempts
to avoid violence on the basis of the pragmatic judgment
that such a policy is the more productive. "When resort is
taken to armed conflict," Niebuhr warned--in the spirit of
such pacifists--"the possessors may have more deadly weapons than the dispossessed."[27] (He was to become somewhat
less sanguine about the virtue of a purely pragmatic pacifism.)

In religious pacifism he recognized a more powerful
claim. He saw it as a "symbolic portrayal of love absolutism in a sinful world" and as such it has "its own value
and justification."[28] In effect, it attempts to proclaim
the relevance of the Christian ethic of love in the historical situation, "to take the law of Christ seriously and
not to allow the political strategies, which the sinful
character of man make necessary, to become the final
norm."[29] While not a plan of action which can hope for
historical success, religious pacifism remains an important
witness, an eschatological sign, for the community of
faith. Niebuhr could therefore write most appreciatively
of its role.

We who allow ourselves to become engaged in war
need this testimony of the absolute pacifist a-
gainst us, lest we accept the warfare of the
world as normative, lest we become callous to the
horror of war, and lest we forget the ambiguity
of our own actions and motives and the risk we

run of achieving no permanent good from this momentary anarchy in which we are involved.[30]

Niebuhr was critical of religious pacifists when they
failed to remember that theirs was a witness to the impossible possibility and tried instead to act as if it were a
political strategy. Thus he was more supportive of the
Mennonite stance than of the Quaker posture which sought to
use pacifism as a social force to restrain oppressors.
Moreover, he warned that religious pacifists were constantly tempted by a self-righteousness which accused others of
apostasy while claiming "to live in history without sin-
ning."[31]

In spite of his genuine respect for it, religious pacifism was not a posture which Niebuhr himself could adopt,
neither on pragmatic grounds nor more deeply on theological
ones. Religious pacifists, he felt, fail to take full account of the fact that we must live our lives under the
conditions of sin.

> Presumably inspired by the Christian gospel, [re-
> ligious pacifists] have really absorbed the Ren-
> aissance faith in the goodness of man, have re-
> jected the Christian doctrine of original sin as
> an outmoded bit of pessimism, have interpreted
> the Cross so that it is made to stand for the ab-
> surd idea that perfect love is guaranteed a sim-
> ple victory over the world.[32]

In terms of the doctrine of grace, the religious pacifist, in Niebuhr's estimation, loses the Reformation emphasis upon justification by faith, opting for sectarian per-
fectionism which assumes "that divine grace actually lifts
man out of the sinful contradictions of history and establishes him above the sins of the world".[33] In short, it
is a position which fails to take seriously enough the
depths of sin, and thus does not recognize "the brutalities

of the conflict of power as basic to the collective history
of mankind."[34]   Coercion and force are inevitable in the
governing of human society. Power must be balanced by power for imbalance breeds injustice. To renounce all force
is to ignore the dynamics of sin and prepare the way for
tyranny. "Power and coercion are not, in short, the simple
devils of the drama of man's age-old struggle to gain community. Coercion is pregnant with both good and evil pos-
siblities--exactly as is freedom."[35]   For Niebuhr, responsible participation in society ruled out an unqualified
disavowal of coercion and of the possible use of violence,
for one cannot responsibly exert coercion unless he or she
also accepts that this could lead to violence.

Religious pacifism also fails, in Niebuhr's mind, when
set in the context of the absolute love revealed in Christ,
the very love which it seeks to express, and herein it
fails at least twice over. It does not recognize that what
it believes to be self-sacrifice may actually be an act of
betrayal. "As soon as the life and interests of others
than the agent are involved in an action or policy, the
sacrifice of those interests ceases to be 'self-sacrifice.'"[36]   That which was seen as an expression of suffering love becomes a failure in love for one's neighbour.
The implications here for pacifism, especially in terms of
the actions of those in authority in society, are obvious.

Furthermore, Niebuhr believed that religious pacifists
were constantly tempted to assume that non-violent resistance was an expression of suffering love, thereby missing
the truly absolute character of that love. Nowhere in
Scripture, he argued, can one find support for this
stance. The social ideal expressed in the love of Christ
is not non-violent resistance but non-resistance.[37]   To
engage in any kind of resistance is to fall short of the
impossible possibility which "refuses to participate in the

claims and counterclaims of historical existence."[38]
Setting the issue in this light, Niebuhr questioned whether
there is a qualitative or only quantitative difference between violent and non-violent resistance. Assuredly, where
it proves effective, there are pragmatic advantages to the
latter. It helps protect the resister against the extremes
of resentment aroused by violent resistance. Moreover, its
use blocks the opponent's claim to represent peace and order in society with the resister presumably championing
disorder and violence. However, non-violent resistance
neither expresses the non-resisting love of the Cross, nor
can it even guarantee that its results will be non-violent. A "non-violent" boycott may lead to the violence of
suffering, poverty and even death for those against whom
the boycott is undertaken. The choice between non-violent
and violent resistance becomes a matter of pragmatic judgment, and not a decision for or against obedience to the
ethic of love.

In summary, Niebuhr offers a forceful Christian apolo-
getic for those who cannot accept a stance of absolute pacifism. It is a position which honours the place and power
of religious pacifism as a witness to the sacrificial love
of Christ, but one which also supports the stance of those
who feel compelled, out of their Christian faith, to engage
in opposition to others, even--on occasion--to the point of
violent resistance.

SOME CRITICAL COMMENTS

Offering now some critical comments upon this ethic, I
do not presume to refute Niebuhr's thought nor do I wish to
raise basic theological questions like whether or not one
should grant such prominence to the doctrine of original
sin. Rather, I shall only raise certain questions within
the context of his own theology, questions which might open

the way for significant modifications in his understanding
of pacifism and faith. In particular, I would re-examine
this understanding of Jesus as the norm for human existence
and his views on the relationship between sin and grace.

Niebuhr, we have seen, views Christ and his relevance
for human history fundamentally through the image of sacrificial love, a love which is an impossible possibility,
given the conditions of sin. John Bennett, I believe, is
rightly concerned that such a view implies "that Christ only could be perfect by being free from the temptations
which accompany the moral responsibilities of most other
men."[39] The perfection of Jesus, in effect, requires
that he not be a participant in the inevitable tension of
power with power, that he be a non-combatant in the una-
voidable involvement of coercion as it seeks to create tolerable harmonies in human society. While accepting the
Christian's call to the risks of social involvement, Niebuhr offers a position which holds too sharp a distinction
between individual and group morality. Jesus becomes the
individual before God rather than the person inevitably
bound up in social structures and in relation to others.
He can write, for example, that "the devotion of Christianity to the Cross is an unconscious glorification of the individual moral ideal."[40] So he proposes that we must
recognize two moralities, individual and social; and asserts that it is "better to accept a frank dualism in mor-
als than to attempt a harmony between two methods which
threaten the effectiveness of both."[41]

The love of Christ which is held up as the ultimate
norm for mankind is , then, a love which relates more to
the single one than to persons in community--a love which
cannot truly be expressed in human history which perforce
is lived in community. Had Niebuhr allowed himself a
larger and more complex picture of Christ, had he imagined

more than suffering love, enriching his vision with the image of Jesus the Clown and Jesus the Rebel, for instance,
he might have developed a fuller model not only of the
Christ but of the meaning and reality of his love in human
history.

While the passion is central to the gospel, Jesus did
confront the Pharisees and drive the money changers from
the temple; he did attend the wedding feast and was criti-
cized as a glutton and drunkard. It may be overstating the
case, as some have done, to claim that Jesus was primarily
a social revolutionary, crucified as a political agitator,
but I suggest that a concentration on the passive suffering
of Jesus alone misses the richness of his life as a model
for mankind. It obscures the fact that in opposing another
we may still be expressing the basic love, the being for
another, which characterized the Son of Man. A fuller image of Christ and his life of love would allow us to consider the role of love in the life of one who must oppose
and the role of love in guiding and setting limits to the
nature of such resistance. (All of this, it may be observed, reflects Niebuhr's far greater sensitivity to the
sin of pride than to the sin of apathy.)

Even if one accepts Niebuhr's sense of the persistence
of sin and the continuing priority of forgiveness, modifications of his views of sin and grace are still possible
which could shed new light on the question of pacifism. To
begin with, one needs to affirm that for the Christian suffering and death, even the suffering of gross social injustice or death at the hands of a cruel tyrant, are not evil
in such an absolute sense that anything and everything is
permitted in opposing them. The central story of the
Christian tradition is indeed the passion, the suffering
and the death of Christ; but the Christian does not believe
that that life was a tragedy. Moreover, the story ends

with the resurrection, the dramatic assertion that God's
options in history are not determined solely by the possibilities of history. Were we to enrich Niebuhr's eschatology with such concepts as we find more recently in Moltmann
and others, this would raise the question of whether the
Christian is not justified in risking more than would seem
acceptable in the light of Niebuhrian realism, whether
there are not richer possibilities for human tranformation
than Niebuhr would allow. Having done so, however, we must
not forget the truth of such realism lest we fall into the
easy optimism which fails to remember the power of sin and
offers the triumph of Easter without the darkness and agony
of Black Friday.

NOTES

[1]Reinhold Niebuhr, "Intellectual Autobiography," in Charles W. Kegley and Robert W. Bretall (eds.), Reinhold Niebuhr: His Religious, Social and Political Thought (New York: The Macmillan Co., 1956), p. 5

[2]Reinhold Niebuhr, "Ten years that shook my world," The Christian Century, April 1939, p. 545.

[3]Reinhold Niebuhr, "What the war did to my mind," The Christian Century, September 1928, pp. 1161-63.

[4]Reinhold Niebuhr, "Pacifism and the Use of Force," The World Tomorrow, May 1928, p. 218.

[5]Ibid.

[6]Ibid.

[7]Reinhold Niebuhr, "Must we do nothing?," The Christian Century, March 1932, p. 416.

[8]Reinhold Niebuhr, "Moralists and Politics," The Christian Century, July 1932, p. 858.

[9]Reinhold Niebuhr, "Why I leave the F.O.R.," The Christian Century, January 1934, pp. 17-19.

[10]Reinhold Niebuhr, The Nature and Destiny of Man (New York: Charles Scribner's Sons, 1949) I: 213.

[11]Reinhold Niebuhr, "A Christian Journal Confronts Mankind's Continuing Crisis," Christianity and Crisis, February 1966, p. 12.

[12]Niebuhr, The Nature and Destiny of Man, II: 45, 87.

[13]Ibid., II: 55.

[14]Ibid., II: 72.

[15]Ibid., II: 49.

[16]Reinhold Niebuhr, Christianity and Power Politics (New York: Charles Scribner's Sons, 1940), p. 2.

[17]Niebuhr, The Nature and Destiny of Man, I: 200.

[18]Reinhold Niebuhr, Moral Man and Immoral Society, (New York: Charles Scribner's Sons, 1932), p. 256.

[19]Ibid., p. 82.

[20]Niebuhr, The Nature and Destiny of Man, I: 267.

[21]Reinhold Niebuhr, The Children of Light and the Children of Darkness (New York: Charles Scribner's Sons, 1953), p. xi.

[22]Reinhold Niebuhr, "Reply to Interpretation and

Criticism" in Kegley and Bretall, p. 437.

[23]Paul Lehmann, "The Christology of Reinhold Niebuhr," in Kegley and Bretall pp. 277-78.

[24]Niebuhr, Christianity and Power Politics, p. 18.

[25]Niebuhr, The Nature and Destiny of Man, II: 125-6.

[26]Niebuhr, Moral Man and Immoral Society, pp. 237-8.

[27]Reinhold Niebuhr, An Interpretation of Christian Ethics (New York: Meridian Books, 1956), p. 169.

[28]Ibid., p. 168.

[29]Niebuhr, Christianity and Power Politics, p. 4.

[30]Ibid., p. 31.

[31]Reinhold Niebuhr, "An Open Letter to Richard Roberts," quoted in John Bennett, "Reinhold Niebuhr's Social Ethics," in Kegley and Bretall, p. 69.

[32]Niebuhr, Christianity and Power Politics, p. 5.

[33]Niebuhr, "An Open Letter to Richard Roberts," p. 69.

[34]Niebuhr, Moral Man and Immoral Society, p. 155.

[35]Reinhold Niebuhr, "Coercion, Self-Interest and Love," Kenneth E. Boulding, The Organizational Revolution (New York: Harper and Brothers, 1952), pp. 241-2.

[36]Niebuhr, The Nature and Destiny of Man, II: 88.

[37]Niebuhr, Christianity and Power Politics, p. 16; An Interpretation of Christian Ethics, p. 166.

[38]Niebuhr, The Nature and Destiny of Man, II: 72.

[39]Bennett, p. 67.

[40]Niebuhr, Moral Man and Immoral Society, p. 82.

[41]Ibid., p. 271.

CHARLES HARTSHORNE

(1897 -   )

by Barry L. Whitney

*Charles Hartshorne's notion that God is love is
central to both his metaphysics and pacifism.
Because God moves persons by loving persuasion
and not by violence, they too should imitate God
and act non-violently. Thus we must see that
Hartshorne's thought on non-violence is central
to his entire philosophical/theological synthesis
because it flows from one of its central principles. B. Whitney indicates the limitations
Hartshorne places on God as persuasive lure, and
shows clearly why he rejects an absolute pacifism
as unrealistic and dangerous because of our weak-
ened nature and the threat it poses to society.
There is, therefore, considerable parallel between Hartshorne's pacifism as unattainable ideal
and Niebuhr's thought.*

During a career that has spanned more than fifty
years, Charles Hartshorne has distinguished himself as one
of the most eminent and increasingly influential of contemporary philosophers. Born in Pennsylvania in 1897, the
son and of an Episcopalian minister (though with a family
history as Quakers), Hartshorne earned his academic degrees
at Harvard University, completing the doctorate in record
time. After two years of research in Europe (with Husserl,
Heidegger, and others) he returned to Harvard to teach
(1925-1928), holding later positions at the University of
Chicago (1928-1955), Emory University (1955-1962), and the
University of Texas (1962-   ). He has held visiting pro-

fessorships or special lectureships at several universities, including Stanford, the University of Washington,
Yale, Frankfurt, Melbourne, Kyoto, and Louvain. His published writings have been prolific, numbering almost four
hundred items, including fourteen books.[1]

While Hartshorne prefers to call his philosophical position "neoclassical metaphysics," he is widely recognized
as co-founder (with Alfred North Whitehead, 1861-1947) of
the school of thought generally referred to as "process
philosophy." Hartshorne has always been a highly original
and creative thinker, and yet his unique contributions in
philosophy and theology have been underestimated. His dependence upon Whitehead in particular has been greatly
overstated. Hartshorne has been a major and sympathetic
interpreter of Whitehead, to be sure, yet he developed
early in his career a unique metaphysical system.[2]

While Hartshorne, like Whitehead, has not been concerned to apply his metaphysics to specifically Christian
theological issues, the next generation of process thinkers
has made this one of its priorities. Process metaphysics,
consequently, is, in the minds of growing numbers of religious thinkers, one rather promising option for addressing
traditional Christian issues. Our task here is to discuss
the applications of this metaphysics to the important issue
of non-violence and pacifism.

THE GOD OF PERSUASIVE LOVE

Hartshorne's philosophy may aptly be called "a metaphysics of love," for he has made St. John's dictum that
"God is Love" central to his entire philosophical scheme.
God's agency in the world is understood as a loving "persuasion." Since, furthermore, God does not act violently
or coercively, and since God, as God, is the standard of
perfection, it is appropriate that *we too* ought to act

without violence in our interrelationships with other human
beings. "God rules his cosmic society (of which we are a
part) by his goodness and his love . . . [hence] it is appropriate for us to ask about *our* goodness and *our* love
for him, for one another, and for the rest of his
society."[3]

Hartshorne's understanding of God as a loving, persuasive "lure" is in direct contradistinction to (what he
and other process philosophers take to be) the more traditional Christian doctrine of divine omnipotence. The traditional doctrine implies that "everything that happens is
either directly caused by God or at least permitted when it
could have been prevented."[4] God is "responsible for
everything that happens in the exact way it happens."[5]
God "actually or potentially . . . [has] all the power
there is."[6]

Whitehead has described the traditional Christian God
as a tyrant,[7] a despot,[8] a dictator,[9] indeed as "the
one supreme reality, omnipotently disposing a wholly derivative world."[10] Hartshorne likewise protests that this
understanding of God as "the power to do anything that
could be done is to equivocate or talk nonsense." "The notion of a cosmic power that determines all decisions fails
to make sense,"[11] for such would deny the reality of
creaturely freedom. God, rather, "guide[s] all things by
the persuasiveness of his sensitivity."[12] He is "a persuasive agency and not . . . a coercive agency,"[13] thereby displaying the "only power capable of any worthwhile
result."[14] Hartshorne is convinced that this understanding of God (largely attributable to Whitehead himself)
"is one of the greatest of all metaphysical discoveries."[15]

Process philosophers insist upon the reality of creaturely freedom and contend, accordingly, that any under-

standing of divine power which negates that autonomy is defective. Process philosophers insist, furthermore, that their affirmation of creaturely autonomy must not be thought to *limit* God's power in any meaningful sense. While "It has become customary to say that we must limit divine power to save human freedom," Hartshorne points out that "to speak of limiting a concept seems to imply that the concept, without the limitation, makes sense." But "The notion of a cosmic power that determines all decisions fails to make sense. For its decisions could refer to nothing except themselves. They could result in no world; for a world must consist of local agents making their own decisions:"[16]

> Instead of saying that God's power is limited, suggesting that it is less than some conceivable power, we should rather say: his power is absolutely maximal, the greatest possible, but even the greatest possible power is still one power among others, is not the only power. God can do everything that a God can do, everything that could be done by "a being with no possible superior".[17]

Not only does Hartshorne reject the traditional Christian understanding of divine omnipotence, but he and other process philosophers reject the traditional conception of divine immutability. If God were statically complete in himself, beyond all change and influence, as the traditional doctrine implies, would not the Bible's revelation of divine love and care for the world be distorted? An immutable God would remain the same whether or not there were a world, whether or not there were an Incarnation, whether or not we pray or worship. How can such a God love us? How indeed can we love such an "indifferent metaphysical iceberg?"[18] "This," writes Hartshorne, "is the paradox at the heart of medieval theism:"[19]

A wholly absolute God derives nothing from the physical or indeed the entire created world; to study that world is to study something that contributes nothing to the actuality of deity; to enrich that world is not to enrich the divine life, which is yet the measure of all value. A wholly absolute God is totally beyond tragedy, and his power operates uninfluenced by human freedom, hence presumably as infallibly determinative of all events.[20]

In place of a God whose reality is conceived as solely immutable, process philosophers argue for a "dipolar" conception of God. In his eternal essence, God may be immutable--in the sense that his existence is an *a priori* necessity and his ethical character is constant; yet God's experience of concrete, historical events constitutes his ever-processive, present reality. God is both immutable and mutable, infinite and finite, absolute and relative, abstract and concrete. Hartshorne has taken great pains to argue that the one set of attributes is the necessary complement of the other.[21] If, on the other hand, God were defined as solely immutable, infinite, absolute, abstract --as traditional Christianity in fact conceives him--we would be faced not with "a metaphysics of love" where God is affected by us and responds to our activities and feelings, but "a metaphysics of indifference" where nothing other than God himself makes any difference to him in his eternal fullness.

The Whiteheadian-Hartshornean conception of God as a loving, persuasive, responsive Reality is intricately related to the processive understanding of the nature of reality itself. All life, from the most insignificant puff of existence to God himself, is understood to be constituted by what Whitehead termed "actual entities,"[22] quantum

units of energy (as modern physics would have it) which are
in constant flux. Complex groupings of these entities appear to our sense perception as fairly stable and continuous objects; yet in reality they are composed of myriads of
microscopic and processive "drops of experience."[23]

All creatures, nevertheless, are not to be considered
merely as random flux: continuity of character and personal identity are accounted for insofar as certain characteristic experiences (mental and physical) repeat themselves
in the processive sequences which constitute all creatures.
In this sense, every creature is "dipolar," for besides its
ever-changing experiences, there remains a more constant
essence or character which gives functional unity and
central direction of purpose to the sequences of the actual
entities involved.[24]   Each creature is autonomous to a
large extent, yet depends upon other actual entities for
its causal data. The world is, as such, a vast and complex
society of beings which are intricately interrelated and
interdependent.

One important implication of this understanding of the
nature of reality is that process philosophers claim to in-
tuit and hence conceptualize God's reality in similar
terms.   God is conceived as processive and dipolar, for he
is (as Whitehead insisted) the chief exemplification of the
metaphysical categories, rather than their exception.[25]
God's nature is both abstract and concrete: he has, re-
spectively, both an immutable essence (his ethical character and necessary existence) and a concrete nature (his
experiences of and responses to every creaturely act and
feeling).

One of God's main functions is to provide creatures
with their "initial aims" and to make available to them
novel possibilities ("eternal objects") which are conceived
by God in his eternal mind.   If these possibilities are

actualized by creatures, the greatest possible value would be achieved at that particular moment in time. God does not coerce his designs upon us, however, but lovingly persuades us toward the ideals which he sees as the best for any particular situation.

While God's persuasive lure is not coercive, it is nevertheless quite effective. God may be but one element in the casual data which in large part determines the new experiences of creatures at every moment, but he is by far the most eminent influence. Hartshorne has illustrated this point by means of his detailed analysis of God's relationship to the world as being analogous to our minds' relationship to our bodies. Just as we are constituted by a body which "is really a 'world' of individuals [i.e., myriads of actual entities], and a mind . . . capable of thinking and feeling . . . [and which] is to that body something like an indwelling God," so likewise is God to be conceived as the World-Mind, the world's creatures constituting his Body. God, therefore, is the central and unifying force.[26]

Such is man's body influenced by its mind, and analogously, such is the world, as God's body, influenced by its mind, God. That this does not imply an all-determining coercion by God is, as noted above, insisted upon by process writers: "actualities can be *contained in other actualities yet retain their own self-decisions.*"[27] God's volitions need not be concretized by his creatures as, analogously, our bodies do not always comply with our wills, as evidenced by muscle spasms and unconscious impulses.

What all of this implies for the question of non-violence and pacifism can be stated quite tersely. Over and over in the process literature we are told of God's loving, persuasive agency, and the implication seems obvious: we too must seek to express ourselves in deeds of loving per-

suasion rather than in violence and coercion. As God allows us to make free decisions, rather than simply making
them for us, so likewise for us "to love another person is
not to make the other's decisions for him; just the contrary, it is to respect his freedom and to accept his decisions as objects of appreciative awareness."[28] God is the
ideal to be emulated, since as "that than which nothing
greater can be conceived" (Anselm),[29] he represents perfection.

As Christians, we are called upon to love God and to
love our neighbors as ourselves. Hartshorne points out,
informatively, that these commandments do not imply that
"some part of us not expressed in the love toward God is to
manifest itself in self-love or neighborly love." Rather,
"[a]ll our being is to be expressed in the relation to
deity, hence any love of neighbor must already be embraced
in this relation, and the second commandment constitutes
not an addition to the first, but only an explication of
part of its meaning." God is the "all-inclusive reality,"
and to love any part of reality is to love God. It is our
religious duty, accordingly, to treat our fellow man with
love and respect.[30]

THE INAPPROPRIATENESS OF ABSOLUTE PACIFISM

While I have suggested that Hartshorne's loving and
persuasive God is the model of pacifism and non-violence to
be emulated by us, there is a rather important qualifying
point to be considered. According to Hartshorne, an "absolute pacifism" which rejects all coercion, no matter what
the particular circumstances, must be forsaken as unrealistic and even dangerous. Only God, he insists, is capable
of acting purely persuasively: "the ultimate power is the
power of sensitivity, the power of ideal passivity and
relativity, exquisitely proportioned in its responsiveness

to other beings." "We," on the other hand, "are radically incapable of such unlimited and universal responsiveness."[31] "We human creatures are very limited in our
passivity, in our willingness and ability to permit others
to mold the content of our experiences. The most sensitive, sympathetic, responsive person you can find is largely unresponsive to all but a very few persons--at a given
moment, at any rate--and his responsiveness even to these
persons has narrow limits."[32] Thus, "Whether we will or
no, we are bound to coerce one another more or less un-
sympathetically."[33] "It is God, not men, who can guide
all things . . . by the persuasiveness of his sensitivity."[34] Hartshorne concludes: "I entirely disagree with
those who hold that the theological conception of love implies the doctrine of absolute pacifism or non-participa-
tion in war."[35]

Not only is man incapable of absolute pacifism, but
there are situations when, according to Hartshorne, coercion is virtually demanded of us! We must act, he insists,
in full cognizance of the weakness of human nature and the
threat this poses. "The extent to which human power or
knowledge is capable of divorce from love measures the
weakness and danger inherent in human nature."[36] "Sentimental humanism might," accordingly, "succeed only in
smoothing the path of the oppressor, who will obliterate
the humanitarian along with his sentiment."[37]

Coercive resistance is not necessarily an unloving or
inappropriate act against those whose coercion threatens
our very freedom or the social order itself: "'love' as
religion intends it is not a mere emotional glow toward
others, nor is it a self-defeating program of attempting to
deal with quarrels by offering appeasement to those who
will not be appeased."[38] Rather, "Social realism . . .
may enable us to see that to hand over the use of force to

those inferior in love is to guarantee that there will be less and less social awareness in the end. To oppose by force is not necessarily to fail in social appreciation."[39] "Indeed a just objection to sheer pacifism is that by making war as such the greatest possible evil it puts discrimination as to wars and their causes to sleep even more effectively than does extreme militarism."[40]

Hartshorne, of course, is aware of the traditional Christian appeal to the example and person of Jesus as a model of strict pacifism.[41] Yet he insists that Jesus' actions cannot be absolutized beyond their particular historical context. That Jesus, for example, was not a soldier does not necessarily rule out fighting in other circumstances: war with the Romans would have been suicidal. Jesus, to be sure, rejected violence and urged his followers to love their enemies. But, as Hartshorne warns, if this maxim were strictly absolutized, "the pacifist must be ready to cooperate with anyone who sets out to take advantage of him." There is, he suggests, "plenty of meaning left to these words [of Jesus] . . . without any such literal absolutism being involved."[42] Indeed:

> It is quite another matter to exclude the use of
> force where no superior method can be found. And
> there are such occasions . . . when those who are
> not in favor of stopping aggression by force of-
> fer no alternative likely of stopping it at all
> until the world is in the hands of the aggressor
> and pacifists will not even be allowed to argue
> any longer.[43]

To secure a just and peaceful world, all means must be pursued, "including force" when necessary:

> The right combination of firmness and generosity
> which alone can really give lasting peace will
> require all the social awareness, all the love,

that can be mustered. But mere generosity to the
aggressor without regard to the need for freeing
his victims will only be generosity coming to the
rescue of ungenerosity as such, that is, it will
be self-refuting.[44]

Hartshorne's position on non-violence, summarily, is
to advocate that we act in a loving, persuasive manner, as
does God, while yet resorting to coercion when our persuasive love is threatened by a coercive, unloving force
(which could destroy our freedom and the very social order
itself). "We must," as Daniel Day Williams[45] has suggested, "distinguish between what love would lead us to
choose in the realm of abstract possibility and what love
may require us to do in the actualities of history."[46]
We cannot escape such involvement in the concrete situation: "Existence in history means involvement in established powers and orders."[47] The "real difficuly in ethical doctrines based exclusively on non-violence is that
they isolate love as spirit and as strategy from the full
context of the situation in which they must work."[48] The
Franciscan renunciation of worldly involvement "is done at
the cost of losing direct effectiveness in the guidance,
restraint and judgment of the structures of power which
shape the social order."[49]

From God's ultimate perspective, pacifism may well always be appropriate, for God has infinite patience in his
luring of the cosmic process toward order and justice.
From man's perspective, however, pacifism would appear to
be the ideal, yet the social realism of the particular situation seems to call, at times, for coercive resistance.
"It is better that many should die prematurely," writes
Hartshorne, "than that nearly all men should live in a permanent state of hostility or slavery."[50]

The problem of defining precisely *when* such coercion

is required and appropriate is, however, left rather vague-
ly stated by Hartshorne. We are told only that coercion is
appropriate in certain circumstances, presumably when our
freedom is threatened or when the social order itself is
threatened. Yet precisely what this implies is left troublesomely obscure by Hartshorne.

The result of this lacuna is, accordingly, to greatly
weaken the force of his pacifist vision and to leave his
readers perplexed as to when pacifism is inappropriate, and
indeed as to how, precisely, we are to respond coercively
to threatening situations.

THE PROCESS GOD: PERSUASIVE OR PARTLY COERCIVE?

Thus far, I have suggested that Hartshorne's conception of God as a persuasive, non-violent, loving agent implies human emulation (Section I), at least to the extent
that it is permitted by the concrete situation (Section
II). I must now draw particular attention to a further
point which demands discussion. It would appear that, for
Hartshorne, it is not only man whose pacifism must be tempered at times by coerciveness, but God himself must often
act coercively!

I readily concede that Hartshorne has always insisted
that his God acts solely persuasively. Yet, as I have argued at length elsewhere,[51] his texts appear to imply the
rather troublesome point that an absolute pacifism is, in
fact, inappropriate even for God. Both God and man appear
obliged to exert coercive force in order to combat potential or actual threats to the very freedom which guarantees
the ongoing existence of the cosmic process. Hartshorne
informs us, for example, that God "tolerates variety [only]
up to the point beyond which it would mean chaos and not a
world: . . . [God] prevents reality from losing all definite character."[52]   "God opposes some of our desires . . .

by balancing them against the main desire-mass of the world
of creatures, somewhat as we may check some of our wishes
by force of other opposing ones."[53] God may act with
perfect "social awareness," an awareness which defines his
loving perfection, yet this would appear to involve some
coercion:

> The divine love is social awareness and action
> from social awareness. Such action seems clearly
> to include the refusal to provide the unsocial
> with a monopoly upon the use of coercion. Coer-
> cion to prevent the use of coercion to destroy
> freedom generally is in no way action without
> social awareness but one of its crucial expres-
> sions. Freedom must not be free to destroy free-
> dom. The logic of love is not the logic of paci-
> fism.[54]

For man, accordingly, "The best expression of belief
in God is an attitude of social awareness which treats all
problems in the spirit of mutuality except where others insist upon treating them in another spirit, at which point
we must in our local way, like God in his cosmic way, set
limits by constraint to the destruction of mutuality."[55]
Hartshorne's God, it would appear, can and must exert coercive force upon the world when we threaten to use our freedom to destroy the very freedom which constitutes our reality.

God has imposed upon us natural laws as the limits to
our freedom. He can also coercively resist any threatening
act within these limits. He can, for example, exercise his
causal influence upon us unconsciously[56] and irresist-
ibly.[57] "There must be," Hartshorne insists, "some mode
of divine power which cannot simply be disregarded."[58]
"God's unique power over us is his partly selfdetermined
being as our inclusive object of awareness;" and "as this

object changes, we are compelled to change in response."[59]
"God molds us, by presenting at each moment a partly new
ideal or order of preference which our unselfconsciousness
awareness takes as object, and thus renders influential
upon our entire activity."[60] "In the depths of consciousness we feel and accept the divine ordering."[61]

I find these (and similar) passages quite puzzling,
for not only do they seem to imply that God acts coercively
at times, despite Hartshorne's insistence to the contrary,
but they seem to imply that God acts coercively, in some
rather ill-defined sense, with respect to *all* of our actions. Hartshorne's central thesis, that God acts solely
persuasively, seems unsubstantiated and problematic, to say
the least.

Yet perhaps what he wants to suggest is that in our
day-to-day decisions within the limits established by God,
the divine causal influence operates as a persuasive lure.
This permits us to decide the minute details of our decisions without divine coercion. Yet God seems also to operate coercively to the extent that he does not permit us to
act beyond certain limits, for this would threaten the very
reality of freedom itself.

All of this, nevertheless, is extremely ill-defined by
Hartshorne and in the process literature as a whole. The
task, accordingly, of assessing the application of this
metaphysics to the question of non-violence and pacifism is
made quite difficult and tentative. I would venture,
nevertheless, to make the following observations by way of
conclusion.

CONCLUSION

Pacifism, for Hartshorne, seems to be the ideal by
which we must seek to act. Non-violent, persuasive love is
God's primary mode of action, and it ought likewise to be

ours. That we are, nevertheless, confronted at times by other human beings who threaten our very freedom would seem to necessitate coerciveness in response, that is to say, where non-violence would be ineffective. And indeed so likewise does God seem to resist threatening creaturely actions. God may value our freedom to the extent that he generally does not overrule us when we exploit that freedom to cause strife rather than harmony. Yet he also seems to act coercively to ensure our freedom does not override its bounds.

When we reject God's persuasive lure, and choose instead the lesser harmony and value, this is a great tragedy for the world and for God himself. Both God and the creature are deprived of the greater harmony to which God was directing us. God, nevertheless, savors whatever value there is in any situation and eternally preserves all that can be saved. God sees all things in perfect perspective, and while this does not undo the evil and violence done by his creatures, it does in a sense overcome it. God, according to Hartshorne (who follows Whitehead here), experiences "not the evil alone, [but] rather the evil with or in its ideal complement of vision." God's experience is "sheer addition, not subtraction or omission."[62]

Evils are not obliterated in God's experience or seen as something other than they are. But rather, "God *adds* to all such evils a content which produces in relation to them, whatever good can be made to result."[63] God's experience of evil is supplemented by his perfect retention of all past values, so that his experience is always "a *net increment* of value."[64] There is, in fact, not only in God's experience but in ours, always a balance of value: "every concrete experience as a whole is a value rather than a disvalue. . . . We wring some kind of satisfaction, however poor or strained, out of pain and frustra-

tion; though we may feel very keenly how much better life
might be."[65]

God, accordingly, is patient to the extent that he is
content to persuasively lure us to actualize good ideals,
at least so far as we do not threaten the very existence of
our freedom. Evil and violent possibilities will surely
continue to be actualized, but not beyond that which God
permits. There is, furthermore, no matter how grim things
are, value and good to be appropriated by us (as it is by
God, more fully) at every moment.

Hartshorne, we may note further, sees no "final end,"
no ultimate good to be attained at the end of history.
Rather, the "creative advance" of the world will simply
continue, hopefully (but not necessarily), toward an increase in good, in value, and in social harmony. Tragedy
is built into the world and it shall remain the world's
constant companion. Every free, creaturely decision, for
example, necessarily excludes (deprives) other potentials
from being actualized.

Yet every creaturely act makes concrete some value:
"the teleology of the world is drafted toward the production of beauty."[66] "Beauty is that which justifies existence, but it is not the outline of a utopia, personal,
cosmic, or social. . . . The experience of creative finitude reveals the delusive quality of progress . . . process
does not promise success; rather, it offers the chance for
a resolute and enriching experience."[67]

We must, accordingly, be patient in our desire for a
more just world: the world cannot be changed over night,
as the truism has it. Rather, we must pursue the pacifist
route and encourage others to follow it, in order to promote greater love and social harmony. Coercion and violence will, at times, be demanded of us (as they are of
God), yet "the one thing we need not and ought not to do is
--to worship it!"[68]

Precisely *when* we are to resort to coercion, however, is left undefined by Hartshorne, and this greatly
weakens the force of his position, causing us great difficulties in applying his metaphysical stance to the pacifist ideal. We may ask legitimately: is Hartshorne's
position really pacifistic? The answer, I believe, is yes,
though in a troublesomely qualifying sense. His vision of
God as a loving, persuasive lure gives rise to the pacifist
ideal which calls for human emulation--this much is clear.
But what is less clear is the extent to which Hartshorne
believes we are capable of pacifism, and indeed, the extent
to which our pacifism is desirable. We must, he insists,
resort to coercion to protect our freedom; yet nowhere has
he explained precisely what this entails.

There is much to do, accordingly, in working out the
implications of the process philosophers' vision of God (as
processive and dipolar and lovingly persuasive) for the
question of non-violence and pacifism. It is, perhaps,
ironic (if not tragic) that their powerful vision of God as
a loving lure has not been more greatly exploited in defence of a pacifist position. Many questions remain unre-
solved: is man incapable of absolute pacifism, as Hartshorne insists? Is absolute pacifism really as dangerous
and naive as Hartshorne suggests? Does God resort to
coercion at times, as would seem to be implied in Hartshorne's texts? In what particular circumstances, if any,
ought we to resort to coercion?

NOTES

[1]For Hartshorne's bibliography to 1976, see _Process Studies_ 6 (1976), pp. 73-93.

[2]For some discussions of the differences between Hartshorne and Whitehead, see the essays by William Sessions, David Griffin, and Lewis S. Ford, in L. S. Ford (ed.), _Two Process Philosophers: Hartshorne's Encounter with Whitehead_ (Tallahasse: AAR Studies in Religion, 1973).

[3]Charles Hartshorne, "God and the Social Structure of Reality," _Theology in Crisis: A Colloquium on 'The Credibility of God'_ (New Concord, Ohio: Muskingum College, 1967), p. 22. See also Hartshorne's _Creative Synthesis and Philosophic Method_ (LaSalle: Open Court, 1970), pp. 55-56.

[4]David R. Griffin, _God, Power and Evil: A Process Theodicy_ (Philadelphia: Westminister, 1976), p. 18.

[5]John B. Cobb, _God and the World_ (Philadelphia: Westminister, 1965), p. 88.

[6]Griffin, _God, Power and Evil_, p. 18.

[7]Alfred North Whitehead, _Religion in the Making_ (New York: Macmillan, 1926), p. 55; pp. 74-75; _Science and the Modern World_ (New York: Macmillan, 1925), p. 266.

[8]Alfred North Whitehead, _Adventures of Ideas_ (New York: Macmillan, 1933), p. 218; _Dialogues of Alfred North Whitehead_, as recorded by Lucien Price (Boston: Little, Brown, 1954), p. 176; p. 198; p. 277.

[9]Alfred North Whitehead, _Modes of Thought_ (New York: Macmillan, 1938), p.68.

[10]Whitehead, _Adventures of Ideas_, p. 213. I am indebted to William Christian for the references in notes 7 through 10; see his _An Interpretation of Whitehead's Metaphysics_ (New Haven: Yale University Press, 1959), pp. 388-390.

[11]Charles Hartshorne, _The Divine Relativity: A Social Conception of God_ (New Haven: Yale University Press, 1948), p. 134; p. 138.

[12]Ibid., p. 154.

[13]Whitehead, _Adventures of Ideas_, p. 213.

[14]Cobb, _God and the World_, p. 90.

[15]Hartshorne, _Divine Relativity_, p. 142.

[16]Ibid., p. 138.

[17]Ibid.

[18]W. Norris Clarke, "A New Look at the Immutability of God," in Robert J. Roth (ed.), God Knowable and Unknowable (New York: Fordham University Press, 1973), p.45.

[19]Charles Hartshorne, Man's Vision of God and the Logic of Theism (Chicago: Willett, Clarke, and Company, 1941), p. 156.

[20]Hartshorne, Divine Relativity, pp. 149-150.

[21]See, for example, Charles Hartshorne and William Reese, Philosophers Speak of God (Chicago: University of Chicago Press, 1953), pp. 1-15.

[22]See Alfred North Whitehead, Process and Reality (New York: Macmillan, 1929; reprinted 1969), pp. 22-75.

[23]Ibid., p. 23.

[24]See Charles Hartshorne, "Personal Identity from A to Z," Process Studies 2 (1972), pp. 209-215.

[25]Whitehead, Process and Reality, p. 405.

[26]Hartshorne, Man's Vision of God, p. 177 and pp. 174-211. Hartshorne recognizes that the "mind-body" analogy (also called the "organic" analogy) is not sufficient in itself to explain the interrelationship between God and the world. An additional analogy is required, the "social analogy", to explain how our minds and bodies interact. To combine the two analogies it is necessary to understand that the mind-body relationship is social, i.e., that the cells which form the body are--to some degree at least--sentient (see pp. 186-188).

[27]Charles Hartshorne, Whitehead's Philosophy: Selected Essays, 1935-1970 (Lincoln: University of Nebraska Press, 1972), p. 72.

[28]Charles Hartshorne, "A Philosopher's Assessment of Christianity," in W. Leibrecht (ed.), Religion and Culture: Essays in Honor of Paul Tillich (New York: Harper, 1959), p. 168.

[29]See Hartshorne, Anselm's Discovery (LaSalle: Open Court, 1965).

[30]Hartshorne, "A Philosopher's Assessment of Christianity," p. 167.

[31]Hartshorne, Divine Relativity, p. 154.

[32]Hartshorne, "A Philosopher's Assessment of Christianity," p. 169.

[33]Charles Hartshorne, Beyond Humanism: Essays in the New Philosophy of Nature (Chicago: Willett, Clark, and Company, 1937; reprinted Lincoln: University of Nebraska Press, 1968), p. 27.

[34]Hartshorne, Divine Relativity, p. 154.

[35]Hartshorne, Man's Vision of God, p. xvii.

[36]Hartshorne, Beyond Humanism, pp. 25-26.

[37]Hartshorne, Man's Vision of God, p. 165.

[38]Ibid.

[39]Ibid., p. 168.

[40]Ibid., p. 169.

[41]Ibid., pp. 170-171. Hartshorne refers to Gandhi as well: see ibid., pp. 171-172.

[42]Ibid., p. 171.

[43]Ibid.

[44]Ibid., p. 172.

[45]See Daniel Day Williams, The Spirit and the Forms of Love (New York: Harper and Row, 1968), a text which Hartshorne once, in conversation, recommended to me as a valuable exposition of the theological doctrine of love with which he basically agrees.

[46]Ibid., p. 271.

[47]Ibid., p. 265.

[48]Ibid., p. 270.

[49]Ibid., p. 264.

[50]Hartshorne, Man's Vision of God, p. 173.

[51]Barry L. Whitney, "Process Theism: Does a Persuasive God Coerce?", The Southern Journal of Philosophy 17 (1979), pp. 133-143.

[52]Hartshorne, Man's Vision of God, p. 265.

[53]Ibid., p. 266.

[54]Ibid., p. 173.

[55]Ibid.

[56]Charles Hartshorne, "Religion in Process Philosophy," in J. C. Feaver and W. Horosz (eds.), Religion in Philosophical and Cultural Perspective (Princeton: D. Von Nostrand, 1967), p. 257.

[57]Hartshorne, Whitehead's Philosophy, p. 164.

[58]Hartshorne, "Religion in Process Philosophy," p. 258.

[59]Hartshorne, Divine Relativity, p. 139.

[60]Ibid., p. 142.

[61]Charles Hartshorne, "A New Look at the Problem of Evil," in F. C. Dommeyer (ed.), Current Philosophical Issues: Essays in Honor of Curt John Ducasse (Springfield: C.C. Thomas, 1966), p. 211.

[62]Charles Hartshorne, "The Immortality of the Past: Critique of a Prevalent Misinterpretation," Review of Metaphysics 7 (1953), p. 106.

[63]Ibid., p. 110.

[64]Hartshorne, Divine Relativity, p. 46.

[65]Hartshorne, "Immortality of the Past," p. 102.

[66]Whitehead, Adventures of Ideas, p. 341.

[67]Joseph Grange, "Whitehead's Tragic Vision: Process, Progress, and Existentialism," Bucknell Review 20 (1972), p. 143.

[68]Hartshorne, Divine Relativity, p. 155.

JOHN HOWARD YODER

(1927 -   )

by Rodney J. Sawatsky

*The writings of John Howard Yoder are a witness
to the non-resistant Gospel. R. Sawatsky indicates that Yoder's pacifism flows from his theological concepts of Church, Christ and world. The
Church is called to absolute obedience to Christ
and so to absolute non-resistance. In replacing
violence by non-resistance Christ revealed God's
will and made pacifism a necessity, not a
choice. The believer is not called to political
realism and efficiency, but to love, patience and
suffering which lead to resurrection. Only the
inner working of the Spirit in the Christian provides the spiritual resources to live with absolute non-resistance. Pacifism is not non-violence, nor is it weakness nor a strategy to attain victory.*

While most religious pacifist spokespersons of note
speak from within traditions at best neutral on pacifism,
not so John Howard Yoder.[1] Yoder speaks for and to a denomination committed throughout its history to pacifism.
Indeed, he is the foremost contemporary Mennonite theologian of pacifism. Elements of Yoder's thought are of
course disputed by brethren in the faith, but no Mennonite
or any other biblically-based pacifist proposal can avoid
the centrality of this man's work.[2]

Even if Yoder's pacifism proceeds from within the context of the Mennonite tradition, its impact is not narrowly
sectarian. The Quakers and the Church of the Brethren, who

join with the Mennonites as Historic Peace Churches, are
not alone in their positive reactions to this theologian's
work.[3]   Roman Catholics entered into dialogue with him
particularly following his posting as a professor of theology at Notre Dame University.[4]   Evangelicals, especially
those deemed new or young,[5] awakened to an evangelical
call for social action[6] and to be sojourners[7] through
the inspiration of Yoder and others.   Yoder's politically-
relevant Anabaptism challenges Reformed scholars to defend
their non-pacifist assumptions.[8]   Others who read Yoder's
writing, notably his most recent, *The Politics of Jesus*,
cannot simply dismiss his arguments as vocational, perfectionist or idealistic.   In contrast to the pacifist apolo-
getics of his Mennonite forefathers, Yoder's perspectives
cannot be dismissed as sectarian, but must be considered by
the larger ecumenical Christian world.

Yoder's ecumenical reception is not entirely accidental; it is essential to his mission.   Speaking historically, Yoder is but a sign of the Mennonite recovery from a
sectarian retreat to an open witness to the nonresistant
Gospel.   The Mennonite Central Committee, a world-wide social service agency which Yoder frequently advises, is a
major incarnation of this trend.   More specifically, Yoder
has been consciously ecumenical.   Already in his doctoral
dissertation he focussed on the disputations between the
Anabaptists and the Reformed,[9] and one of his first publications, *The Ecumenical Movement and the Faithful
Church*, challenged Mennonites to ecumenical participation.[10]   His is not, however, an ecumenism which weakens
the tradition, rather the very opposite is true.   It is the
imperative to call all Christians to unqualified obedience
to Jesus Christ that motivates this ecumenical dialogue.

Despite the larger context of his theological work,
symbolized by his appointment at Notre Dame, John Howard

Yoder is very much a son of the Mennonite Church. Born in 1927, he was raised and nurtured in the Oak Grove congregation in Smithville, Ohio. His intellectual formation, under the tutelage of such creative Mennonite minds as Guy F. Hershberger and Harold S. Bender at Goshen College, was challenged and enriched, but not overthrown, by doctoral studies in Basel with the likes of Karl Barth.[11] A relief worker with the Mennonite Central Committee in France, a professor of theology at Goshen College Biblical Seminary, an administrator with the Mennonite Board of Missions and Charities—these were and are the areas out of which he speaks and writes.

The church is central, not only to Yoder's life and work, but also to his faith and order. The church, he says, is the community which by faithfulness has been ordered throughout the ages on the model and in the power of the life, death and resurrection of Jesus Christ. This new creation is fundamentally different from the world and its structural incarnations which do not seek first the kingdom of God. The essential mark of this messianic community is unmitigated obedience to its Lord. Since the way of Jesus is absolute nonresistance to the point of crucifixion, so too an obedient disciple has no choice but to live a life of pacifism if he would be truly Christian.

The task of the following pages is to place Yoder's pacifism within the context of his larger theological system. This is both an easy and difficult task. It is not difficult to locate where pacifism arises from his theological reflections; it is difficult to isolate areas where it does not apply. Almost all Christian concepts, according to Yoder, have ethical implications, which in turn are inevitably nonresistant or pacifistic. Yet to help limit our exercise four main areas will be examined: the church, Christ, the world and pacifism. On each of these topics we

shall allow Yoder to speak in his own words as much as possible because our purpose is not to analyze or critique his
work, rather it is only to delineate his pacifist reflections in theological context.

Before entering into Yoder's theological perspectives,
several terms require clarification. In contrast to most
other chapters in this book, the terms pacifism or nonresistance are used rather than non-violence. This is the
case because Yoder defines non-violence as a method, not as
a theological stance. Non-violence, according to Yoder, is
always preferable to violence. Yet because it need not be
premised upon pacifist assumptions, it may yield to violence when it proves unworkable. Yoder would differentiate
his system from such a programmatic posture although he
would advocate non-violence in concrete situations.[12] In
twentieth century Mennonite thought sharp distinctions have
also been made between pacifism and nonresistance, but
since Yoder uses both terms to label his own position, that
differentiation is not developed here. In what follows,
pacifism and nonresistance are used interchangeably.

THE CHURCH

Pacifism is derived from Yoder's theology, not vice
versa. The constituent parts of this theology are carefully crafted into a logical, consistent whole. Analysis
could begin at a number of points in the system. However,
his ecclesiology demands consideration first, not because
it is systematically fundamental, but because it is pro-
grammatically central. All else is connected to the doctrine of the messianic community in that it is the church
which is the bearer of the Gospel's ethical imperative, and
ethical obedience to Jesus the Christ is the essence of
man's response to the good news.

Yoder stands four-square in the Anabaptist-Mennonite tradition with reference to his high view of the church. Against Protestant individualism he posits a visible community of believers, fully real in its immanence and not merely a transcendent ideal. Against the Roman Catholic duality of priest and layman, all Christians are saints, called to fulfill all that Jesus has commanded.

The church lost its soul with the Constantinian Revolution, says Yoder. In order to redeem itself from this fall, it must again be the church as it was prior to being co-opted in the third to fifth centuries by a fundamentally antithetical force--the force of the world incarnated supremely in the state. The true church is a free church, free from the principalities and powers of this world, and hence free to be obedient to its Lord.

The first step of obedience to God is for the individual to commit himself to the people of God, an act which is symbolized in adult baptism because it must be an act of adult decision. A continuity of God's people reaches back throughout the ages to Abraham.

This is the original revolution; the creation of a distinct community with its own deviant set of values and its coherent way of incarnating them. Today it might be called an underground movement, or a political party, or an infiltration team, or a cell movement. The sociologists would call it an intentional community. Then they were called Hebrews', a title which probably originally meant, 'the people who crossed over'.[13]

Jesus created a society in this same Hebrew tradition, yet with significant differences. For one, Israel had misdirected the original revolutionary community by turning the peoplehood of God into a nationalistic entity.[14] Secondly, God's incarnation of Jesus modelled a standard heretofore unavailable in such clarity and profundity.

The primary social structure through which God works
in the world is the church. Accordingly, Christians locate
their primary sociological entity for identity and loyalty
in the church. It is within the context of a "binding" and
"loosing" community that social relationships are built,
relationships that are essential to personal self-defini-
tion as well as to the new humanity.[15] Yoder details the
nature of this society Christ founded thus:

1. This was a voluntary society: you could not
be born into it. You could come into it only by
repenting and freely pledging allegiance to this
king. It was a society with no second generation
members.

2. It was a society which, counter to all pre-
cedent, was mixed in its composition. It was
mixed racially, with both Jews and Gentiles;
mixed religiously, with fanatical keepers of the
law and advocates of liberty from all forms; with
both radical monotheists and others just in the
process of disentangling their minds from idolatry; mixed economically, with members both rich
and poor.

3. When He called His society together Jesus
gave its members a new way of life to live. He
gave them a new way to deal with offenders--by
forgiving them. He gave them a new way to deal
with violence--by suffering. He gave them a new
way to deal with money--by sharing it. He gave
them a new way to deal with problems of leader-
ship--by drawing upon the gift of every member,
even the most humble. He gave them a new way to
deal with a corrupt society--by building a new
order, not smashing the old. He gave them a new
pattern of relationships between man and woman,

between parent and child, between master and
slave, in which was made concrete a radical new
vision of what it means to be a human person. He
gave them a new attitude toward the state and toward the 'enemy nation'.[16]

Insofar as, but only insofar as, the church is loyal
to its mandate from its Lord,[17] it is called "to be the
conscience and the servant within human society."[18] This
means among others being "a model society,"[19] contributing "to the creation of structures more worthy of man,"[20]
discerning the social structures of our times,[21] declar-
ing judgment upon the world,[22] proclaiming the Lordship
of Christ,[23] breaking down the barriers that separate man
from man and God,[24] and exhibiting true international unity.[25] Nation, race, ethnic group, clan, even family--
all are secondary to this new creation. Traditional paro-
chialisms, which are at the base of all warfare, are thus
dethroned as this international organism gains its legitimate place in the social order of those claiming to be
Christian.

The church is not to be equated with the kingdom of
God. "The kingdom is inexorable. Whether it comes or not,
it is not up to us to decide."[26] The church by contrast
is exorable; it is dependent upon Christian obedience. It
is at best a sign or a foretaste of the kingdom. The
faithful church signifies in microcosm the purposes of God
in history which will ultimately, in God's own time, embrace the macrocosm. Then the kingdom will have come.[27]

The messianic community is thus an eschatological community. It awaits the kingdom and knows that victory is on
its side, but it realizes that patience and suffering characterize the interim. The church renounces attempts to
govern or direct history; neither is effectiveness its
norm, for "the cross and not the sword, suffering and not

brute power determines the meaning of history. The key to
the obedience of God's people is not their effectiveness
but their patience."[28] Or again "the relationship between the obedience of God's people and the triumph of
God's cause is not a relationship of cause and effect but
one of cross and resurrection."[29] The church exists in
the confidence of the resurrection, but in the interim
lives and works in the shadow of the cross.

JESUS THE CHRIST

Obviously the church is nothing without the life,
death and resurrection of Jesus Christ. Yoder derives all
else in his theological structure from his Christology.
Faithfulness to Jesus is normative, says Yoder, for any
theology or ethic which would claim to be Christian. Indeed, his "position collapses if Jesus be not Christ or if
Jesus Christ be not Lord".[30]

Yoder's Christology is fully orthodox if Nicaea is
considered normative. Jesus is understood as both God and
man not merely for the sake of orthodoxy, but for the sake
of Christian ethics. In his deity Jesus revealed how God
responds to evil, namely, by coming among men, labeling
sins and injustices, taking upon himself the suffering men
inflict upon one another, and doing all this nonresistantly
to the point of his own death.[31] In his humanity Jesus
prescribed God's purposes for man. The unity of Jesus with
his father is correctly understood, not in terms of substance, but rather of will and deed, that is, of perfect
obedience to the will of the father. For example, in sid-
ing with the poor and rejecting the sword and the throne,
Jesus reveals the will of God. "This is by the same token
a revealed moral imperative for those who would belong to
and obey him."[32]

Yoder brings the two natures of Jesus together in
dramatic fashion.

Jesus was not just a moralist whose teachings had
some political implications; he was not primarily
a teacher of spirituality whose public ministry
unfortunately was seen in a political light; he
was not just a sacrificial lamb preparing for his
immolation, or a God-Man whose divine status
calls us to disregard his humanity. Jesus was,
in his divinely mandated (i.e. promised, anoint-
ed, messianic) prophethood, priesthood, and king-
ship, the bearer of a new possibility of human,
social, and therefore political relationships.
His baptism is the inauguration and his cross is
the culmination of that new regime in which his
disciples are called to share. Men may choose to
consider that kingdom as not real, or not relevant, or not possible, or not inviting; but no
longer may we come to this choice in the name of
systematic theology or honest hermeneutics. At
this one point there is no difference between the
Jesus of *Historie* and the Christ of *Geschich-
te*, or between Christ as God and Jesus as Man,
or between the religion of Jesus and the religion
about Jesus (or between the Jesus of the canon
and the Jesus of history). No such slicing can
avoid his call to an ethic marked by the cross, a
cross identified as the punishment of a man who
threatens society by creating a new kind of community leading a radically new kind of life.[33]

Not only is the church, the messianic community, returned
to centre stage, but its political importance is rein-
forced. Essential to this new politics is the politics of
Jesus.

    Yoder directly challenges three alternative proposals
in his representation of Jesus as radically political, and

therefore socially relevant. Against his own Mennonite
tradition, which posited an apolitical Jesus as the legitimation for social non-involvement and sectarian withdrawal,
Yoder cites Jesus confronting the powers in the midst of
the world.[34] Against Christian realism, epitomized in
the work of Reinhold Niebuhr, Yoder presents Jesus as the
Messiah who refused to adapt (in his concern for political
responsibility) the demands of *agape* to the realities of
sin. Rather, Jesus proclaimed a new political order, namely the church, where *agape* is fully normative.[35]
Against Christian liberationists, who with the Zealots of
old, would bring in a new order through violence, Yoder in-
troduces a Jesus who rejected the Zealot option, not because it changes too much, but because it changes too little.[36]

Yoder's Mennonite, realist and liberationist friends
gain momentary relief by realizing that the politics of
Jesus are in a sense an "anti-politics" or a "counter-politics." Jesus challenges the very notion of political realism and power with the cross--the symbol of the politics of
the messianic community. But that comfort is shortlived,
for this politics of a counter-politics is lived in the
midst of the world not separated from it; is ever relevant
as the real alternative, not as a mere impossible ideal;
and is available as the most practical and profound solution to the yearnings of the oppressed.

Here Christology necessarily moves quickly to soteri-
ology. The possibility of responding positively to the
political Jesus, that is, of being ethical in a Christian
way, requires personal transformation. "Only through the
reorientation of the personality which Jesus and His first
followers called repentance," can one act ethically as a
Christian. "Repentance initiates that true human experience to which all men are called."[37] With such repent-

ance comes a transformation of perspective to those who accept Jesus as their Savior and Lord. According to Yoder,
biblical terms such as "justification," "new creature,"
"being in Christ," etc., have profoundly relational implications.

> [Their] accent lies not on transforming the on-
> tology of the person (to say nothing of trans-
> forming his psychological or neurological equip-
> ment) but on transforming the perspective [in
> terms of social relationships] of one who has ac-
> cepted Christ as his context.[38]

Yoder emphasizes the sacrificial death of Jesus as important for redemption. Yet against a one-sided emphasis
on the blood of Jesus, he also presents Jesus as a teacher
and example. Although "the exemplary quality of Jesus humanity is . . . a model of our social ethics," there are
limits to the imitation of Christ.[39] The *imitatio
Christi* applies only

> at the point of the concrete social meaning of
> the cross in relation to enmity and power. Serv-
> anthood replaces dominion, forgiveness absorbs
> hostility. Thus--and only thus--are we bound by
> New Testament thought to 'be like Jesus'.[40]

The Christian is not redeemed by imitating first century Christianity, but rather by gaining victory over the
divisions of man through suffering rather than violence.
How is such transformation attained? It is attained by
"the acceptance of the cross." Yoder means by this that
"the full cost of utter obedience to the loving nature of
God" is accepted as "the path to the accomplishment in history, not of perfection, but of action which can please God
and be useful to men."[41] This process results in "a
change of motives so basic as to be called a new
birth."[42] Secondly, such a change is the work of a gra-

cious God who, through the resurrection of Christ, both forgives sin and enables obedience.[43] Thirdly, the Holy Spirit empowers transformation.

> The coming of the Spirit means the imparting of power, and that power is not a mythological symbol for the infinite perfectibility of human rationality but rather a working reality within history and especially within the church.[44]

Accordingly, Yoder, adds, "Christian ethics calls for behavior which is impossible except for the miracles of the Holy Spirit."[45]

Reference to the Holy Spirit gives cause to pause briefly at Yoder's trinitarian theology. Critics have implied that Yoder's theological orientation focuses unduly on Jesus the Redeemer and thereby shortchanges God the Creator, with the result that the orders of creation, including the state, are shortchanged in God's divine economy. He is fully aware of this contention and discusses the issue particularly as it is formulated in H. Richard Niebuhr's trinitarian motifs.[46] Yoder's most telling rejoinder is to recall the notion of the eternal existence of the Son. What that doctrine means, he says, is that God "has not revealed a different purpose of character through creation than what we encounter through Jesus."[47] Because of the unity of the godhead, emphasis on the normativity of Jesus can not be heterodox.

The source of our knowledge of Jesus is the Bible. In fact, the Bible and its correct interpretation are critical for theology, particularly since Jesus is not only intercessor, but also exemplar and teacher. In his approach to scripture, Yoder is neither a fundamentalist nor a liberal. He identifies with the biblical realist school represented by a person such as Paul Minear. With that school, Yoder seeks to read the Bible "on its own terms." The

Bible, then, is seen as essentially a "testimony clustering around the saving events of human history in which God has called to Himself a people around His Son as their Lord."[48]

If biblical scholars find a "real Jesus" fundamentally different from the one presented in the documents as they presently stand, Yoder says his interpretation would suffer a setback. Yet he is confident that scholarship will confirm "the believability of those elements of the picture" which are critical for his interpretation.[49] The problem, according to Yoder, is not that the Bible is unclear, but that people refuse to respond positively to the obvious message. Every attempt is made to obfuscate the clear biblical message of Jesus.[50]

One such mechanism to erode the normativity of Jesus is the frequent and illegitimate appeal to the Old Testament as equally normative as the New. The proper relationship of the Old and New Testaments is the relationship of promise and fulfillment. Yoder obviously identifies with the Anabaptists who, he says, saw "movement within God's purposes which brings the biblical witness to its high point in the work of Jesus himself, and which sees His continuing work in the life of a disciple people."[51] Jesus is not judged by Old Testament ethics; Old Testament ethics find their perfect fulfillment in Jesus. Other procedures have been used by theologians to avoid the normativity of Jesus ever since Constantine. These procedures have sought to give credence to the Constantinian error which illegitimately fuses the church and the world.

THE WORLD

Jesus Christ introduced a new age represented by the church. Yet, the old aeon, incarnated variously but most notably in the state, remains in the interim until all things are made new.

The New Testament sees our present age--the age
of the church, extending from Pentecost to the
Parousia--as a period of the overlapping of two
aeons. These aeons are not distinct periods of
time, for they exist simultaneously. They differ
rather in nature or in direction; one points
backwards to human history outside of (before)
Christ; the other points forward to the fullness
of the kingdom of God, of which it is a foretaste. Each aeon has a social manifestation:
the former in the 'world', the latter in the
church or the body of Christ.[52]

Yoder thus works with a two-kingdoms theology. The duality
proposed here is not one in which the victor in the cosmic
battle awaits determination. Christ is Lord over history
and the powers; yet the world does not recognize his lordship. With Oscar Cullman, Christ is triumphant even if
evil still prevails for a time.[53]

The corollary dynamics to church and world are faith
and unbelief.

The 'world' is neither all nature nor all humanity nor all 'culture'; it is structured unbelief,
rebellion taking with it a fragment of what
should have been the Order of the Kingdom. It is
not just an 'attitude', as is supposed by the
shallow interiorization of attempts to locate
'worldliness' in the mind alone. Nor is it to be
shallowly exteriorized and equated with certain
catalogued forbidden leisure-time occupations.
There are acts and institutions which are by
their nature--and not solely by an accident of
context or motivation--denials of faith in
Christ.[54]

Yoder is obviously convinced that H. Richard Niebuhr se-
verely distorts the fundamental antipathy of the world to
Christ by his use of the ambiguous label "culture" to de-
signate that other power to which the church must respond.[55]

Yoder interprets the New Testament as saying that
those structures which govern the world are the principalities and powers referred to especially by Paul. With
Hendrik Berkhof, Yoder identifies these powers as those
religious, intellectual, moral and political structures
which are integral to a good creation.[56] People need
these powers in order to avoid chaos. Yet, because they
absolutize themselves, they enslave the individual and society, and thus make free, loving life very difficult.[57]

The powers are fallen. People create them and in turn
become victim to them. The state is the supreme example of
these powers. Rather than serving people, people serve the
state, as is evidenced in their willingness to die for it.
Despite their fallenness, the powers are not outside God's
sovereignty. God does not "create" or "institute" or "or-
dain" these powers for they have existed since the beginning of human society. He "orders" them and thus gives
them their proper place. Such ordering is a realistic appraisal of the powers, not necessarily approval of all
their activities.[58] God does not take responsibility for
the existence of the powers, only for ordering them to
serve his purposes.

God's purposes for the state, the most noteworthy member of Yoder's powers pantheon, are to protect the good and
punish the evil in such a way that chaos is avoided and the
church can carry out its mission. The fact that the very
authority of the state depends ultimately on force, on
bearing the sword, does not mean that it cannot be used by
God. In fact, God does use it. Nevertheless, because of

its necessary coercive character in pursuit of a "tolerable
balance of egoism," it cannot respond freely in obedience
to the non-violent Jesus. To do so would mean to deny its
own existence. Yet God uses this fallen power by ordering
it to serve his ends.[59]

Yoder understands history since the time of Christ to
be marked by two kingdoms--the idolatrous and the freed.
An ethic is operative in both and both are within God's redemptive purposes. It is very important to notice, however, that these two operative ethics do not constitute an
ethical dualism, but rather a duality of responses to Jesus
Christ.

> The difference between Christian ethics for
> Christians and a Christian ethic for the state is
> therefore due to the duality not of realms or
> levels, but of responses.[60]

Only the Christian has the spiritual resources necessary to
respond to the full demands of the Christian ethic.[61]
Others respond, but because of their idolatry and unbelief
can respond only in limited fashion. Yoder uses the cate-
gory "middle-axioms," borrowed from John C. Bennett, to describe the maximum ethical level attainable by the world as
long as it remains outside the perfection of Christ.[62]

The essential duality between the church and the world
was and is still obscured by Constantinianism. The victory
of Constantine ended the persecution of the church. Yet,
Yoder argues that it also marked the defeat of the church.
Once everything was baptized, nothing was of the world.

> It was perfectly clear to men like Augustine that
> the world had not become Christian through its
> compulsory baptism. There therefore sprang up
> the doctrine of the invisibility of the true
> Church, in order to permit the affirmation that
> on some level somewhere the difference between

belief and unbelief; i.e. between church and
world, still existed. But this distinction had
become invisible, like faith itself. Previously
Christians had known as a fact of experience that
the Church existed, but had to believe against
appearances that Christ ruled over the world.
After Constantine one knew as a fact of experience that Christ was ruling over the world, but
had to believe against the evidence that there
existed a believing church. Thus the order of
redemption was subordinated to that of preserva-
tion, and the Christian hope turned inside
out.[63]

This reversal necessarily required that the Christian ethic
be radically diluted. Since everything was Christian, virtually nothing was un-Christian. Even making war was
Christianized.

Justification for this new state of affairs proceeded
apace and continues unabated. Natural law, orders of creation, just war, Christian responsibility and similar categories are used to rationalize the Constantinian assumptions which continue to dominate Christian thought. An essential step to recovering truly Christian ethics is to un-
mask Constantinianism and to return to the biblical understanding that the church and the world are two separate,
visible identities within history. Having done that, categories such as natural law can be useful for analysis; but
they will no longer be allowed to obfuscate the normativity
of Jesus for the church and for the world.[64]

PACIFISM

Yoder's understanding of Christ, the church and the
world leads inevitably to a pacifist ethic. If Jesus
Christ in his teachings, life, death and resurrection is

normative for the Christian, then pacifism necessarily follows. If the church is the body of this self-giving, suffering and victorious Lord, then it must incarnate his pacifist ways. As well, if the church is significantly different from the world--not the world's chaplain, but its
judge and structural alternative--then ethics is not accom-
modated to the world's warmaking, but is consistent with
Christ's peacemaking. All this does not mean a simplistic
turning the world into the kingdom with the liberal pacifists, nor withdrawing from it to perfectionist enclaves
with the separated Mennonites. It requires a strategy of
involvement in the world which calls for obedience to
Christ without proving inconsequential or compromised.

Pacifism begins with the love of Jesus Christ.

> Christ is *agape*; self-giving, nonresistant
> love. At the cross this nonresistance, including
> the refusal to use political means of self-de-
> fense, found its ultimate revelation in the un-
> complaining and forgiving death of the innocent
> at the hands of the guilty. This death reveals
> how God deals with evil; here is the only valid
> starting point for Christian pacifism or nonre-
> sistance. The cross is the extreme demonstration
> that *agape* seeks neither effectiveness nor jus-
> tice, and is willing to suffer any loss or seem-
> ing defeat for the sake of obedience.
>
> But the cross is not defeat. Christ's obe-
> dience unto death was crowned by the miracle of
> the resurrection and the exaltation at the right
> hand of God.[65]

The disciple of Jesus is called to incarnate this same
love, as Yoder also indicates.

> Every strand of New Testament literature testi-
> fies to a direct relationship between the way

> Christ suffered on the cross and the way the
> Christian, as disciple, is called to suffer in
> the face of evil.[66]

Therefore, discipleship means nonresistance even if this
requires suffering and death.

Such love extends even to the supposed enemy. Love
here does not mean the denial of normal human preferences,
but it does require a clear perspective as to ultimate loyalties.

> The Christian loves one's enemies not because he
> or she thinks they are wonderful people, nor be-
> cause it is thought that love is sure to conquer
> them; and not because the believer fails to re-
> spect one's native land or its rulers, nor is un-
> concerned for the safety of one's neighbors, nor
> because another political or economic system may
> be favored. The Christian loves his or her enem-
> ies because God does and he commands his follow-
> ers to do so; that is the only reason, and that
> is enough. Our God, who has been made known in
> Jesus Christ, is a reconciling, a forgiving, a
> suffering God.[67]

Loyalty to God as revealed in Jesus requires the Christian
to love even the unlovely.

Love of this kind is "perfect love." Yoder does not
avoid the perfection called for particularly in the Sermon
on the Mount, but his definition contrasts significantly
with the one typically applied by both the perfectionist
and anti-perfectionist schools of Christian ethics. Perfection, he says, "is not flawlessness nor impeccability,
but precisely the refusal to discriminate between friend
and enemy, the in and the out, the good and the evil. It
is revealed to man in the indiscriminateness in which God
loves the good and the evil alike."[68] Love, he adds, "is

not the fruit of long growth and maturation; it is not in-
conceivable or impossible." It can be activated as soon as
man grasps and is "grasped by the unconditionality of the
benevolence of God."[69] To Luther's strong objection to
such a stance Yoder has a ready response: "*Simul justus
et peccator* is allowable as an historical observation; but
it is illegitimate in the realm of faith and ethics."[70]
It is a fact of history, but not a determinant of theology.

No Christian is excused from God's kind of love.
"Pacifism is not the prophetic vocation of a few individuals." According to Yoder "every member of the body of
Christ is called to absolute nonresistance in discipleship
and to abandonment of all loyalties which counter that obedience."[71] Yoder rejects that interpretation of Christian pacifism found within and without the Mennonite brotherhood which deems pacifism a denominational uniqueness or
a vocational calling. Even as he rejects an ethical dualism which posits a different ultimate norm for the world
than for the church, so also he rejects vocational pacifism.

Although Yoder does not accept the label "vocational"
for his understanding of Christian pacifism, neither is he
prepared with liberal pacifists to apply simplistically the
ethic of Jesus to the entire society. His critique of liberal pacifism shares much with neo-orthodoxy. Yet, in
marked contrast to the Niebuhr brothers and their ethical
kin, Yoder refuses to circumvent the biblical mandate to be
like Jesus in order to develop an ethic applicable to the
entire society.[72] Against such Constantinianism, John
Yoder insists that Christian ethics is first and foremost
for Christians, because only Christians have the resources
to love as God loved in Jesus. Only the Christian has the

> resources of love, repentance, the willingness to
> sacrifice, and the enabling power of the Holy
> Spirit, within the supporting fellowship of the

church. Whether or not, or in what sense, non-
Christians or the non-Christian society *should*
love, forgive and otherwise behave like Christians is a speculative question. The spiritual
resources for making such redeemed behavior a
real possibility are lacking.[73]
Accordingly, only Christians can be Christian pacifists,
for only they are empowered to that end.

Probably the major stumbling block for the non-Christian with the pacifism of Jesus is the real possibility of
suffering, or what may be perceived from a worldly perspective as defeat. With Jesus, Yoder believes, the Christian
should anticipate a cross as the logical culmination of his
style of life.

This Gospel concept of the cross of the
Christian does not mean that suffering is thought
of as in itself redemptive or that martyrdom is a
value to be sought after. Nor does it refer
uniquely to being persecuted for 'religious' reasons by an outspokenly pagan government. What
Jesus refers to in his call to cross-bearing is
rather the seeming defeat of that strategy of
obedience which is no strategy, the inevitable
suffering of those whose only goal is to be
faithful to that love which puts one at the mercy
of one's neighbor, which abandons claims to justice for oneself and for one's own in an over-
riding concern for the reconciling of the adversary and the estranged. I Peter 2 thus draws direct social consequences from the fact that
Christ "when he suffered did not threaten but
trusted him who judges justly."[74]
The problem of such a stance to the unbeliever is that it
renounces distinctions between the near neighbor and the

distant enemy. It sets aside a supposed responsibilty to
act on behalf of the lesser evil. All must be loved equally even if the result is suffering for oneself and for
those who are held most dear.[75]

Such an attitude assumes that maintaining life in and
of itself is not the ultimate good. Yoder's is an ethic
based neither on squeamishness over the sight of blood nor
on the painfulness of death. Rather it assumes the abandonment of an egocentric definition of the good. One's own
preferred situation, be it personal or national, must be
set aside. "Personal survival is for the Christian not an
end in itself; how much less national survival."[76] Following this line of reasoning, Yoder is also prepared to
argue that war is not preferable to tyranny.[77] Accepting
suffering is Christian; causing suffering is not.

Using Quaker language, Yoder refers to readiness to
suffer as the "war of the lamb." Essential to this war is
identification with the tactic of Jesus, who through "powerlessness" or "revolutionary subordination" defeated evil
on the cross. Such a tactic is not a matter of weakness.
It is the "voluntary subordination of one who knows that
another regime is normative" and that the present "powers"
have no ultimate strength.[78] Neither is it a calculated
mechanism to gain victory as in non-violence theories.

> The key to the ultimate relevance and to the tri-
> umph of the good is not any calculation at all,
> paradoxical or otherwise, of efficacy, but rather
> simple obedience. Obedience means not keeping
> verbally enshrined rules but reflecting the char-
> acter of the love of God. The cross is not a
> recipe for resurrection. Suffering is not a tool
> to make people come around, nor a good in it-
> self. But the kind of faithfulness that is will-
> ing to accept evident defeat rather than complic-

ity with evil is, by virtue of its conformity
with what happens to God when he worked among
men, aligned with the ultimate triumph of the
Lamb.[79]
The "war of the lamb" is the willing subordination to the
powers that be which use violence to gain their ends, not
because these powers are indeed powerful, but because "The
willingness to suffer is . . . in itself a participation in
the character of God's victorious patience with the rebellious powers of his creation."[80]

The opposite of suffering is violence. Yoder per-
ceives the use of violence to be our way, in the name of
social responsibility, to force history, to make it come
out right. Jesus' way was to disregard concern for effectiveness by accepting the cross. The cross responds to the
human predicament in foolishness, not in terms of obvious
relevance. In God's time, eschatologically, it gains relevance. So also, the rejection of violence is irresponsible
from the human point of view, but eschatologically it is
the way of victory. This is not to say that pacifism always works; it may not. Yoder's pacifism is not based on
pragmatic calculation, but on Christ's cross. It is a pacifism which gains meaning only in partnership with Christian eschatology.[81]

Despite Yoder's strong critique of those who in the
name of managing society and directing history legitimate
violence, he does not commit the messianic community to silence.[82] The church, which is obedient to the suffering
Christ, can and must witness to the state, which is by definition required to manage society. The church is to be a
model society. Its ethical norms cannot be "transposed directly into non-Christian society . . . yet by analogy certain of its aspects may be instructive as stimuli to the
conscience of society."[83] The result is a "moral osmo-

sis" which has a powerful effect on Western society.[84]
Secondly, the church is called to bear an evangelical witness, in the narrow sense of the word. It is to call the
"statesman to be reconciled with God."[85] Speaking more
broadly, the church's evangelical task is to seek the wel-
fare of its neighbors.

> The more sweeping the state's claims, and the
> more self-conscious its manipulation of social
> and economic mechanisms, the more self-evident
> does its effect on our neighbors' welfare be-
> come. Not only does this add a dimension to our
> understanding of what it is that drives a Chris-
> tian to testify against injustice; this consider-
> ation further reminds us that 'human welfare' is
> in itself a value, a criterion, which, although
> not always abstractly definable, is usually self-
> evident in a given context of need. When Jesus
> instructed us to love our neighbors as ourselves,
> He did not mean to enjoin a certain measure of
> selfishness, either undergirding or counterbal-
> ancing our altruism; the point is much more sim-
> ply that I know very well, in looking at myself,
> what I consider to be 'good'.[86]

The church must also witness to the state from the
vantage of knowing the proper function of the state in
God's providence.

> Thus the church's prophetic witness to the state
> rests on firmly fixed criteria; every act of the
> state may be tested according to them and God's
> estimation pronounced with all proper humility.
> The good are to be protected, the evildoers are
> to be restrained, and the fabric of society is to
> be preserved, both from revolution and from war.
> Thus, to be precise, the church can condemn meth-

ods of warfare which are indiscriminate in their
victims and goals of warfare which go further
than the localized readjustment of a tension.
These things are wrong for the state, not only
for the Christian. On the other hand, a police
action within a society or under the United
Nations cannot on the same basis be condemned on
principle; the question is whether the safeguards
are there to insure that it become nothing more.
In practice, these principles would condemn all
modern war, not on the basis of perfectionist
discipleship ethics, but on the realistic basis
of what the state is for.[87]

In brief this means that the church does "not ask of the
government that it be nonresistant," but rather "that it
take the most just and least violent action possible."[88]

What are the ethical criteria from which the church
recommends the least possible violence? The state is judged and condemned by that perfect love incarnated in Jesus
and imitated by the church. However, because of its fallen
condition, it can only be expected to achieve a level of
response referred to as a middle axiom. Such axioms are
the highest level of ethical response attainable by moral
agents outside the church. They translate Christological
ethics into politically applicable categories. They make
relevant supposedly impossible ideals.[89] On the basis of
these middle axioms, Yoder condemns just war rationales,
revolutionary proposals, nuclear warfare and capital punishment. On the same basis, he supports international law,
international government and economic justice.[90] With
this model of critique, Yoder gives the obedient church a
vehicle to remain "relevant," not by compromising itself,
but by challenging the state to the very best it can possibly obtain.

CONCLUSION

John Howard Yoder formulates a pacifism premised on obedience, the obedience of the messianic community. This messianic community is the real presence of the body of Christ in the midst of the world. As such, its norm can only be Jesus himself, both in his teaching and example. This norm is the kind of love which encounters all forms of violence with suffering, even to the point of a cross. Such pacifism allows evil its day with the knowledge that resurrection follows the cross, that Christ is Lord, and that in God's own time the kingdom will come and His will be done even on earth.

Yoder's understanding of the Christian gospel is rich, but surely not exhaustive; creative, but deserving careful critique. Even if entering into dialogue with Yoder has not been the purpose of this paper, hopefully it will contribute to further serious consideration of his thought. Yoder, like his Anabaptist forefathers, is a prophet, or possibly an evangelist. He is less interested in theological speculation for its own sake than in being a preacher of obedience--obedience to Jesus Christ, in the context of the messianic community. To rightly "hear" Yoder, he would tell us, is to live and love like Jesus.

NOTES

[1]This is a distinction Yoder himself makes in Never-theless: The Varieties of Religious Pacifism (Scottdale, Pa: Herald Press, 1971), p. 125.

[2]Mennonite and other sympathetic scholars gathered in Kansas City, Missouri, on October 7-9, 1976, to discuss with Yoder his recently published work, The Politics of Jesus (Grand Rapids, Michigan: Wm B. Eerdmans Publishing Co., 1972). A published document of this conference, which indicates the importance of Yoder's work to Mennonite the-ologizing, is John Richard Burkholder's, Continuity and Change: A Search for a Mennonite Social Ethic (Akron, Pa.: Mennonite Central Committee, 1977).

[3]The Quaker, T. Canby Jones and Brethren theolo-gians, Dale Brown, Donald Durnbaugh and Arthur Gish are among those responding appreciatively to Yoder's work.

[4]Stanley Hauerwas, a professor of theology at Notre Dame, has become a strong advocate of the insights to be gained from J. H. Yoder. Two of Hauerwas' articles on the subject have informed my reading of Yoder, namely: "Messi-anic Pacifism," Worldview (June 1973), pp.28-33 and "The Nonresistant Church: The Theological Ethics of John Howard Yoder," Vision and Virtue (South Bend, Indiana: Fides Press, 1974), pp. 197-221.

[5]Richard Quebedeux in The Young Evangelicals (New York: Harper and Row, 1974) develops these categories.

[6]Yoder participated in the 1973 Thanksgiving Work-shop on Evangelicals and Social Concern which produced the Chicago Declaration. See: Ronald J. Sider, ed., The Chic-ago Declaration (Carol Stream, Ill.: Creation House, 1974).

[7]Yoder is a contributing editor of the periodical Sojourners published in Washington D.C. by a group of Evan-gelical social activists.

[8]Richard J. Mouw, a political philosopher at Calvin College, Grand Rapids, Michigan, is the leading Reformed respondent to Yoder. See esp. his Politics and the Bibli-cal Drama (Grand Rapids, Michigan: Wm. B. Eerdmans Pub-lishing Co., 1976). Yoder's two unpublished papers on the subject are available from the author: "The A Priori Dif-ficulty of 'Reformed-Anabaptist Conversation'," 1977 and "Reformed Versus Anabaptist Social Strategies: The Limits of a Typology," 1979.

[9]Taüfertum and Reformation in Gespräch (Zürich EVZ-Verlag, 1968) and Taüfertum and Reformation in der Schweiz (Karlsruhe: H. Schneider Verlag, 1962).

[10]Focal Pamphlet Series No. 3 (Scottdale Pa.: Herald Press, 1958).

[11]Although Yoder's theology is frequently considered to be Barthian, the limit of his agreement with Barth in the area of ethics is documented in his Karl Barth and the Problem of War (Nashville, Tenn.: Abingdon Press, 1970).

[12]Nevertheless: The Varieties of Religious Pacifism, Chapter V and The Original Revolution: Essays on Christian Pacifism (Scottdale, Pa,: Herald Press, 1972), pp. 48, 124.

[13]The Original Revolution: Essays on Christian Pacifism, p. 28.

[14]John Howard Yoder, The Christian Witness to the State (Newton, Kansas: Faith and Life Press, 1964), p. 10.

[15]The Politics of Jesus, p. 157.

[16]The Original Revolution, p. 29.

[17]The Christian Witness to the State, p. 21.

[18]The Politics of Jesus, p. 158.

[19]The Christian Witness to the State, p. 20.

[20]The Politics of Jesus, p. 158.

[21]John Howard Yoder, "The Otherness of the Church," Mennonite Quarterly Review XXXV (October 1961), p. 287.

[22]The Politics of Jesus, p. 159.

[23]Ibid., p. 160.

[24]Ibid., pp. 223, 225.

[25]The Original Revolution, p. 130. cf. John Howard Yoder, "What is Our Cross?," Sojourners (May 1977), pp. 17-19.

[26]John Howard Yoder, "The Healing Professions in the Disciples' Church," (unpublished paper available from the author, n.d.), p. 8.

[27]The Christian Witness to the State, pp. 9, 17, 39.

[28]The Poiltics of Jesus, p. 238.

[29]Ibid., p. 238.

[30]Nevertheless, p. 126.

[31]"The Healing Professions in the Disciples' Church," p. 4.

[32]The Original Revolution, pp. 136-37.

[33]The Politics of Jesus, pp. 62-63.

[34]See especially, Nevertheless, chapters XIII to XVI.

[35]John Howard Yoder, Reinhold Niebuhr and Christian Pacifism (Washington D.C.: The Church Peace Mission, 1966), c.f. The Politics of Jesus, pp. 110-13 and elsewhere.

[36]The Original Revolution, p. 23. c.f. numerous relevant sections in The Politics of Jesus.

[37]Nevertheless, pp. 125-26.

[38]The Politics of Jesus, p. 228.

[39]Ibid., p. 131.

[40]Ibid., p. 134.

[41]Reinhold Niebuhr and Christian Pacifism, p. 22.

[42]Ibid., p. 21.

[43]Ibid., P. 20.

[44]Ibid., p. 22.

[45]The Original Revolution, p. 121.

[46]The Politics of Jesus, pp. 103, 147. c.f. Glen H. Stassen, "The Politics of Jesus--Moving Toward Social Ethics," unpublished paper presented Oct. 8, 1976, available from the author.

[47]John Howard Yoder, "Glory in a Tent," (duplicated sermon preached in Goshen, Indiana, 1974), p. 10.

[48]John Howard Yoder, "The Message of the Bible on its Own Terms," (photocopied paper presented at Berkeley, California, New College Summer Session, 1978), p. 45.

[49]The Politics of Jesus, p. 24, footnote 14.

[50]The Politics of Jesus, chapter 1.

[51]John Howard Yoder, "The Recovery of the Anabaptist Vision," in Virgil Vogt, ed., Radical Reformation Reader (Scottdale, Pa.: The Concern Group, 1971), p. 20.

[52]The Original Revolution, p. 58.

[53]The Christian Witness to the State, p. 9.

[54]"The Otherness of the Church," p. 293.

[55]"The Otherness of the Church," p. 293. c.f. The Politics of Jesus, pp. 103, 147.

[56]Hendrik Berkhof, Christ and the Powers, trans by J. H. Yoder, (Scottdale, Pa.: Herald Press, 1962).

[57]The Politics of Jesus, p. 146.

[58]Ibid., p. 203.

[59]The Christian Witness to the State, pp. 12-13, chapter 8.

[60]Ibid., p. 32.

[61]Ibid., p. 29.

[62]Ibid., pp. 32-35.

[63]"The Otherness of the Church," pp. 288-89.

[64]This perspective is most clearly developed by Yoder in "The Otherness of the Church"; The Original Revolution, ch, III; and "The 'Constantinian' Sources of Western Social Ethics, "Missionalia: The Journal of the South African Missiological Society 4 (Nov. 1976), pp. 98-108.

[65]The Original Revolution, p. 57.

[66]Ibid., p. 60.

[67]"What is Our Cross?," p. 18.

[68]The Politics of Jesus, p. 231, footnote 16. c.f. 119-20.

[69]The Original Revolution, pp. 47-48.

[70]John Howard Yoder, "What Are Our Concerns?," in Paul Peachey, ed., Concern IV (June 1957), p. 23.

[71]The Original Revolution, p. 76.

[72]Reinhold Niebuhr and Christian Pacifism, p. 17.

[73]The Christian Witness to the State, p. 29.

[74]The Politics of Jesus, p. 243.

[75]The Original Revolution, pp. 84-85.

[76]Ibid., p. 86.

[77]Ibid., p. 86.

[78]The Politics of Jesus, p. 192.

[79]Ibid., p. 245.

[80]Ibid., p. 213.

[81]See esp. The Original Revolution, ch. III, which was originally published as "Peace Without Eschatology?"

[82]Politics of Jesus, p. 235. cf. Richard Mouw's discussion of his critique in Politics and the Biblical Drama, pp. 107-11.

[83]The Christian Witness to the State, p. 17.

[84]Ibid., p. 40.

[85]The Original Revolution, p. 76; The Christian Witness to the State, p. 76.

[86]The Christian Witness to the State, p. 14.

[87]The Original Revolution, p. 78.

[88] *The Christian Witness to the State*, p. 42.
[89] Ibid., pp. 32-33.
[90] Ibid., chapter 6.

THE MOVEMENT FOR A NEW SOCIETY
(1971 -   )

by George H. Crowell

The Movement for a New Society is a Quaker-based movement committed to building community and working by non-violent means to bring about radical social change. It is an ecumenical organization committed to developing universal community. Its origins and spirituality are deeply rooted in the Christian tradition. Many of the principles it follows in its own organization and in the development of non-violent strategies to bring about change flow from basic Quaker spiritual principles and practices. By emphasizing the strategies of the Movement, G. Crowell's article adds an interesting dimension to the book because it moves from the theological and spiritual foundations for a life of non-violence to the application of this spirituality.

In the Movement for a New Society (MNS), the non-violence which is central to Christian spirituality has gained vital and active expression. MNS membership is not limited to Christians, nor does MNS present itself solely and explicitly as Christian, because in a pluralistic society, and indeed in a pluralistic world, it sees an urgent need to press beyond the limits of parochial communities, Christian and others, to a universal human community. Perception of this need itself arises not only from the pragmatic requirements of the situation, but also from the Christian imperative to transform the world into a peaceful, just, and loving community. While MNS does not stress its Chris-

tian heritage, it is clearly rooted in Christian spiritual-
ity, especially of the Quaker tradition. This Christian
Quaker influence can be seen at every point in the life of
MNS.

The Movement for a New Society is a network of groups
committed to work through non-violent action for social
change in the direction of justice and peace. With MNS
non-violent action is not only an abstract ideal, but a
reality to be known in experience and to be lived out in
ongoing struggle to transform the social order. In its
short life, MNS has developed a complex array of organizations and activities, all of which are intended to bring
into concrete human reality the non-violent way of life.
The hopes and dreams of MNS are audacious. They extend to
the entire human community. The goal of MNS is a global
order in which human beings live in harmony with each other
and with their environment, an order in which human conflicts of whatever scale are consistently resolved by non-
violent means. While the vision is global, MNS members
concentrate their energies on tasks within reach, yet well
beyond the expectations and imaginations of most people in
our society. An illustration of this principle is the action campaign in the midst of which MNS was launched.

In the fall of 1970, a group of people primarily from
Quaker backgrounds, who shared an intense concern about the
perilous social problems confronting the human community a-
long with a passionate desire for justice and peace, gathered in Philadelphia for a series of meetings to discuss
future directions that they might take together. They had
gotten to know and to trust each other in the past through
participating in the civil rights struggle which had been
led chiefly by Martin Luther King, Jr., and in efforts to
bring an end to the Vietnam war. Some had worked with that
effective Quaker instrument of social concern, the American

Friends Service Committee, and some with a voluntary, non-
violent social change organization, A Quaker Action Group.
They shared a keen desire to create an ongoing community
which would support themselves and others in non-violent
political action.[1]

As discussions about estabishment of their "Life Center" continued into June of 1971, news reports appeared
describing brutal attacks by West Pakistani troops on the
Bengali people of East Pakistan. Thousands of terrorized
refugees were fleeing to India which had no adequate resources to care for them. When the planning group discovered that the United States was in the process of shipping
military equipment to the West Pakistani regime which was
slaughtering defenseless Bengalis, they began to grope toward some action that would call into question the U.S.
role in supporting the injustice.

The action chosen was a non-violent campaign featuring
an attempt by a fleet of canoes and kayaks to blockade the
port of Baltimore against entry of ships intending to load
armaments for shipment to West Pakistan.[2] This campaign
played a key (although indeterminable) role in achieving
the November 8, 1971, State Department announcement that
all licenses for export of weapons from the U.S. to Pakistan were being cancelled.[3] Even in a society which up-
holds citizen participation, this campaign extended well
beyond ordinary imagination about possibilities for citizen
participation in social change. While the prompt results
it helped to achieve could not be expected with any assurance to flow from this or any other similar campaign, it
was a highly encouraging note on which to begin MNS.

This campaign also helped to establish for the future
of MNS the priority of social action in its life even over
the very important task of community building. While the
Philadelphia Life Center, whose founding marks the formal

beginning of MNS, was opened in the fall of 1971 in the
midst of the Pakistan campaign, the task of starting the
Center took second place to the social action effort.[4] In
its fundamental commitment to action, MNS reflects the persistent activism of its Quaker forebears.

QUAKER ROOTS, ECUMENICAL THRUST

Clearly MNS has its roots in the spirituality and in
the life of committed Quaker communities. The considerable
body of literature published by MNS members, and made a-
vailable to the public by MNS, makes this fact clear without making it a direct claim, and without pursuing the matter in any precise way.[5] Finnerty describes the Philadelphia Life Center as

> a radical pacifist community made up of some one
> hundred members living together in fifteen house-
> holds. Although it is a secular community, it e-
> volved from a Quaker base and thus has many of
> the attributes of a spiritual community, and its
> prime reason for being is to provide a center of
> support for people who want to change our socie-
> ty.[6]

To call the Life Center and hence MNS a "secular community," however, is misleading. It is really an ecumenical community whose ecumenism draws upon the spiritual resources of the entire Christian commmunity, and which goes
beyond to include secular humanists and members of other
religious traditions as well. All are drawn together in
their common commitment to non-violent struggle for global
justice.

In a pluralistic American society and in a far more
pluralistic world, this non-violent struggle cannot possibly be carried on effectively by members of a single sectarian group. Active support must be sought from people of

all traditions and views compatible with the struggle. MNS has no wish to limit its membership to people of Quaker background, but strives to draw in people from a wide spectrum of backgrounds, Christian and non-Christian. This need for a global ecumenism is abundantly clear to non-violent activists who could hardly have achieved their present stage of development without the powerful resources of loving, non-violent action that Gandhi drew from the Hindu tradition. For those who wish to see the way of non-violence actualized in human history, such a global ecumenism is an inescapable pragmatic requirement. Few enough of the world's people are Christian, much less Quaker. Nevertheless, the Quaker Christian influence remains potently present in the life of MNS.

The fundamental tenet of Quaker faith is the conviction that God is present in the spirit of every human being. While some persons acknowledge this inner presence less fully than others, and some even deny it, the Spirit of God as revealed in Christ is nevertheless present in every person. This conviction has radical implications for the way in which human beings relate to each other. It means that everyone as bearer of the divine must be treated with profound reverence. This requires a complete rejection of violence toward anyone, and even toward the enemy in whom also the divine is present. It further requires a radical equality among all. The Quakers from the very beginning of their history under the leadership of George Fox were vigorously active in attempting to express these principles in daily life. The active quest for equality and the struggle for justice by non-violent means, which have long characterized Quakerism, remain vital in MNS which inherited these concerns from its Quaker founders.[7]

While MNS people draw strength from their own Christian roots, they welcome the spiritual resources of other
traditions when they, too, contribute to the non-violent
movement toward peace and justice. During the Bangladesh
campaign, a worship service was held in a Washington, D.C.
park to commemorate the lives lost as a result of U.S. and
Pakistani government actions.

It was a deeply moving experience to sit across
from the White House and to reflect on those who
had died and would still die, while as we meditated, a Moslem Bengali read from the Koran, a
Hindu Bengali read from the *Bhagavad-Gita*, and
a Christian minister read from the Bible. At the
close of the service, we passed around bowls of
rice and water, a symbolic "communion" through
the elements that were the refugees' rations.[8]

Both the Quaker Christian roots and the ecumenical
thrust of MNS are evident in its participation in a movement for simple living. The impulse for this movement came
not from MNS, but from a meeting of Christian retreat center staffs in 1973. They wrote and signed the Shakertown
Pledge which calls for ecologically sound life styles of
reduced consumption, sharing wealth with the world's poor,
and working for a more just global society. While all
these concerns were thoroughly rooted in the authors'
Christian convictions, the Pledge was worded without explicit reference to the Christian faith so that it would
appeal to a common human concern which Christians share
with all people.[9] It was widely published and evoked
wide-spread support, especially from church groups across
North America.

In 1977 the Simple Living Collective of the American
Friends Service Committee in San Francisco (a Quaker, but
not an MNS group) published a handbook, *Taking Charge*,

which is highly useful for group discussion of creative simple living.[10] Already giving expression to simple living in its lifestyle, a theme rooted in the Quaker rejection of excesses in clothing and in other worldly goods, MNS through its Churchmouse Collective and through its Minneapolis group, contributed actively to this broadly ecumenical effort.[11]

COMMUNITY BUILDING

In order to support persistent, non-violent action for social change, which our society urgently needs, MNS founders recognized the necessity for the sustaining power of ongoing community life. As MNS members put it:

Working in earlier years as isolated individuals, we found we were quickly "burning out": we often felt lonely, overwhelmed and discouraged. Realizing that we needed more support and encouragement from each other, we began exploring with others more cooperative ways to live and work together.[12]

As a result there are now two basic ways in which MNS people come together, two basic types of community through which they organize and affirm their lives. There are residential collectives, people living in households together, and there are working collectives, groups with specific tasks. Their memberships usually differ, but may often overlap.

Into both types of community life, MNS people have put an enormous amount of effort to assure that they function effectively. Even when people come together with clearly defined common goals, as they do in MNS, tensions, resentments, and conflicts can rend their unity. MNS seeks a collective life that is fully democratic and egalitarian. This is difficult to achieve in our culture which takes for granted male-dominated, hierarchical, racist, elitist ways of organizing human relationships. But these taken-for-granted assumptions go to the very heart of the social problems which imperil our future. Only through overcoming the culturally promoted inequalities in their own communal life, MNS people recognize, can they most effectively challenge them in the wider society.

The high value which MNS places on the development of community derives partly from the direct observation and experience of members, and partly from their awareness of the vitalizing and transforming power of Christian communities dating back to the early Church as described in the Book of Acts. A key factor in the MNS commitment to overcome all expressions of inequality is rooted in the MNS Quaker heritage, with its doctrine of the indwelling Spirit. Springing from this doctrine is the style of the Quaker meeting which, rejecting the authority of any formal clergy or other office, always remains open to the possibility that the Divine Spirit may speak through any person present.

Moreover, Quakers insist upon making decisions by consensus, refusing to override the views and consciences of some members even by the seemingly democratic procedure of majority vote. The Quaker meeting, with its fully egalitarian structure, has long served as a potent bulwark against authoritarian and hierarchical tendencies. The experience from childhood of the founders of MNS with Quaker meetings has provided MNS with much of the wisdom about group processes which has enabled it to struggle effectively with the problems which endanger community life in households and task forces just as they endanger the wider society.[13]

Although each of the two types of MNS collective has its unique problems, most of the MNS wisdom about group processes applies to both types. Especially relevant to both is the wisdom that has been accumulated, largely from the Quaker tradition, for running group meetings. A participant in MNS meetings highlights their dynamics.

My first MNS meeting: in a circle, with big wall charts showing what was planned . . .; two women as "facilitators" (not "chairpeople" with the implication of unequal power) asking all of us if we accepted the agenda and if the times allotted to each item seemed reasonable. When energy slumped, we all jumped up and did some crazy physical activity for a moment. When someone became upset, there were people to give supporting attention and to help with a resolution of the anger/fear. Strangely, there was not much jockeying for attention, little domination by a few. . . . We sang, laughed, and got a lot of work done without voting once! . . .

Our meetings are usually lively but also caring. We open with songs or games, and share what has recently been exciting in our lives. We also may "check in" with each other about how we're feeling and to see if anyone needs help or attention from the whole group. We may close with hugs or with an arms-around-each-other circle where we appreciate our being together. . . .

We make decisions by consensus. . . . This is not the same as unanimity! I may prefer another course, but I would block consensus only if I had a major (and often principled) objection. Full and freely flowing communication is what makes consensus decision-making lively, productive and really democratic. This means lots of talk, but with good process it's amazing how much we can communicate per hour. . . .

We get incredible amounts of work done at
each meeting. There's lots of confidence building. . . . Countering the idea that only through
competition can excellence be had, we find that
working cooperatively is energizing and highly
creative, as well as supportive to us all.[14]

In its published materials, in far greater detail than
could possibly be included here, MNS has described its
techniques for running meetings,[15] and for coping with
the wide range of problems which arise in close-knit communities.[16] Employing Quaker Christian wisdom and insights from depth psychology along with friendship, love,
and common sense, MNS members offer each other, again with
a number of carefully worked out techniques, effective personal counseling. In their households and task-oriented
collectives, they have learned to deal gracefully with issues arising from members' falling in and out of love, and
with their moving into marriage. They have faced head-on
problems related to homosexuality and to homophobia, the
fear of homosexuality.[17] When parents share responsibility for their children with others in their communities,
all concerned work together to develop beneficial styles of
childrearing. Sex-role stereotyping frequently arises as a
problem, and MNS communities constantly struggle to overcome it with its damaging effects on both men and women.

MNS has often struggled with tensions concerning how
much priority should be given to personal growth and how
much to political action. It recognizes the temptation to
withdraw into personal concerns--community living, mutual
support, and child development--especially since so many
people in our society need therapeutic help. But thus far
MNS has maintained its commitment to non-violent social action for which it gains support from its ongoing community
life.[18]

This community life is based primarily on the workings of small, intimate groups, but is integrally related to a wider network of collectives. Through both informal and formal means, including an annual meeting, the collectives of MNS maintain contact with each other, cooperate on actions, support each other's initiatives, and continually offer each other encouragement.[19] In keeping with the principles of democratic egalitarianism, and full participation by all, the network is decentralized. It steers clear of bureaucratic, hierarchical structures. MNS writer Richard Taylor sees this commitment to equality rooted in the biblical insistence upon a radical equality among all members of the human family, and especially within the Christian community. He quotes the Apostle Paul:

As a matter of equality your abundance at the present time should supply their want, so that their abundance may supply your want, that there may be equality (II Corinthians 8:14).[20]

SOCIAL ANALYSIS

A shared passion for justice in human affairs first brought together the founders of MNS. Their sensitivity to the destructive power of current injustices had been nourished by the biblical passion for justice. Integral to this passion for justice, as MNS writer Taylor makes clear, was the biblical drive, expressed especially by the prophets and by Jesus himself, to trace particular expressions of injustice to their roots in exploitative institutional structures, and also to expose the rationalizations which were used to buttress them.

Indeed, Taylor effectively employs biblical insight to expose a contemporary rationalization for injustice. The ideology of free enterprise economics has been used to justify systems which promote vast inequity between the rich and the poor. This ideology argues that each individual (or firm) seeking his own selfish economic advantage contributes through the working of an "invisible hand," as Adam Smith put it, to the well-being of all. Taylor's comment:

> Can we imagine Jesus walking through Galilee, urging everyone to pursue his or her own selfish interests, to seek personal financial gain and not worry about the needs of others? Would it not be nearer the spirit of Christ to say that everyone should lovingly pursue the well-being of each member of the human family, thus cooperating with God in assuring the common good? The only invisible hand in Christian teaching is the hand of God, and when we grasp it, we are led away from self-interest to love our neighbor as ourselves.[21]

Nourished, therefore, largely by the biblical, Christian commitment not only to express indignation at injustice, but also to uncover its sources, MNS does thorough analyses of the roots of social injustices, and shrewd appraisals of the power realities which undergird them. One of the earliest and best developed disciplines of MNS is social analysis, or as they themselves label it, "macro-analysis." Out of shared participation in macro-analysis grew both the Bangladesh action and the founding of the Philadelphia Life Center, which essentially remains at the heart of MNS. Just as a deeply shared perception of social realities was initially essential for bringing people together to create MNS, so it continues essential for invigorating and expanding the movement. MNS members meet frequently to renew and to deepen their macro-analysis, especially in view of insights brought to light through their social action. Moreover a key component of their outreach

to others is their offering, virtually wherever requested,
"macro-analysis seminars."

As the MNS manual, *Organizing Macro-Analysis Seminars*, puts it:

Macro-analysis seminars are democratically-run
study groups that attempt to increase the participants' awareness of the ecological, political,
economic, and social forces that are shaping our
global society. They are designed for people who
are concerned about the environmental deteriora-
tion and the injustice and oppression that exist
all around us, and to help people do something
about it. It is our hope that the macro-analysis
process will lead to increased understanding--and
that the increased understanding will lead to
collective action for social change.[22]

The macro-analysis seminar format apparently presupposes of its participants a rather keenly devloped sense of
the injustices which presently prevail, and of the perils
which threaten the human community. The suffering that human beings undergo as a result of injustices can only be
known either through direct personal experience or through
empathy with others at a deeply personal level.[23] Macro-
analysis builds on this awareness and concern at the personal level, and pushes beyond to uncover the social roots
of the suffering. In doing so, the macro-analysis process
leads to the discrediting of widely held assumptions.

For example, it is commonly believed that vast numbers
of people in the world suffer the agonies of malnourishment
and starvation because there are too many people and too
little food. The fact is that the world produces enough
grain alone (not to mention fruits, vegetables, beans,
nuts, seafood and pasture-fed animals) to feed every human
being the world over some 3,000 calories a day--more than

enough. Indeed every country has sufficient arable land to
feed its own people. Why, then, are people hungry? They
starve because they do not have control over land to produce their own food, nor control over other economic resources enabling them to buy their food. Land is concen-
trated in the hands of very few, and this concentration of
land is increasing as giant corporations extend their control over land, especially in the Third World. These large
landholders seldom produce food to feed the hungry. Rather
they produce food and other commodities for sale in affluent markets.[24]

As in this case, when the real roots of the problem
are revealed, it often becomes apparent that the discredited explanation effectively obscured or rationalized certain
powerful vested interests, which would prefer the truth not
to be known. If the truth is known, appropriate change can
be initiated. This is the fundamental assumption behind
macro-analysis.

If the widely held assumptions which obscure the truth
are to be effectively discredited, then a great deal of evidence must be marshalled to support a true explanation.
MNS macro-analysis seminars take on this responsibility by
providing rich bibliographical references, only a few of
which have been produced by MNS itself. The seminars,
therefore, impose a demanding academic discipline. But it
is a discipline which requires voluntary commitment. In
keeping with its anti-hierarchical, democratic principles,
MNS structures macro-analysis seminars to avoid traditional
authoritarian teaching styles. Both teaching and learning,
along with group facilitation, are fully shared among participants, and great pains are taken to assure that no
strong personalities dominate the group. The empowerment
of all is a key goal of MNS, sought assiduously even
through its first outreach contacts, which are very often
macro-analysis seminars.

While a single broad problem like world hunger might provide a focus for initiating the macro-analysis seminar process, such an issue becomes an opening to understanding interconnections among a great variety of social issues, such as environmental degradation, depletion of resources, racism, sexism, militarism, torture, and many others. While all problems could not possibly be analyzed thoroughly even in a normal seminar of 24 three-hour sessions, a key goal of macro-analysis is to indicate how all kinds of human suffering in the social dimension can be traced again and again through their interconnections to the same basic institutional roots. Once the tools and techniques for uncovering the roots of one major injustice and its interconnections with others are mastered, they can readily be applied to any injustice with new attention to revealing specific detail. Since new details must be mastered in order to understand each injustice as it develops in different times and places, macro-analysis is a continuing discipline for MNS people who are struggling to prepare themselves for healing social action.

While the bulk of time in macro-analysis seminars is ordinarily given to *analysis* of social injustices as outlined above, two additional foci for study and discussion are also included. These are *vision* and *strategy*.[25] By "vision" is meant looking toward possibilities for a new society. How can human interaction be realistically organized to maximize possibilities for loving, harmonious human relationships and to assure reverent care for our environmental life-support systems? "Strategy" refers to the means for achieving a new society. How can people realistically and effectively move the human community away from its terrifying involvement in practising and in threatening violence to a loving, non-violent social order? In presenting its vision for the future and its strategy for get-

ting there, the special sensitivity of MNS to non-violence
in theory and in practice becomes notably evident. Since
vision and strategy embody the same basic insights concerning non-violent action, they can be dealt with together under that heading.

NON-VIOLENT ACTION

Especially striking in the MNS commitment to the non-
violent way of life is the willingness of MNS writers to
argue consistently for the superiority of non-violence over
violence *on pragmatic grounds*. When the argument runs
into obstacles, there is no retreat to some transcendent
ethical norm immune from pragmatic tests. There may be an
admission that in some cases a choice between violent and
non-violent actions is very difficult. More evidence may
be necessary to make a stronger case, but the commitment to
a pragmatic approach persists.

So persistent is this commitment, however, that it reveals its basis in religious conviction. The MNS commitment to non-violence has not simply been derived from pragmatic analysis of human interactions. It is ultimately
rooted in the Quaker Christian faith that God, however hidden He may be, is present in every human person, and therefore that all persons must be treated with the reverence
that can only be adequately expressed in non-violence.
This faith precedes the pragmatic investigation. Indeed,
it is this faith which assures that, despite all the evidence which is available to justify violence, nevertheless
all possible pragmatic evidence supporting non-violence
will be assiduously sought out.

Further support for this MNS commitment to a pragmatic
approach can be found in Christian tradition. The Christian position is accepted as true not only because it is
believed that God revealed it, but also becuase it is vali-

dated in experience. One of the tasks of Christian theology has long been to show that the Christian position can be validated by the realities of human life and history. In its pragmatic arguments for non-violence, MNS is making a key contribution to this task. It is also using an argument which has the widest possible appeal. In arguing along these lines, MNS writers demonstrate impressive insight into the workings of power in human affairs.

An oppressive order, they point out, is a violent order. Violence is the inseparable companion of oppression. A world like ours in which the prevailing institutional structures give to a few elites power to dominate and to exploit other people and resources is inherently violent. It comes into being and preserves itself through violence.[26] It is utterly incompatible with an order in which people live in harmony with each other and with the environment, an order in which they treat each other and the natural world with gentleness and reverence.

The MNS vision of a new society calls for a high degree of equality among human beings both in use of limited resources and in exercise of political power. As George Lakey puts it:

> We believe a just economic order will stress cooperation, not competition; relative equality of income, not wide disparity; democratic self-management, not dictatorial management by others; self-reliance and initiative, not dependence on bureaucracies.[27]

Rejecting both the media-manipulated politics represented by the liberal, "democratic" United States, and the bureaucratic centralism epitomized by the "socialist" Soviet Union, Lakey proposes a political alternative:

> Decision-making in the new society should be rooted in the face-to-face discussions of the

citizenry, starting on the neighborhood level.
As many decisions as possible should be made on
the local level; economic decentralization
should be matched by political decentralization.[28]

This vision for a new economic and political order is elab-
orated in considerable detail by MNS writers, and with a
keen appreciation of the objections that can be raised a-
gainst it.[29]

MNS insists upon a high level of democratic participation as essential for a new society free of oppression and
violence, a society characterized by non-violent reverence
for all life. In harmony with that *vision*, it insists
upon a *strategy* that maximizes democratic participation
in the struggle toward a new society. In order to be effective, the non-violent movement must necessarily maximize
participation from the very beginning. A revolutionary
movement that turns to violence, however justifiable this
may be in view of the oppression that it attempts to overcome, unavoidably creates conditions in which further oppression will flourish. Even successful violent revolu-
tions, even those which bring a much greater degree of justice than the older order, as in the case of China, invariably sow seeds for further oppression and violence.[30]
The reason is that violent movements necessarily include
strongly anti-democratic elements.

Since oppressive regimes possess military and police
power to crush insurrections, violent revolutionary movements must necessarily plan in secret. Only small elites
can participate in the planning. The majority of oppressed
people must be excluded. Thus the people fail to develop
the capacity for active participation in shaping their future.

Secrecy brings divisiveness into movement life because there must always be those who know and those who do not know. Those who are outside feel resentful; those who are inside develop feelings of superiority.[31]

Even within the inner group, the danger of spies and *agents provocateurs* creates suspicion and undermines trust. The danger of betrayal is keen, and increases if a member of the inner circle should be arrested and tortured.[32]

Oppressive regimes have often demonstrated their preference for violent rather than non-violent opposition. They have planted *agents provocateurs* in non-violent organizations, urging upon them violent adventures which the regime could legitimately crush.[33] Even in responding with brutal repression to a violent uprising, an existing regime can usually pose successfully as the guarantor of order against a threat to public safety. Moreover, by its violence a revolutionary movement may quickly alienate the very people whose grievances against the regime would otherwise have led them to support the movement.[34]

To most of us who have absorbed the prevailing values of our culture, the prospect of overcoming through non-violent action a brutal dictatorship appears too remote for serious consideration. Unfortunately few of us know that it has been done. In 1944, for example, first in El Salvador and then in Guatemala, the expanding of various kinds of non-violent resistance into general strikes led to the overthrow of dictators who had been ruthless in their use of military and police power to suppress their people.[35] Expressed here was a key principle of non-violent struggle --*non-cooperation*. Even the most oppressive regime depends upon the cooperation of its subjects. If that cooperation is withdrawn, even dictators can be overthrown.[36]

This is not to say that non-violent revolutionaries
can expect to be immune from violent retaliation. They
must be willing to accept suffering and even loss of life.
However, as Lakey puts it:

All I will say is that, other things being equal,
there will be *less* suffering to be endured by
the people when a non-violent strategy is used
than when a violent strategy is used.[37]

The cases of El Salvador and Guatemala indicate how
much can be accomplished when a spontaneous, non-violent
insurrection erupts against a brutal dictatorship. But in
each case the insurrection came in a moment of public rage,
and the people were not prepared to consolidate their
gains. Old habits of submission remained. A new capacity
for self-determination had not developed. Capacities for
leadership and organization had only begun to germinate and
had not been widely disseminated. Strategy for non-violent
revolution must include thorough preparation of people for
active participation in public life.[38]

This raises a key question. In a regime which is so
repressive that it does not even allow people to meet for
discussion without danger of arrest and torture, how can
people develop organization and communication, or even sufficient clarity about the issues, much less the strategy
that could be used, even to begin a movement against the
regime? Here is a point at which MNS writers acknowledge
that it is difficult to press on with a fully convincing
pragmatic argument.[39]

Certainly we are not saying that there is a
nonviolent revolutionary answer in every situation. There has never been a nonviolent revolution in history, in the sense we mean. . . .[40]

Can an oppressive situation be so desperate that nothing but violence offers any hope of change? If so, then

the new order, while it may be an improvement, will retain elements of violence that must still be overcome.

A violent revolution creates a violent structure in which, having killed one's enemies, it is all too easy to kill one's friends for holding "wrong positions." Having once taken up weapons, it is difficult to lay them down.[41]

If it is argued that our position is utopian and that people can turn to nonviolence only after the revolution, we reply that unless we hold firmly to nonviolence now, the day will never come when all of us learn to live without violence.[42]

The challenge we make to our nonpacifist friends in the liberation movements is to develop the outline of a nonviolent strategy for revolution before rejecting it out of hand. If you see violence as a last resort, then first put time and energy into the next-to-last resort. If you see yourselves as practical people choosing among alternative courses, then *create* a nonviolent strategy so your choice will have meaning.[43]

In North America today, with the political freedoms that prevail, violent social action is not only unnecessary, but would be "a strategic disaster."[44] But even here, where freedom to organize and to initiate non-violent actions is very broad, people have barely begun to develop their creative imaginations for non-violent tactics. Beyond such strategies as strikes, demonstrations and sit-ins, most have little awareness of the enormous range of possibilities. One study, much used by MNS, has classified more than 190 different types of non-violent action.[45]

Once people have seen in rich detail the potentialities for non-violent strategies, they are much more likely

to set aside violent options. The discovery can be exhilarating. Into the often grim business of struggling for
justice, creative non-violent actions can even bring a note
of delightful humor. In Buenos Aires, Argentina in 1902,
for example, in the context of numerous efforts to repress
labor, the police chief ordered all the jobless arrested,
claiming that anyone willing to work could find a job.
When throngs of workers applied for jobs at the police
chief's home, the order was rescinded.[46] In pointing,
through its literature and in its macro-analysis seminars,
to the virtually unlimited possibilities for creating non-
violent tactics, MNS encourages people to devise non-violent options for social action that they would never before
have imagined.

Some reject the non-violent approach as irrelevant in
the case of a nation invaded by an aggressor. MNS people,
however, argue compellingly for non-violent civilian defense,[47] although space is lacking to include their argument here. In a world faced with the alternative of military defense that leads to nuclear holocaust, there is urgent need to take such proposals seriously.

The MNS vision of a new society, unlike the Marxist,
is not utopian. It does not expect even under the best
imaginable conditions, that conflict among human beings
will ever be ended.[48] But conflicts might be waged non-
violently, with police forces functioning only to assure
that violence is kept out of the struggles. An example of
conflict carried on non-violently comes from the independence movement in India in 1930. The police, having found
violent repression ineffective, stopped a large demonstration from marching to central Bombay by blocking their
route.

About 30,000 men, women, and children sat down
wherever they were on the street. Facing them

sat the police. Hours passed but neither party
would give in. Soon it was night and it began to
rain. The onlooking citizens organized themselves into volunteer units to supply the Satya-
grahis with food, water, and blankets. The Sat-
yagrahis, instead of keeping the supplies for
themselves, passed them on to the obstructing po-
licemen as a token of their goodwill. Finally,
the police gave in, and the procession culminated
in a triumphant midnight march.[49]

When contending groups can escalate their level of non-violence, then, in radical contrast with the destructiveness
of violence, creative, life-affirming forces essential for
a new society have come into play.

MNS IN SOCIAL ACTION

In its brief history MNS has developed and nourished a
wide range of skills and activities which it sees as essential to the struggle for a new society. While stressing
community building and educational tasks, it maintains its
commitment to action for social change. MNS members recognize the hazard of coming to see themselves as trainers who
train others to train still more trainers. They identify
themselves as social change activists.[50] MNS began in
the midst of the Bangladesh campaign, and continually expresses its commitment to social action.

MNS people were active in the Wounded Knee crisis of
1973. They have joined in the struggle of the United Farm
Workers.

They have demonstrated against the B-1 bomber and
the Trident submarine. They seek to educate people about the dangers of S-1, the criminal code
revision. They participated in the Continental
Walk and trained marshalls for the Bicentennial
counter celebration in Philadelphia.[51]

Since 1973, they have been involved in various actions against nuclear power. Especially notable was MNS participation in the anti-nuclear protests at Seabrook, New Hampshire in 1977 and 1978, where their range of experience and skills made an especially valuable contribution.

On April 30 and May 1, 1977, a large crowd of protesters occupied the nuclear power plant site at Seabrook. In a sense their challenge to the system was quite mild, since they made no attempt to block plant construction. Nevertheless, 1,400 people were arrested and jailed, vividly witnessing to the sacrifices that citizens were willing to make in order to express their urgent convictions concerning the perils of nuclear power.

The occupation had been planned months in advance by the local Clamshell Alliance which asked an MNS team of some forty people to provide intensive training several days in advance, especially in non-violent tactics. MNS experience with democratic group process played a key role in organizing participants into "affinity groups" of ten to fifteen people each, who accepted a common non-violent discipline, and who took on special responsibility for each other during the occupation. Each group chose a spokesperson to participate in the overall group decision-making. Through role-playing they prepared for virtually every eventuality--relating to police, facing arrest, responding to the media, dealing with *provocateurs*, coping with emotional strain and tiredness. At the same time, they worked to overcome elitist and sexist tendencies, with the result that responsibilities of all kinds were broadly shared, with exhilarating impact on the participants. A tribute to the effectiveness of this preparation was paid by Governor Thompson, when he labelled the occupation as "one of the best planned mass criminal conspiracies in American history."[52]

MNS, rooted in Christianity of the Quaker tradition, does not emphasize its Christian heritage. It has chosen to strive toward a universal human community transcending particular religious traditions. Nevertheless, it is extraordinarily faithful to that fundamental element in Christian spirituality which requires active struggle to transform the world in the only way that is really effective--through non-violent action.

At the beginning of this article, the hopes and dreams of MNS were described as audacious, but, in a sense, they are the hopes and dreams of all of us. Indeed, we can hardly expect to survive on this globe unless such dreams prevail.

NOTES

[1]William Moyer, "MNS Structure and Strategy: Comments and Suggestions," (MNS mimeographed paper, April 1976), pp. 23-24. This item and others cited here, unless otherwise specified, are published by the Movement for a New Society, 4722 Baltimore Avenue, Philadelphia, Pennsylvania, 19143.

[2]See Richard K. Taylor, Blockade (Maryknoll, New York: Orbis Books, 1977).

[3]Ibid., pp. 94-101.

[4]Moyer, "MNS Structure and Strategy," p. 24.

[5]See, for example, Taylor, Blockade, pp. ix-xi, 6-7, 19, 28, 46; George Lakey, Strategy for a Living Revolution (San Francisco: W.H. Freeman and Company, 1973) p. xv; Moyer, "MNS Structure and Strategy," pp. 23-24; MNS Service Collective, "Building the Good Life," Doing It!, October 1976, p. 10.

[6]Adam Daniel Finnerty, No More Plastic Jesus: Global Justice and Christian Lifestyle (Maryknoll, New York: Orbis Books, 1977), p. xiii.

[7]Interview with Sandra Boston and Robert McClellan of MNS Churchmouse Collective, May 10, 1980.

[8]Taylor, Blockade, p. 90.

[9]Finnerty, No More Plastic Jesus, pp. 95-104.

[10]Simple Living Collective, American Friends Service Committee, San Francisco, Taking Charge (New York and Toronto: Bantam Books, 1977).

[11]Moyer, "MNS Structure and Strategy," pp. 12-13.

[12]Virginia Coover, Ellen Deacon, Charles Esser, and Christopher Moore, Resource Manual for a Living Revolution (Philadelphia: New Society Press, 1977), p. 3.

[13]Interview with Boston and McClellan.

[14]Pete Hill, "MNS Group Process," Dandelion, Summer/Fall 1979, pp. 13-15.

[15]See especially Resource Manual for a Living Revolution, pp. 43-99.

[16]Ibid., pp. 101-27; Peter Woodrow, Clearness, (MNS, 1976); Training/Action Affinity Group, Building Social Change Communities (MNS, 1976).

[17]The Gay Theory Work Group, Gay Oppression and Liberation (MNS, 1977).

[18]Moyer, "MNS Structure and Strategy," pp. 7-8.

[19]For a list of MNS collectives and contacts, see Dandelion, Summer/Fall 1979, pp. 16-24, and Resource Manual for a Living Revolution, pp. 321-39.

[20]Richard K. Taylor, Economics and the Gospel (Philadelphia: The United Church Press, 1973), pp. 19-20.

[21]Ibid., p. 12.

[22]The Philadelphia Macro-Analysis Collective, Organizing Macro-Analysis Seminars: A Manual (Philadelphia: MNS, Third Edition, 1975) p. v.

[23]Awareness of suffering at the personal level is seen as a first step in "consciousness raising" in Resource Manual for a Living Revolution, pp. 129-31.

[24]Frances Moore Lappé and Joseph Collins, Food First --Beyond the Myth of Scarcity (Boston: Houghton Mifflin Company, 1977), as cited in William Moyer and Erika Thorne, Food/Hunger Macro-Analysis Seminar (New York: Transnational Academic Program, Institute for World Order, 1977).

[25]Resource Manual for a Living Revolution, pp. 33-41.

[26]Susanne Gowan, George Lakey, William Moyer, Richard Taylor, Moving Toward a New Society (Philadelphia: New Society Press, 1976) P. 194.

[27]George Lakey, A Manifesto for Nonviolent Revolution (Philadelphia, MNS, 1972) p. 12. (Reprint from WIN Magazine, November 15, 1972).

[28]Ibid., p. 14.

[29]See especially, ibid., pp. 10-17; Lakey, Strategy for a Living Revolution, pp. 146-66, 186-96; Moving Toward a New Society, pp. 163-216.

[30]Lakey, Strategy for a Living Revolution, pp. 156-58.

[31]Ibid., p. 97.

[32]Ibid., pp. 98-99.

[33]Ibid., pp. 57, 98.

[34]Ibid., pp. 130, 138-40.

[35]Ibid., p. 37-44.

[36]Ibid., p. 45. Bob Irwin, Gordon Faison, and David H. Albert, Why Non-Violence? (Special Dandelion issue, MNS, 1978), p.3.

[37]Lakey, Strategy for a Living Revolution, p. 112.

[38]Ibid., pp. 44-65.

[39]Ibid., p. 99.

[40]Lakey, A Manifesto for Nonviolent Revolution, p. 25.

[41]Ibid., p. 25.

[42]Ibid., p. 24.

[43]Ibid., p. 25.

[44]Lakey, Strategy for a Living Revolution, p. 99.

[45]Ibid., p. 179. Lakey refers to Gene Sharp, The Politics of Nonviolent Action (Boston: Porter Sargent Publishers, 1973).

[46]Lakey, Strategy for a Living Revolution, p. 141.

[47]Ibid., pp. 180-86; Moving Toward a New Society, pp. 208-15.

[48]Ibid., pp. 202-03.

[49]Quoted in Lakey, Strategy for a Living Revolution, p. 160, from Gene Sharp, Gandhi Wields the Weapons of Moral Power: Three Case Histories (Ahmedabad, India: Navajivan, 1960), p. 167.

[50]William Moyer, "Building Local MNS Networks" (MNS mimeographed paper, June 1977), p. 4.

[51]"Building the Good Life," p. 11.

[52]David H. Albert, "Seabrook in Retrospect," Fellowship Magazine, July/August, 1977.

LIST OF CONTRIBUTORS

MURRAY BODO, O.F.M.   holds an M.A. from Xavier University, Cincinnati, Ohio. He is currently an English Instructor at Chatfield College, Ohio, and writer for St. Anthony Messenger Press. Father Bodo has published five books: Francis: The Journey and the Dream; Walk in Beauty: Meditations from the Desert; Song of the Sparrow; Clare: A Light in the Garden, and Sing Pilgrimage and Exile, as well as articles and poetry in Catholic Update and St. Anthony Messenger. For several summers he has done research and lectured on the spirituality of St. Francis in Assisi.

GEORGE H. CROWELL   holds a Th.D. from Union Theological Seminary, New York. He is an associate professor in the Department of Religious Studies, University of Windsor, Windsor, Ontario. His publications include a book, Society Against Itself, and articiles in Explore and Rethinking Social Ministry. Dr. Crowell's special vocational commitment is exploring motivation for social action. He is active in social education and action projects.

EDWARD J. CROWLEY   holds an S.T.L. from The Catholic University of America and an S.S.L. from The Pontifical Biblical Institute, Rome. He is a professor and former chairperson of the Department of Religious Studies, University of Windsor, Windsor, Ontario. He published a commentary on The Books of Lamentation, Baruch, Sophonia, Nahum and

Habacuc, was one of the translators for The Encyclopedic
Dictionary of the Bible, and annotated the Books of Joshua,
Judges, Ruth and Esther in The Oxford Study Edition of The
New English Bible with the Apocrypha. He was also a con-
tributor to The New Catholic Encyclopedia and The Encyclopedic Dictionary of Religion as well as publishing an article in Catholic Library World. Professor Crowley is active
in Amnesty International.

JOSEPH T. CULLITON, C.S.B.   holds a Ph.D. from Fordham
University and is a professor and chairperson of the De-
partment of Religious Studies, University of Windsor, Wind-
sor, Ontario. He has published two books: A Processive
World View for Pragmatic Christians and Obedience: Gateway
to Freedom, as well as articles in The Basilian Teacher,
America, The Catholic Biblical Quarterly, The Homiletic and
Pastoral Review, The Teilhard Review, Thought, and The Na-
tional Apostolate with Mentally Retarded Persons Quarterly.
He also contributed an article to the monograph, Working
Papers on the Theology of Marriage.

ROBERT J. DALY, S.J.   holds a Dr. Theol. from Julius Maxi-
milians Universität, Würzburg. He is an associate professor and chairperson of the Department of Theology, Boston
College, Chestnut Hill. His publications include two books:
Christian Sacrifice: The Judaeo-Christian Background before Origen and The Origins of the Christian Doctrine of
Sacrifice as well as articles in Theological Studies, Catholic Biblical Quarterly, American Ecclesiastical Review,
Studia Patristica, Biblical Theology Bulletin, Emmanuel,
National Institute for Campus Ministry Journal, Origeniana
and other monographs. Fr. Daly's research focuses on the
biblical and patristic origins and development of Christian
theology. He has taught and published on the topic of war
and peace.

JOHN C. HOFFMAN   holds a Ph.D. in chemistry from McGill
University and a Th.D. from Union Theological Seminary, New
York. He is a professor and former chairperson of the De-
partment of Religious Studies, University of Windsor, Wind-
sor, Ontario. He has published a book entitled, Ethical
Confrontation in Counseling, and articles in The Canadian
Journal of Theology, Studies in Religion, Humanitas, Sound-
ings, Religion in Life, New Catholic Encyclopedia and the
Canadian Journal of Chemistry. He has worked extensively
on the relationship between theology and the social sciences in articulating theology and upon the writings of
Reinhold Niebuhr in this context.

J. NORMAN KING   holds a Ph.D. from The University of St.
Michael's College, University of Toronto. He is an associate professor in the Department of Religious Studies, University of Windsor, Windsor, Ontario, and has published an
article in Thought as well as contributing chapters entitled Catholic Social Work: A Contemporary Overview, and
Many Futures: Many Worlds to two books. He also has two
books presently in press: The God of Forgiveness and Healing in the Theology of Karl Rahner and Experiencing God All
Ways and Every Day. One of his major areas of interest and
teaching is relating spiritual development and social responsibility in the thought of Thomas Merton and Karl
Rahner.

CHARLES C. McCARTHY   holds an M.A. in theology from The
University of Notre Dame and a J.D. in Law from Boston College, Chestnut Hill. He is spiritual director at St. Gregory's Byzantine Catholic Seminary, Newton, Mass. He is
author of The Stations of the Cross of Non-Violent Love and
has done a fifteen part video-tape series entitled, The
Theology of Christian Non-Violence. He is also Founder and

Director of The Center for the Study of Non-Violence at the
University of Notre Dame and has been actively committed to
fostering the Christian tradition of non-violence for the
past fifteen years.

RODNEY J. SAWATSKY   holds a Ph.D. from Princeton Universi-
ty and is currently an associate professor of Religious
Studies and History at Conrad Grebel College, University of
Waterloo, Waterloo, Ontario. He was co-editor of the book,
Evanglical-Unification Dialogue, and contributed chapters
to three books: The Believers Church in Canada; A Time for
Consideration, and Call to Faithfulness. As well, he has
published articles in Theology Today, Mennonite Life and
The Canadian Journal of Sociology. Dr. Sawatsky has taught
courses in the history and thought of Christian pacifism.

WILLIAM D. WATLEY   holds a Ph.D. from Columbia University,
an L.L.D. from Edward Waters College, Jacksonville, Florida
and a D.D. from Payne Theological Seminary, Wilberforce,
Ohio. He is a former president of Paul Quinn College,
Waco, Texas. His doctoral dissertation was written on
Martin Luther King Jr.'s non-violent ethic. He has published in the Black Studies Program; Volume II of the Pastor's Manual of the A.M.E. Church, and the 1977 edition of
Meditation for Liberation and Unity, as well as being a
speaker on the album "Partners in Mission," Dave Nelson Co.

BARRY L. WHITNEY   holds a Ph.D. from McMaster University,
Hamilton, Ontario, and is an associate professor in the Department of Religious Studies, University of Windsor, Windsor, Ontario. His publications include articles in The
Southern Journal of Philosophy, Studies in Religion and
Horizons, as well as a chapter in the monograph, The Reality of God in the Contemporary World. He specializes in
process thought, especially that of Charles Hartshorne.